For Bob and Sandy

Ken Greenberg

Always the best to you —

A Tiger by the Tail

Kenneth R. Greenberg

A Tiger by the Tail:

Parenting in a Troubled Society

Nelson-Hall *nh* Chicago

ISBN: 0-911-012-77-X

Library of Congress Catalog Card Number: 73–93103

Manufactured in the United States of America

To
lovely Cindy,
loving Scott,
and
loyal Kacey

Contents

Foreword

This book is being written in a time of national crisis. Society is faced with internal problems that threaten to destroy the unity of a country whose birth was brought about by the need to be united. This is a time of dissension, violence, and disrespect for controls. It is a strange mixture of the unbelievable scientific successes of man, coupled with a regression to social chaos and a loss of personal security. Most tragically, it is a time of fear. The future points in two opposite directions. It looks to the excitement of what man will learn about himself and his universe, and it looks helplessly and dejectedly into the faces of the poor, the uneducated, and the deprived. It is a future that offers hope in solving technological mysteries and futility in coping with social injustices. Man is the core of society. He is the product of many influences and wears both the crown of society's glories and the scars of society's disgraces.

There is a need for the people who make up our society to take an objective look at themselves. Such an evaluation would involve an exploration of the philosophy and practices of its members. Many of our youngsters have already begun such an appraisal. Using crude and oftentimes primitive forms of rebellion, they are seeking to isolate themselves from their culture. They have identified their parents with the culture, and in rejecting the culture they feel they must put aside the parents. Their actions have forced the parents to come out from behind their newspapers and television sets and take notice. Although many of the youngsters' complaints and arguments are critical rather than constructive, many of their feelings are considered justified. The controversy does not center around *what* young people are talking about, or what changes they seek, but rather the methods whereby they are attempting to bring about such changes. Many of their questions are embarrassing. It is as if the generation that was encouraged to think and raise questions has stumbled upon the skeletons that have been hidden away in closets for years. We are uncomfortable because they have not feared to open the closets, and we tremble because they have dared to handle the bones of the skeletons. They ask how an intelligent and civilized nation can permit social injustices to continue without solutions on one hand, while boasting of huge economic successes on the other. They ask how a country that is so education-conscious can be content with an educational system that discourages so many youngsters from taking part. And they ask the most difficult of all questions, "What's it all for?"

The expressions on the faces of parents today are indicative of the worry and apprehension about the present and future direction of their children. In the attempt to create an affluent middle-class society, parents have created a child who rejects controls, rebels against the traditional sacred cows of our culture, and demands unrealistic autonomy. Many adolescents have become disenchanted with parental hypocrisy, parental values, and parental methods. They are prepared to leave their secure two-car families and can do so without feelings of guilt or a sense of obligation to the family. They are convinced that they can show their parents that there is a better way to live. Most of this group will learn the hard way that there may be a better way to live, but they will not have found it. Many youngsters have already done irreparable damage to their lives with the use of harmful drugs and subsequent attitudes of lethargy and indifference. Many more youngsters will, unfortunately, follow their lead.

The parents of the adolescent are continually advised of the generation gap, the communication gap, and a so-called credibility gap. Although they may not be able to define these terms with precise language, the implication of these gaps spells out the isolation and separation that exists between the parent and the child. Parents have become fearful of the potentially destructive weapons their child has learned to use against them. They are frustrated by their inability to control the youngster who appears determined to bring physical or emotional harm to himself. They are upset by the child's contemptuous attitudes towards authority and parental roles. And, they are fearful to speculate on the generation of children that their children will produce.

The parents of younger children also fear. They fear the effect the teenager has already had on their growing and impressionable child. They fear the early signs of rebellion, both in the home and in the school. They fear the streets and the cities where their children will grow up. And they fear that they, too, may be powerless to direct the moral and social conduct of the child.

Nor can the parents of the very young child relax and enjoy watching their child grow to maturity. They are constantly made aware of the potential hazards that lie ahead of their infant or toddler. They see education as an ill-defined series of obstacles for the child to overcome. They see a society that is being torn and divided in a multitude of directions by angry groups, each of whom maintains that it possesses the solution to our ills. They see the prospects of prohibitive college costs, the consequences from an approaching sexual revolution, the growing competition that has become a pressure-producing way of life, and most of all, they see the threat of man's total destruction by nuclear power.

At no time in our history has there been such a critical need to be aware of and understand what is going on. If we deal with each of the problems singularly, we will be guilty of concentrating on symptoms and ignoring causes. If we emphasize the causes and ignore the symptoms, we will be guilty of neglecting issues that are vital and pressing. The solution would have to include attention to the specific problems without losing awareness that the underlying causes will require the greatest effort.

The first task would be to determine the root or source of the problem. Taking the position that social behavior is learned, and feeling that parents are the first teachers of the child, this book will examine the role of parents in preventing problems, identifying the early signs of trouble, and coping with the behavior of their children.

The rationale for this as the point of departure is not to point the accusing finger of blame at parents for all that has happened to society, but to indicate the importance of parental training in shaping the behavior of the child. Many of the problems of children can be traced to parental procedures which involve inappropriate methods of training, inconsistent actions, and hostile attitudes towards the child. Many of the problems of the child are, in reality, problems of the parents which have been superimposed upon the child. Some of the issues that need to be raised are: What should a parent be? What can parents do to promote stable and self-confident behavior in their child? What do parents do that encourages misbehavior? What events have occurred in the historical past that have produced our turbulent and restless youth generation? Is the parent powerless to help the child who seems to be heading towards a disaster? What are some guidelines for the parents of infants and young children, for parents of pre-adolescent children, for parents of adolescents? What impact is public education having on the child? Why are schools faced with serious crises, and in what ways do parents contribute to educational problems?

Finally, a thought about a question that is not thought about enough: What kind of relationship should exist between the child and his parents after the child is married and has become a parent? This book addresses itself to these issues with the optimistic belief that certain improvements and changes can be brought about.

Until the child reaches a legally prescribed age, the parents are responsible for the welfare of the child. At some point in time they will be required to relinquish their direct power and control and let the child pursue his own direction in life. This separation can occur gracefully when the child matures into young adulthood and feels ready to assume independence. It can also occur abruptly if the immature adolescent rebels against parental standards and authority and escapes into an uncertain future. Regardless of how the separation takes place, as long as the parent is maintaining some controls over the child, he is, figuratively speaking, holding a tiger by the tail. Once he lets go of the tail, he may be in great danger of being hurt by the freed animal. Whether the parent will walk with the tiger or whether he will be forced to run from it will be determined by what he did to the tiger while he was holding its tail.

Kenneth R. Greenberg

- 1 -

The Tasks of Parenting

Take a little girl who is supposedly made of "sugar and spice and everything nice," and a little boy who is a combination of "frogs and snails and puppy dog tails," and age them twenty years. Let them meet, fall in love, and get married. Then, let them become parents and observe what the blend produces. What are parents made of? *Worry and fears and hearts filled with tears*, is one possibility. Another is *joys and pleasures in a home filled with treasures*.

There is much that parents can do to determine which definition will describe their feelings about being parents. How parents define their role as parents and what they actually do as parents are the best predictors of which definition will apply. The personality of each parent plus the blend produced by the marriage explains why the parents have developed into the kind of parents they are. The effects the parents will have on their child are likewise predictable. Calm and relaxed parents will probably have a child who is relatively calm; tense and nervous parents will produce an anxious child. By early childhood parents will get a glimpse of the personality traits the child is acquiring. Some parents will enjoy what they have helped to produce; others will wish they could turn back the years and begin again.

If parents reap the joys and pleasures, it will be largely due to what they have put into their roles as parents. It will be because they have been unselfish as parents, consistent in their training, and more important, good models for the child to copy. They will also have been patient, understanding, and respectful of the child's dignity and self-worth. They will have helped the child develop confidence in himself and encouraged him to set realistic goals for himself. Parents who can provide the child with an environment that offers love and trust and in which the child can feel rewarded by his successes will give themselves the best protection against the *worry and fears and hearts filled with tears*.

What is Parenting?

In considering the role of parents today, the most accurate way of describing the functions of a parent is to say that a parent *is* what a parent does. Parental roles range from a devoted and loving relationship with a child to a basic caretaking function providing little more than the essentials for survival. Parental roles vary from one culture to another, from one generation to another, and from one socio-economic level to another. The individual's attitude towards being a parent is the result of an interaction of many factors, most important of which are his own experiences as a child and his impressions and memories of his parents. Parental attitudes are also influenced by such things as the pressures of society, educational and vocational levels, the personality of the parent, parental expectations, the number of children in the family, and cultural norms. The responsibilities a parent assumes for a child, as well as the manner in which they are carried out, depend largely upon the way the parent's role is self-defined.

Since being a parent involves specific actions and attitudes, the term *parenting* can be defined as just what it is the parent does in the process of being a parent. The vast differences that are found in parental behaviors reveal that parenting is both an *action* and an *attitude* towards rearing children. Changing a wet diaper is an action. How often it is changed and how the parent reacts to changing it is an attitude. Telling a child to pick up his toys is an action on a verbal level. How the child is told and how often the child has to be told indicate the attitude the parents have towards child training and reveal their parenting practices.

Parenting develops from the personal beliefs and values the parent has about himself and others. The expression of a personal code of conduct governs the parental response to the child in an observable way. Parenting is a reflection of the personality of the parents and is usually predictable. Fun-loving and enthusiastic parents will show their zest for life in their parenting through their ability to see the pleasant side of life and by showing an optimistic view about things. Their parenting will encourage the child to become involved in activities that offer enjoyment and interest because as parents, they will be active and interesting people. Likewise, tense and insecure parents will carry their fears into parenting and reveal to the child a world that is characterized by apprehension, restraint, danger, and doubt.

Parenting can be many things. It can be consistent, inconsistent, or hypocritical. It can represent a full commitment, an occasional awareness, or a non-involvement. It can be viewed as a challenge, a threat, or a distasteful chore. It can be enjoyed, tolerated, or avoided. In short, it can be a variety of things in varying degrees. What parenting becomes, however, will be the most significant factor in predicting the later behavior and attitudes of the child.

It is doubtful that a person can fail to show the impact of early childhood experiences. The parent will reveal the influence of his parents even though his method of child rearing appears to be different from that he experienced. Parents often find themselves acting like their own parents, despite efforts to avoid duplicating behavior they disliked in their own parents. Whether or not they want to be models for their child, the child will see them as models. When the child later becomes a parent, he will copy, reject or modify the models he has known. He may admire and repect his own parents, or dislike and resent them. He may also react to them with ambivalence, feeling simultaneous like and dislike towards them. A person's attitude towards his parents, whether one of love or hatred, honor or denial, pride or shame, is determined by the parenting he has experienced.

The Decision to Become a Parent

Unfortunately, it cannot be said that every parent wanted to be a parent. A large number of infant births are the result of accidental pregnancies. Pressure pregnancies account for another large number of babies, whose parents decided to have a child because of social

4 A TIGER BY THE TAIL: Parenting in a Troubled Society

pressure, religious beliefs, or parental influences. People have also become parents to save a faltering marriage, to relieve a wife's boredom, to satisfy a discontented spouse, or because it was just assumed that becoming a parent was a natural consequence of marriage.

A recent trend in society is to regard having children as a matter for decision. Ideally, it should be a mutual decision based upon the readiness, willingness, and ability of the couple to provide for the physical and emotional needs of a child. Having subsequent children also involves a decision, which again should be based upon the criteria of readiness, willingness, and ability of the couple to provide for more than one child. Providing the first child with a playmate is not a sufficient reason for enlarging a family. *Wanting* more than one child is a more valid reason than feeling you *should* have more than one child.

Despite the fact that young married couples today are very much aware of planned parenthood, and even though there are effective ways to control the size of a family, many unwanted children are born. Fortunately, the majority of these unplanned children are accepted and loved. It is a tragedy when they are not. The unplanned pregnancy requires another decision; namely, to develop positive attitudes towards the child that is soon to be born, or to live with resentment that inevitably turns into guilt. It is essential that both parents have good feelings about a forthcoming birth. When they do not, they should obtain professional counseling before the infant's birth in order to prevent the "unwanted child syndrome." The unwanted child grows to feel rejected by his parents, resentful of their attitude, and isolated from them. He feels alone in a big world.

The only requirement for becoming a natural parent is the individual's biological and physical ability to produce either the egg or the sperm cell. By way of contrast, there are a number of prerequisites for adoptive parents. Typically, they must demonstrate evidence of maturity, reliability, stability, and social acceptability. They must first express a desire to become parents and prove their financial ability to provide for the child. There are even follow-up visits by case workers to determine whether or not the adoptive parents are doing a good job of parenting. None of these qualifications are required of the natural parents. Consequently, there is no way to assure each newborn that his parents will be responsible adults—or even adults.

Parent Training

In our highly specialized and automated society we have come to look upon training and preparation as an essential prerequisite for any task. The amount of training is usually determined by such factors as the complexity of the job, the kind of knowledge that will be needed, and the amount of responsibility that is demanded by the job. Relating this to the task of parenting, a valid question is "How much, and what kind of training is needed for the job of being a parent?"

We would all agree that some preparation is necessary. There is less agreement when it comes to deciding the nature of the preparation. There is no reason to feel that the training of the mother should be different from that of the father, for both should assume a responsible role in the training of the child. There are some differences, though, for it is best for the child when mother can be in the home during the early years of the child's life. When mother must work, someone else assumes the role of the mother. Until the child is in school, the mother is the model the child should see most. Unlike the baby sitter or all-day nursery school, she gives the child personal love and develops training standards that are compatible with the values of the home. Until the child is about six years old, the child needs a mother to be where he can see her.

The child needs a father, too—one who supports and reinforces the efforts of the mother, who is committed to assuming an active role in the rearing of the child, and who is capable of loving and enjoying a child. Too often the father is willing to let his wife assume the entire responsibility for the early years of child training, excluding himself from the day-to-day problems in child training by using his busy schedule as an excuse.

Increasing numbers of expectant parents have enrolled in baby care programs sponsored by the Red Cross. A large number of high schools have incorporated prenatal care classes in health programs. Some hospitals offer instruction to the expectant mother and new mother, but the focus of their programs is on the physical care of the infant. Instruction and training for social and emotional development in children has largely been ignored and parents who seek advice on such matters are told to consult their busy pediatrician.

Books, pamphlets, and periodicals on raising children are available in both libraries and bookstores, but reading an article on the control of temper tantrums is not as meaningful as being able to discuss what you have read with a professional or experienced person in the field of child development. There is a great need for parent training classes that deal with the social and emotional issues of childhood. Problems such as weaning, thumb sucking, toilet training, excessive crying, temper tantrums, needs for structure, and management of discipline can form the subject matter of parent training programs that are relatively nonexistent today.

In most communities there are adult education classes that are sponsored by the public schools or local colleges. Classes in child development or child psychology are helpful, and small parent discussion groups that involve both mothers and fathers can be directed towards training issues. However, if we are to be successful in educating parents to the social and emotional problems of childhood, a broader program of training must be developed that will reach the many parents who do not avail themselves of the already existing programs.

Much of the child's basic personality is developed by the age of six. Because many of the child's behavior patterns and action tendencies are formed by this age, *early* training for parents must be available. Cities must begin to address themselves to this important task, and either existing agencies or newly created ones should provide direction for parents. Within the existing structure, state universities, local colleges, and public schools can form the nucleus for instruction. Community child welfare agencies can implement parent training classes, churches can encourage parent discussion groups, and hospitals can expand their facilities to include more programs that deal with the problems of child raising. If enough parents ask for such services, the community will be forced to respond. One of the tasks of parenting is to become an informed parent. Reading about children, enrolling in courses that are related to children, attending discussions on children's problems and sharing experiences with other parents are ways to become more informed. These actions also discourage parents from taking the tasks of parenting for granted.

Parental Tasks

The awareness that the complete destiny of a newborn lies within the hands of its parents is awesome. The infant is helpless and completely dependent upon others for all of its needs. In the process of growing from infant to toddler to child to adolescent, there is a continual reduction of dependence and a corresponding increase of independent behavior. Nevertheless, at any stage in the development of the child there are specified parental obligations and responsibilities. The greater number of parental tasks occur during the child's early years, for these are the critical years in which child training is essential. They are designated parental tasks since no one else is in a position to carry them out as effectively.

Foremost, parents are *teachers*. What kind of teachers they are or what they teach the child will be partially reflected in the personality the child acquires. From the day of the first contact between the parents and the child, the teaching begins. It can be subtle or direct, by word or example. It can be deliberate or accidental, appropriate or inappropriate. Each interaction the child has with his parents carries with it some teaching. When the newborn is picked up every time it cries, it learns a lesson in effective manipulation of parents. If the toddler is promised a big red balloon and later the parent changes his mind or forgets to buy it, the child learns a lesson in mistrust. When the child is witness to frequent arguments between his parents, he learns the lessons of weak self controls, inappropriate ways of dealing with frustration, a basis for feeling insecure within his environment, and fear of one or both of his parents.

Similarly, the child will learn love when his mother and father show affection and interest in him. He will learn respect when his parents are fair. He will learn trust when his parents are consistent. And, he will learn self-confidence when his parents offer him encouragement and show confidence in his ability.

All that the child learns, however, does not come from the parents, nor is it always what the parents want him to learn. The child learns from all of his contacts and experiences. Although most parents are aware of the "monkey-see-monkey-do" concept, many parents forget their roles as teachers and expect that the child will only copy their desirable traits.

The double standard is one of the biggest dangers in early child training. What better way to teach a child to become aggressive and hit others when he becomes angry or frustrated than to permit him to see parents act this way when *they* become angry and frustrated? When parents have temper tantrums and revert to physical violence or shouting, they are teaching a lesson that they cannot be proud of. If parents attempt to explain to the child that it is all right for adults to act this way, but not children, they are confusing him. Parents are models for their children and as such are required to demonstrate what they are teaching. The home is really a teaching laboratory.

The same holds true for other things the parents want the child to learn. If they want their child to learn honesty, consideration for others, cooperation, and respect, the parents should insure that he sees these behaviors in the home. It is not sufficient for parents to simply talk about what they want their child to develop; they must lead the way. This requires behavior that supports their beliefs. Parents will be more successful if they first decide what values are important to them, then demonstrate them to the child. Parental values can be identified and clarified through discussions between the husband and wife, ideally before the couple makes the decision to get married. Compatible values are necessary for a good marriage as well as for good parents.

For the parent to be a teacher he need not become a lecturer. Many parents are unaware that they are lecturing or criticizing their child instead of teaching him. For teaching to be effective and for learning to take place, certain conditions must be present. As the learner, the child must feel that he can trust, respect, and be comfortable with the teacher. As the teacher, the parent has to develop rapport with the child. The parent who is an effective teacher will be one who has established a good relationship with his child.

A second parental task is that of being a *love object*. The parents should provide security for the child. Early security results from the trust that develops between the parents and the child. Initially, security means physical comfort. Later, security means emotional comfort to the child. A child feels secure when he knows that parents will provide for, protect, and help him, and when the parents communicate to the child through their actions that he is an important person to them. When this feeling has been conveyed to the child, the child's security *with* the parents turns into his love *for* the parents.

The parents as love objects afford the child an opportunity to feel needed and wanted. At the same time, when the child feels secure, he is free to experiment, to test parental limits, and to try out freedoms without fear of rejection or a withdrawal of parental love. Because the child finds this security and love gratifying, he is reluctant to do anything that might cause him to lose it. Soon, he will have to test the limits to see how far the parents will allow him to go. Even the young child can evaluate the potential danger of his actions through the parental responses. The child who is afraid to test limits, namely, the child who might be termed the "perfect child," may be this way because he fears the consequences or the disapproval from the parents. Fearing what the parent might do, and not trusting his love, the child becomes overcontrolled and inhibited.

Conversely, the child who is continually testing the limits and who frequently goes beyond them, may feel as if he has nothing to lose by incurring the anger of parents. Such a child conveys a lack of relatedness to love objects and a disassociation from parental controls. For a variety of reasons, it has become more important for this child to displease parents than to please them. A need to punish parents and seek revenge is one of the more common reasons for this behavior.

The child who is comfortable with his parents as love objects has a strong need to please them. This child enjoys his feelings of security with parents and consequently feels good about himself. Even so, he will have to try out his early needs for independence and satisfy his curiosities and will therefore occasionally rebel. When limits are set by parents, the child has to test their elasticity. If he chooses to go beyond the limits, he should be made aware that he has not pleased his love objects. He then has a clear choice of whether to surrender his autonomy and need for self-assertion, or experience a rather painful isolation from the security which he knows can be so comforting. *Only because he has known love and security does he have the desire to please parents.* For this reason he usually accepts parental controls. The wise parent understands when these controls can be reduced and relinquished. As the child approaches adolescence, the number of these controls should be minimal, and the judgment shown by the child should suggest to the parents how many controls are needed.

The love object role of parents is not only a responsibility to the child but a need for the parent. However, the child's needs for someone to love and the opportunity to love the parents are of greater importance to the child's development than is the parent's satisfaction or pleasure in loving the child. Initially, the parents give love and the child receives it. Soon the child begins to return love, and the parents get gratification and fulfillment. The cycle repeats itself, for when the parents feel love, they give more love. The child who receives this love is able to return love. Ultimately, the cycle becomes one of mutual pleasure in giving and receiving.

Whereas the parents have experiences preparing them to begin loving their child at once, the child has to learn to love before he can develop love for his parents. It follows that the child's need for parental love differs from the parental need for the child's love. Love, for the child, grows out of his needs for acceptance, reassurance, comfort, security, and belonging. Physical contact is one way these needs are met; the positive regard the parents have for the child is another. As love objects, the parents should be available to satisfy, but not satiate the child's needs.

A third critical function of the parent is as a *provider*. The parent provides food, shelter and clothing; he is also responsible for providing motivation, encouragement, and experiences. Motivation is the impetus for making an effort. When it is strong, much can be accomplished; when it is weak, even basic survival is jeopardized. Without motivation there is no purpose, goal, or direction. The child who is unmotivated to cooperate with parents will not, or, when he does, his efforts will be minimal and his resistance will be obvious.

There are degrees of motivation. People who lack strong motivation to produce can, with pressure, force themselves into producing. The youngster who really doesn't want to do homework, but after much procrastinating and external pressure ends up doing it, has some degree of motivation. The child who flatly refuses to do an assignment is showing no motivation for that particular task.

Motivation can be external or internal. It is external when outside forces or pressures are the stimulus that makes the person respond. It is internal when the need to respond comes from within the individual, without promptings from outside sources. A child may not want to join the Boy Scouts, but he may be aware that his father will be pleased if he does join. If his desire to please his father is strong, or if he will be allowed to go to a summer camp if he joins the scouts, his motivation to become a scout is based on external pressures. Much of the young child's motivation is external. Yet, frequently what starts out to be external motivation will become internalized. A child may read a book because his parents have requested him to. He may find that he enjoys the book and begin reading spontaneously. For such a child, motivation for reading has become internalized.

One notion about motivation suggests that every child is born with only a potential for motivation, rather like a pilot light.

When the early environment protects the flame, and provides encouragement and incentives for growth, the flame becomes a small fire and ultimately a roaring blaze. However, it is easy to snuff out the flame of motivation while it is still small. Convince the child that he can't do anything right, ridicule or insult the child, develop so much fear within the child that he cannot act spontaneously, or degrade the child through harsh or cruel punishment, and the tender flame of motivation will flicker and possibly go out. It may never be turned on again, at least to the force that it could have been. The child with a broken spirit, the severely depressed and withdrawn child, the extremely fearful child, may have undergone an irreversible extinguishing of motivation.

One task of the parent should be to insure that the child's motivation will grow. What occurs within a child's developing motivational system will determine whether the child feels adequate to pursue and persevere, or whether he feels apathy, indifference, and an unwillingness to even try.

Encouragement does not mean false praise or forcing when an interest is not there. When parents get the idea that their child should learn to play piano and proceed to buy a piano and arrange for piano lessons, this is not necessarily encouragement. Unless the child has initiated the idea or has responded favorably to the suggestion, the parents could be forcing rather than encouraging. Piano lessons for the child frequently serve to gratify the ego of the parent rather than to fulfill a need within the child.

Encouragement permits the child to feel free to make a spontaneous response or show a natural interest in something. From the cues that the child gives through expressed interest or enthusiasm, the parents can provide the appropriate encouragement. This should not be interpreted to mean that when the child announces that he wishes that he could play the piano the parents should rush out and buy one. Preliminary talk about what is involved in learning to play the piano is important, as is determining the degree of interest. The child's known personality patterns with respect to perseverance and impulsiveness should also be considered if and when there is talk about buying a piano.

Encouragement means letting a child make some mistakes by himself. Failure to do this has a discouraging effect for the child. If, for example, a child feels that his way of doing something is best and the parent knows it is not the best way, as long as safety, health, or other critical factors are not involved, the parent can provide encouragement to the child to learn for himself by merely standing by. When the child is always told how something should be done, and is denied opportunities to solve problems for himself, he becomes discouraged to make attempts at problem solving. Encouragement is also a reinforcement. Many times verbal reinforcers are more effective than giving a material reward to the child. Many people are quick to criticize but neglect to praise. The parent is often guilty of doing both at the same time, for instance when he tells the child that he did a good job of cleaning his room, then adds, "but the next time . . ." Saying, "but the next time . . ." negates the praise. Research has shown that immediate reward is better than delayed reward, suggesting that it is better to praise the child at the time he has done something praiseworthy than to wait and do it later. The same is true for punishments.

In order to encourage the child, the parent must be prepared to provide experiences for him. The parent should be willing to expose the child to a variety of situations, giving him an opportunity to repeat those experiences which he enjoyed. If we learn best by doing, then nothing can replace the live experience gained by going places and doing things. Certainly, selected television programs, which many parents use to give the child experiences, can have some positive effects, but television is not an adequate substitute for direct contact. Providing experiences for the child requires the efforts of both parents. For the mother, it means organizing the day to include time for such opportunities. For the father, it may mean giving up an occasional Sunday football game on television or a weekly golf game.

In addition to being teacher and model, love object, and provider, the parent has at least one other critical responsibility to the child. This is the dual function of being a *friend and counselor*. The word friend should not be confused with the terms playmate or companion. Nor should the word counselor imply that the parent should tell the child how to live his life.

The parent as friend can establish a relationship with his child that is comfortable, safe, and consistent, for both the parent and the child. He can be a confidant with whom the child feels willing to share parts of his life. He can be the person the child will turn to, not because there is no one else to turn to, but because the child knows that the parent is sincerely and deeply interested in him. The parent as friend is a special type of friend who will not interfere or compete with the child's other friendships. The friendship will parallel the love relationship, and will be founded on a mutual respect for one another.

Many parents seek to become "buddies" with their children. They appear to want to grow up with their child or possibly to recapture a part of their own childhood. Such child-parent relationships, especially when the parent wants to be the child's constant companion, may initially be comforting to the child, but later, as he gets older, they can be embarrassing. As the child grows he will come to have more in common with peers than with parents. Ultimately, he will hurt the parent by rejecting the relationship. To seek a "buddy" relationship with a child is to deny the child the only child-parent relationship he will ever have, as well as his chance to observe his parents as models.

As counselor to the child, the parent should be a source of information, a guide, a reflector of feelings, ideas and opinions, and someone who helps the child see things accurately. The parent-as-counselor can help the child gain insights into problems and their solutions. As counselor, the parent does not seek to live the child's life for him nor relive his own life through him; rather he gives the child the opportunity to think things through clearly and realistically. When it does become necessary to provide direction for the child, the parent is in a position to offer suggestions rather than demanding specific responses. Initially, the parent-as-counselor function is a way to foster social training, moral and value teaching, or encouragement in solving problems. Later, it can be an assistance in goal setting, a sounding board for ideas, or a chance to experiment in handling life problems.

One of the most important attributes of the parent-as-counselor is one that is difficult for many parents. The parent as a counselor must become a good listener. The child should be given the opportunity to talk freely and without fear of frequent interruptions, critical comments, or negative reactions. It is not necessary that the parents agree with everything the child says, but it is necessary that the child be encouraged to express his opinions and feelings. In this way, the child learns that talking with parents is safe even though discussion does not always result in mutual agreement or approval.

Much has been said and written about the communication gap that exists between the child and his parents. The gap usually begins when the child learns or feels that the parent does not care enough to listen to what he is saying. If what the child is saying is ignored, rejected, or ridiculed by the parent, the impression the child gains is that what he is saying is not important because only a child is speaking. Conversations with parents then become parental lectures; lectures turn into repetitious monologues, and the monologues become boring. Protectively, the child learns to turn the parents off! Much of the communication gap could be avoided by the parents. By not requiring the child to become defensive, by showing respect for what the child is saying, whether or not he agrees with him, by encouraging the child to "get something off his chest," by not frustrating the child by terminating the conversation before he has had his chance to say what he wanted to say, and by trying to understand the feelings of the child, the parent can leave the lines of verbal communication open.

Often, for the satisfaction of having the last word, the parent destroys a vital link that could serve to unite him with his child. It is easy for the child to see the parents as bullies. When the child perceives that the parents are loaded with ammunition that can be used against him, he has the choice of either submitting passively and withdrawing, or fighting the parent through the development of an arsenal of his own. At this point the "cold war" turns into a shooting war, and both the parents and the child lose.

A final requirement for the parent-as-counselor is fairness, implying both parental consistency and mature judgment. If the parents respond unfairly to the child or punish by impulsive threats, the child loses faith in their fairness. Promises that are repeatedly broken have a devasting effect on the child's concept of fairness. So does punishing one child for having done something but not another child who has done the same thing. The child who feels his sibling is "getting away with something" will accuse parents of favoritism. Unwarranted or harsh punishments, deceiving a child, hypocritical behaviors on the part of the parents, and falsely blaming a child are all unfair.

Being consistent is part of being fair. Consistency is exhibited when an individual feels comfortable with his own actions or is strong in his beliefs. When you are consistent about something, you do not doubt your rationale for doing it. If you consistently brush your teeth in the morning, you know why you do it. If a person is consistently punctual, he is announcing his strong belief in punctuality.

When a parent feels strongly that stealing is an unacceptable behavior, and if he needs no one to convince him that it is wrong to steal, he will be consistent in punishing for stealing. Furthermore, this parent will feel comfortable in punishing since he knows that he is right. But, if the parent says that it is wrong to steal from a poor little shop owner but that a big grocery store won't miss one little apple, his attitude toward stealing is hazy. Such a parent may have difficulty in punishing acts of thievery with consistency. Saying to a child, "OK, but don't do it again," tells the child that it must not have been a very bad thing to do or his parent would have acted more forcefully. It also conveys to the child that the parent is willing to overlook some things, usually encouraging the child to repeat his performance. Of course, if the father who admonishes the child for stealing brings home something he "procured" from the office, regardless of what he says to justify his actions, the child sees him exposed as a hypocrite.

Consistency is necessary for fairness. Consistency teaches a child what to expect and thereby helps define limits to a child. It is fair because the child has been told what to anticipate as a consequence of his behavior. But, a parent cannot be consistent until he has defined his own beliefs and values. Many husbands and wives should first discuss values and behaviors with each other until there is some resolution of differences or until specific practices can be agreed upon. It would be ideal to have many of these issues resolved in advance of their occurrence, so the first parental response to the child's behavior can set the precedent for future actions.

Parental Anticipations

There are many situations that can be anticipated by parents. The parents who feel the second child will be better because they have learned from their mistakes with the first child are parents who did not or could not anticipate behaviors. They acted without preparation and impulsively made wrong judgments and decisions. As usual, it is the child who ultimately suffers from parental mistakes.

Parents of infants and young children can anticipate a number of issues that they will probably have to face. To anticipate their occurrence allows time for thought as to how they will be handled and avoids some of the doubts and dangers of hasty decisions. Some of these issues are:
— What should our approach be towards picking up the newborn when it cries during the day? When it cries at night?
— When and how should we approach weaning and toilet training?
— What do we do when the child has a temper tantrum at home? In public?

— What do we do when the child hits another child?
— How do we answer his early questions about sex?
— What is our attitude about the amount and type of television the child can watch?
— How can we avoid excessive jealousy when a brother or sister is born?
— How many and what kind of toys should be bought?
— What do we say when the child wants us to buy what the neighbor child has?

Parents of the older child can anticipate a different set of issues:
— What should we do about an allowance?
— When do we let the child attend boy-girl social functions?
— How much television should we permit?
— What is our policy about checking homework?
— What chores and responsibilities should we expect from the child?
— How do we punish?
— What kinds of rules should there be in the home?
— What should bedtime be?

The parents of the adolescent could anticipate other kinds of issues:
— What rules should govern the use of the car?
— What curfews should there be on school nights and weekends?
— What responsibilities should the adolescent assume?
— Should the parents insist on a "dress code?"
— What will the parents do if the child is caught using illegal drugs?
— What is the parental attitude towards smoking and the use of alcohol?
— What role should parents assume when it comes to selecting a college?
— How should criticism be handled?

The lists could be ten times longer, and it is not important that you have complete answers for any of these questions. What is important is that you develop a guiding philosophy that is both consistent and fair. It is not too soon for the parents of a 14-year-old boy to begin discussing, between themselves, a tentative attitude towards driving lessons, use of a car, etc., etc. Sooner or later the child will bring it up, and unless there has been prior parental discussion, the child will hear those two words that turn hope into frustration: "We'll see."

Parental Structuring

In many ways, one simple decision made before problems develop can go a long way to avoid many problems. Parents should face and find an answer to the question of who trains whom. Parents who can say, "We train the child," and mean what they say, may go through a few anxious periods, but eventually they will be more relaxed and more gratified than parents who want peace at any price and let the child train them. Parents who put off answering this question will find that the child will answer it for them. Without structure in the home the child will take over. His wants, needs, and demands will control the parents, for without a recognized structure the child knows no limits and will have no reason to develop self-control or a tolerance for frustration.

Parents should determine the amount and type of structure. The possible range would be from total permissiveness to complete authoritarianism. Either extreme would be devastating, first to the child and eventually to the child's parents. The kind of family controls will be determined by the personality, temperament, experiences, and philosophy of both parents. When there are serious differences between the parents on this dimension of child rearing, the actions of one parent offset the actions of the other parent. When one parent is unusually harsh to the child, the other parent will frequently compensate for this by being unusually lenient. The outcome is confusion for the child. The child may grow to fear one parent and have little respect for the other, or to avoid one parent and play upon the sympathy of the other.

The question as to the kind of family structure should be discussed and any major differences should be resolved. If the parents are in conflict, it may help to trace the consequences of each parent's practice or philosophy according to the expected outcomes it would produce. The basic question parents must discuss is, *"what kind of a child are we seeking?"* Some predictions can be made of the effects of various approaches. If parents want an independent child, they will have to allow him to make decisions for himself. If parents want a child who is fair in his relationships with other people, they will have to provide a home in which the child can see justice. If parents are encouraging the child to exert self-control, they will have to remain calm and controlled themselves. Once parents have decided on the kind of a child that will please them, they can examine the family practices to be sure that these practices have a good chance of producing the kind of person they want the child to become. When in doubt, read, research, or ask. Much has been written about children and adolescents. Although it may not always relate to the specific problem you are having, the literature does provide information that is helpful in understanding children. Reading and researching should be as automatic and necessary for parents and parents-to-be as consulting a cook book is to the wife who is baking her first cake, or reading the automotive manual to the husband who is trying to repair his carburetor. The reading and researching, however, should not be a replacement *for* thinking. Instead, it should result *in* thinking. Reading may answer questions by giving specific information; however, it should also generate ideas and raise questions. Parents would be advised to read from several sources, since the "experts" reflect their personal philosophies. For example, the philosophy of this author with respect to children is that a child:

— is a unique individual
— has personal dignity and is entitled to respect
— is born with an innate capacity to grow
— will need help to achieve his full potential
— learns from what it sees and experiences
— prefers satisfaction and seeks pleasure
— needs direction from responsible adults
— seeks an identification with parents
— is most susceptible and responsive to early environmental training

The views expressed in this book are a reflection of these beliefs and the recommendations that are made are, likewise, developed from these principles. Other writers with another viewpoint may make other recommendations. It is left to the parent to decide what forms a solid basis for an approach to child training.

Parenting is a mother-father task that begins at conception and continues, in some manner, as long as the parent lives. In our society we are able to give our children many comforts, opportunities, and luxuries. We can offer them protection and security, education and training. And yet, the one thing that we can do for a child that encourages the development of his full potential is to start him off in life with parents who are dedicated to the many tasks of parenting.

- 2 -

Society's Impact on Parenting

As teachers, models, love objects, providers and counselors, parents exert the most significant influence on the development of the child's personality and his subsequent behavior. Yet, the impact that society has on parents, and therefore their parenting, cannot be overlooked. Socially accepted values and the behavior that is prevalent in society define morality and determine both the rewards offered for conformity and the punishments given for resistance.

Parents are aware of the pressures that society creates for them. They are also aware that serious conflicts in the home can arise when the values of the parents are being challenged by opposing practices in society. Parents become upset when they cannot condone the changes they see, and become frustrated when they feel powerless to change what they cannot accept. Parental frustration over unacceptable changes that have affected their children can lead to aggression, often directed against the child who symbolically represents his generation. The child is caught in the middle, punished by his parents for identifying with the changes, or punished by his peers for rejecting the changes. In this way, conflicts between parents and society become conflicts between parents and child.

Society is in the process of examining attitudes towards many social issues, including sexual equality, capital punishment, abortion, the penal system, and busing as a means of achieving racial balance in schools. There is confusion as to whether certain practices should be socially accepted, condoned, or condemned. Many sexual issues come under this category. Is it emotionally healthy for the individuals or for society when a man and woman live together without being married? What should society's position be with regards to homosexuality, extra-marital relationships, inter-racial marriages, and surgical procedures that alter the sex of an individual? Does providing a shelter for runaway children encourage a rebellious child to run away? Should marijuana be legalized because we cannot control its use by an estimated 26 million people? What changes in the present welfare system can be made that would decrease, rather than increase, the number of welfare recipients?

We would be naive to believe there could be complete agreement as to how to resolve these issues, but we are negligent if we sit back and wait for more people to be hurt before initiating actions to clarify, reduce or eliminate social problems. In a final analysis, everything that happens in society has an effect on parenting in one way or another. The current exploitation of sex through "X-rated" movies, topless dancers, and erotic magazines has an effect on parenting. So do laxity on liquor sales to minors and the increased number of traffic accidents due to carelessness, alcohol, or unsafe vehicles. Low standards in schools that fail to discourage truancy and undiscouraged use of illegal drugs on campuses affect parenting. Even the granting of amnesty to people who have destroyed property or hurled rocks at the police has a direct effect on parenting.

Cause and effect relationships are both perplexing and challenging. Would we say that feelings of insecurity are *caused* by a fear of failure, or is insecurity the *effect* of repeated failing? If the latter statement is accurate, then fear of failure is the cause of feeling insecure; if the former, we would say that fear of failure is the product of not feeling secure.

Would it be accurate to say that problems in the home are being caused by trouble in society? Or would it be more valid to say that the troubles in society are a reflection and hence the effect of problems in the home? Regardless of which came first, one thing is certain: we are having difficulties both in the home and society.

Although being a parent has never been an easy task, current troubles in our society have complicated an already difficult role. Present conditions have made anxiety—the fear of some impending danger that cannot be identified easily—a common denominator for parents. Because the conditions that exist in society are reflected in the home, and because the social problems have an impact on parents, it is important to look at some of the social issues that affect parenting.

Changes in Society

The big challenge in society today is learning to cope with the large number of changes that are taking place. Customs and practices heretofore unquestioned have been subjected to the scrutiny of a social microscope. Few have been able to pass the test of acceptability. The result of this analysis, for many people, has been dissatisfaction, discontentment, disillusionment, and disgust. For parents, the effects have been serious concern for the present, pessimism for the future, and feelings of bewilderment and helplessness.

Since neither time nor mankind stands still, growth and change must be anticipated and accommodated. Our life in the planetary age encourages change, for as man's horizons are extended, his needs are increased. Because progress results in the development of new commodities, the number of things man wants is also increased. Our society is a mixture of people who lack the basic needs of survival and people whose basic needs are satiated and who now pursue new needs. While the poor seek money for food, shelter and clothing, the non-poor seek new ways to spend their money.

Some of the changes in society have primarily affected those who have been unfairly treated by an affluent society. Other changes have improved the living conditions of most Americans. Changes have resulted in work-saving and time-saving devices and in opportunities to travel more, eat more, and enjoy more recreation. We have changed from a work-oriented culture to a work-play society in which many tolerate their work in order to experience their pleasure.

Even though not all of the changes have been well received by each member of society, the challenge to society is not caused simply by the changes themselves, but rather by the rapidity, frequency, and nature of the changes. We must be prepared to anticipate changes, but the number of recent changes and the speed with which we have been expected to accept them contribute greatly to the confusion, doubts, and fears seen in society today. The limits of man's adaptability have been strained, for it is difficult to concentrate on changes from too many directions at one time. Modern man awakens with the question, "What changes must I adjust to today?" He goes to bed with an equally disturbing question, "What can I do about the changes that I don't like?" Such questions produce anxiety, and anxiety cannot establish a stable society.

Social change is healthy when it improves the conditions in society, when it replaces something that is outmoded or impractical, when it is fair to all concerned, and when people are not hurt by it. Change is unhealthy when the motivation is simply change for its own sake, when it occurs so fast that people are neither prepared nor willing to accept the change, when it weakens or fails to improve a situation, and when the consequences of change either retard or impair emotional or intellectual growth.

Many of the changes that have taken place in our society and in some homes must be seen as unhealthy. Changes weakening law enforcement agencies and giving criminals the freedom to repeat their crimes have made city streets unsafe and crimes involving violence too common. Changes easing abortion laws and making birth control pills easily accessible have contributed to the epidemic of venereal diseases. Changes lessening the penalties for the sale, use, or possession of potentially dangerous drugs have increased the number of drug addicts and have done irreparable harm to the lives of countless numbers of adolescents who have become indifferent, hypercritical of society, and without direction for themselves. Legislative changes without attempts to educate people or prepare them for the changes have caused much of the racial tension we continue to face. Changes in the philosophy and practices of schools have created an atmosphere of student apathy and serious parental concerns. Changes increasing the pace of living, as well as the cost of living, have made it necessary for people to turn to mechanical or chemical ways of coping with themselves and society. The widespread use of alcohol, tranquilizers, mood elevators, and cigarettes indicates our dependence on artificial adjustment methods.

Changes that offer a person the freedom to which he is entitled are healthy. But changes that encourage the abuse of freedom by depriving others of their rights for freedom are not healthy. When one person's freedom to carry a pistol constitutes a threat to another person's right to live without fear of being shot, there is a need to consider changes that protect the person without the gun.

The Social Dangers of Progress

Our society demands constant striving for progress and achievement. Whereas achievement can be measured in terms of knowledge and ability, progress is more ambiguous. The term can be used to describe continuous improvement or advancement towards beneficial objectives, but there is a tendency to measure progress in terms of productivity, expansion, or the increased speed with which something can be accomplished, regardless of the impact it has on the individual. Large stores call themselves progressive when they use computers to do their billing. Yet, from the customer's point of view, computers make shopping more impersonal and errors in billing extremely difficult to correct. Highways are already dangerous, and every year nearly 60,000 people can be expected to lose their lives in highway accidents. Is it progress to have more cars on the road, to travel faster, if highways are no safer? Is the development of a new nerve gas progress? Society is adversely affected, and parenting is made more difficult, when progress is accompanied by insensitivity, exploitation, or madness. Progress must be defined in terms that are protective of the dignity and safety of the individual.

The child is adversely affected when progress creates inappropriate expectations, dangerous conditions, and questionable goals. It is progress when we can expect a child to develop his intellectual potential through a meaningful school curriculum that is supported by researched innovations in teaching, but not when a lack of structure and an overly permissive school system result in student indifference and an abuse of freedom. Developing a drug that can calm a person who is emotionally upset is progress. But, when this drug is used on pregnant women and results in deformed children, progress has dangerous side effects. Our current problems of pollution, ecology, and what to do with nuclear power have developed as a result of questionable goals that were attained in the name of progress.

Progress in child rearing practices can be shown when better health care facilities and preventative medicine produce a healthier child. It is also progress when young children can be exposed to an exciting world of learning through educational toys, television programs that focus on teaching, libraries that have books for children of all ages, and travels that make pictures in books come alive.

Man's need for progress, and the successes he has had, have provided us with the potential for doing and enjoying many things. Society is the direct recipient of man's progress, and at times, the victim. If unemployment is high because technology has made the unskilled laborer unnecessary, was it progress to develop the machine that could do the work of ten men? It can be argued that people are needed to manufacture and design the machines, but the ten men who are displaced by the machine can neither design nor manufacture it, neither can they be trained nor retrained to do it. Many of our troubles in society can be linked to the impact of progress and many people feel they have been reduced to a social security number and a zip code.

The Abuse of Liberalism

This country was founded on the principles of freedom and the need to govern itself. From our beginnings in 1776 we have grown continually because of the value we have placed on improvement and productivity. The founding fathers of this country were both independent and liberal thinkers, and both the Declaration of Independence and the Constitution attest to the fact that our forefathers did not feel bound by traditional ideas or values.

"Liberal" is defined by the American Heritage Dictionary as: "1. having, expressing or following political views that favor non-revolutionary progress and reform;" and "2. having, expressing or following views or policies that favor the freedom of individuals to act or express themselves in a manner of their own choosing." These can be beneficial traits. It was progressive thinking that shaped this nation and liberal views that continue to point us in the way of changes for the betterment of all. But, liberalism, like any philosophy or doctrine, can be distorted and abused. What started out to move our society in a forward direction now seems to be turning us around. At some point we seem to have stopped progressing and are now in danger of regressing.

There are at least three forms of liberal abuse which can affect society and ultimately the child: selfish liberalism, lax liberalism and unthinking liberalism. The selfish liberal is primarily concerned with doing those things that have a high probability of returning some personal gain. In the home, a parent may be a selfish liberal if he refrains from disciplining a child because he wants to be popular with the child. The parent may rationalize that a child has to learn things for himself, but his liberalism is selfish if based upon the need to protect his own image. The selfish liberal in society could be the political figure who proposes or supports legislation that makes him a champion of a cause, not because of a genuine feeling about the cause, but because it is a good way to gain popularity or win votes.

The lax liberal seeks to avoid or deny responsibility and justifies negligence on the basis that it teaches others to be responsible. Lax liberal parents may operate their home in a very permissive and unstructured manner. There may be no designated meal time or bed time for the children. No rules may govern how much or what kind of television programs can be watched, and no consideration may be given to the language that is used in the home, either by parents or children. The young child may be left alone while the parents are visiting neighbors and will rarely be told what to do. Such parents may try to justify their methods by saying they encourage children to become self-sufficient and independent. In reality, the parents are negligent and unwilling to devote the time and energy required to supervise the child's activities or become involved with the child. They have placed their need to be free from responsibility over the child's need for loving and caring parents.

Unthinking liberalism, the third form of liberal abuse, is seen in the person whose intentions are good, but who fails to consider the total impact of liberal decisions. By definition, liberalism seeks to maximize the individual freedoms that are guaranteed by law. But unthinking liberalism can account for repeated criminal acts when a suspected rapist is released on his own recognizance and commits another crime. In the home, unthinking liberalism could cause a parent to sanction birth control pills for a teenaged daughter whose sexual behavior suggests she will become pregnant. But, should the parental sanction encourage promiscuity that results in the daughter contracting gonorrhea, the parental failure would have been due to their inability to see the full implications of their decision.

Liberal thinking ceases to be progressive when it creates more problems than it resolves and when it encourages or condones a lower standard of values. In studying children who were designated middle-class and lower-class, McCandless[1] developed a partial list of values and made the following observations which are summarized in table form on pages 28 and 29.

Many of the values represented by the lower-class population are becoming popular in today's society. When parents who call themselves liberal encourage or permit their children to adopt these practices, they distort the principles of liberalism and by so doing lower the standard of our society. Because of the abuse of liberalism there has been a rejection of traditional values and ideas which have helped our society improve. Many adolescents who come from middle-class homes have adopted lower-class standards. Parents who have abused liberalism have permitted this to happen. The reluctance to provide children with structure and to establish and enforce standards has brought about an intolerance for parental values and a disrespect for parental authority.

This kind of liberalism, both in the home and in society, has created conditions in which offenses are pushed aside or almost ignored. Both the child in the home and the adult in society has been able to exceed the limits, for without respect for controls it is safe to disregard the feelings of others in order to maximize personal pleasure. The child expects his parents to conform to his standards, and many parents have been all too willing to comply, with no better reason than a desire for peace at any price.

Many parents envy the freedom their children have and because they have allowed the child to have so much freedom, feel they have been better parents than their own parents were. They have taken the position that they should not allow their values to influence their children, for they feel the child should be free to make his own decisions. But, freedom that is given to a child too early fails to protect him from his own impulses, impulses that can cause serious problems later in the child's life. Parents who have allowed the ten-year-old child to have the freedom to decide when it is time to go to bed may find it impossible to tell him to be home by midnight when he is fourteen and has begun to socialize.

There are parents who do nothing to discourage their children from insulting or directing obscenities at them. Even when the parents are not guilty of initiating the verbal abuse, they reason that words are harmless and do nothing more than ask the child to

---

[1]McCandless, B. R., *Children, Behavior and Development.* New York. Holt, Rinehart, and Winston. 1967.

stop using unacceptable language. What they do not comprehend is that they are sanctioning disrespect and should not be surprised when the child continues to be insulting and disrespectful to people other than parents. Parents who have abused liberalism have condoned violations of society's moral code by rationalizing that it doesn't hurt a child to learn things the hard way. But, the child may end up paying a severe price for the parents' liberal views.

It has become increasingly difficult for parents who do not have liberal views about parenting to hold to their own position. Assuming they can withstand the pressures from their child, they must also contend with the problems that develop because of pressure from other parents. The less liberal parents run the risk of isolating their children and making them vulnerable to insults and abuse from their peers. Because the child naturally seeks acceptance from his peers, and since group pressure is often more meaningful for the child than parental pressure, the child whose parents are less liberal is caught in the middle. He is expected to obey his parents, and he wants to conform to his peer group. Parents see the dilemma this causes, and many have abandoned their efforts to control their children and have lowered their standards.

Parenting in our society today demands thinking and planning that goes beyond day-to-day maintenance. It is not sufficient for the father to simply bring home the money to buy the family essentials, or for mother to see that the house is clean and that there is food on the table. Parenting today expands on the traditional essentials of food, shelter, and clothing, and includes equipping the child with the stamina and direction needed to survive in and cope with society. In order to counteract the trend to abuse liberalism, parents must have more clearly defined values and goals, more insights into the impact of society, and more determination not to yield to forces that will not produce a more stable child. Certainly, the parent of today is aware that he cannot rear his child in a vacuum, devoid of external influences. For this reason, it is incumbent on parents to place great emphasis on the early value training the child receives. In this way, the child will be in a better position to evaluate differences between what he has been taught and what he is exposed to in society.

The decision that parents must make is, in reality, no decision at all, for they must answer the question, "Do we assume responsibility for rearing our children, or do we allow others to determine their morality and direction?" Because of changes in our society, parents who used to hear their child ask, "Why can't I use the

Differences Between Middle-Class and Lower-Class Values in Children

Value Considered	Middle-Class Attitude	Lower-Class Attitude
Religion	Belief in God, frequent church attendance.	Less frequent church attendance.
Personal cleanliness	Emphasis on cleanliness of clothes, body, teeth, hair and fingernails.	Much less emphasis.
Thrift	Belief in thrift, savings, planning, punctual payments. Possessions are status and represent security.	There is no money to save. No comprehension of thrift or savings. "Grab while the grabbing is good."
Controls	Intellect should preceed emotion. Reason and common sense are important.	No comprehension of reason. Reacts with emotion instead of intellect. Stress on action for survival.
Expression of strong emotions	Restraint and an attempt to avoid. "People should live peacefully and chastely together."	No restraint. Freedom to express desires in aggressive ways. Open aggression can confer status with peers.
Expression of aggression	Verbal expression is socially acceptable. Physical aggression is rare. May express aggression in subtle ways such as in driving a car, but poor manners in driving are frowned upon.	No restraint. Verbal expression of aggression not as effective as physical means.

Sex	Sexual restraint. Many taboos.	No repression of sexual impulses. Few taboos. Early exposure and experience.
Language	Clean and correct. Swearing not condoned, especially in front of children. Proper language used between the sexes.	Not concerned with bad language, or grammar. Communication more important than form.
Use of alcohol	Restraint and temperance. Firmer for women.	No restraint. Early exposure to alcohol and parents who drink excessively. This often leads to subsequent open sexuality and violence.
Honesty	Professed belief in honesty, even though it is not always practiced.	Professed belief. Values similar to middle-class.
Work attitude	Belief that hard work and self-discipline bring about success. Delay of immediate impulses for later and bigger goals.	No reason to believe that hard work will produce success. Their work is regarded as *hard work*.
Doing one's duty	Seen as a virtue. Should live up to expectations. Hard work is good for you.	No virtue in working hard or to capacity. No incentive to do your duty.
Learning	Learning for learning's sake. School a way to get ahead. College is a virtue, despite any practical use of it. A school drop-out is disgraceful. Girls need education. Too much learning is viewed with suspicion.	Seeks more immediate pleasure than that obtained through studying. Less a virtue, and less value placed on school attendance.

car Saturday night? Bob's parents let him use their car." may now hear, "Why can't I smoke dope? Bob does, and his parents know it!" Parents today must think through their position carefully and decide what they feel is the best thing for their child.

Liberalism is not the problem, but the abuse of it is. By its very nature, liberalism seeks progress and reform. It is obvious that many conditions in society are in need of both progress and reform. Liberal parents give their child the choice of determining when he prefers to do his homework. Lax liberal and unthinking liberal parents leave the entire matter of homework up to the child. Selfish liberal parents do likewise, because it is easier on them. They say that school work is the child's responsibility, and he will have to pay the price for failure. But, if failure should result, they typically berate and belittle the child for being irresponsible. These parents assume that the child knows what is best for him and give the child the freedom to do whatever he wants. They force a child to be responsible for himself even though he is not mature enough to assume this responsibility. The child who has been encouraged to make major decisions for himself regardless of their appropriateness will be prepared to tell his parents, "It's my life, and if I want to hurt myself by dropping out of school and leaving home, it is my decision." When the child makes that statement, it is probably too late for his parents to stop him.

Tragically, many schools are adopting the same practices. The child is offered choices beyond his maturity and knowledge as to what is best for him. He is given the freedom to take courses that *he thinks* are best for him. He is not bound by rules or restrictions, for he knows that the authority of the school can be questioned. Without the authority to enforce standards, schools are unable to accomplish their basic responsibility; namely, to teach children. Many high school students are indifferent to school and many feel that schools have little to offer them.

A large number of college students are apathetic and resentful of academic policies. Student leaders are angry, bitter, and defensive and look upon the administration as their enemy. College students have been allowed to intimidate university presidents, deans of colleges, and members of the faculty. They have demonstrated that they can be violent, destructive, and powerful. Their success is due, in part, to the willingness of administrators and professors to yield to the pressure of individuals or groups who are prepared to threaten and make a lot of noise in order to get their own way. The student makes a demand, and the university is afraid of what will happen if it is not met. The same is happening in junior and senior high schools.

The same trend has made it safe for the rebel in society to call a policeman a "pig," knowing the policeman can do nothing about it. However, the policeman knows that if he returns the insult he will be reprimanded and could even face a charge of inciting a riot. The abuse of liberalism enables a person to use a deprived or underprivileged life as an excuse for violence, placing the blame on society instead of himself. Needless to say, this trend has not deterred the criminal and could even encourage him.

There is much that is known about why people become anti-social, why they turn to alcohol, drugs, and promiscuity. Liberal thinking can free us to develop more effective ways of dealing with these and other problems, but the abuse of liberalism perpetuates and increases the troubles within our society.

Emphasis on the Negative

Another trouble in society is the tendency to view the "establishment" in a one-sided and narrow way. Much criticism is leveled at society for its weaknesses, but little praise is offered for its strengths. Many people talk as if there is nothing good about our society. They want to see it destroyed or completely overhauled. They dwell on injustices and ignore virtues; they focus on prejudice and overlook attempts to correct the problem; they point out deficiencies and negate progress. The negative thinker cannot allow himself to see things objectively, for seeing something good challenges his negative views. In order to defend his position, the negative thinker must deny and distort the positive elements in society.

Unfortunately, many people have learned distorted views of society. Their pessimism fails to take into account the many improvements that have been made. A more objective outlook would recognize that we are far from a Utopian society and we are frustrated because it has taken us so long to resolve a number of our social ills. However, we can feel proud of many constructive accomplishments and feel encouraged by our continued willingness to seek social improvements.

One way to overcome the tendency to dwell on the negative aspects of society is to focus more on positive things. It is not necessary to destroy society in order to improve upon it. It is possible to build on existing strengths and remove current weaknesses. It will take time, cooperation, and careful planning. Society's image is not a good one, and there is no public relations firm that can be hired to boost its image by promising an improvement in services. Parents can help by talking positively about society to their children when there is reason to do so; social and civic groups can help by instituting pride in the community through campaigns that advertise positive actions that improve conditions for people. Reinstating patriotism as a meaningful value can help to unite people and give them common goals and a spirit of brotherhood. The source that offers the potential for the greatest impact on society's image is the news and entertainment media, for it has the capability of influencing all who are exposed to it.

Impact of the News and Entertainment Media

The medium having the greatest influence on society is television. More people watch television than read newspapers and magazines or listen to radio. What is shown on television—whether it be news, entertainment, or commercial advertisement—has an impact on the thinking and behavior of the viewer. For this reason, it is important that all forms of news and entertainment be more aware of their effect on society. This holds true not only for the television industry, but also the newspapers, magazines, motion picture studios, radio and commercial advertisers who are able to exert a significant influence on society.

A question that can be asked is, "Have the news and entertainment media done all they can do to improve the conditions in society?" A more controversial question is, "Have the news and entertainment media contributed to the problems in society?" A riot can command front page headlines; the discovery of a vaccine gets less coverage. Motion pictures that depict violence get awards and will be seen by millions of people; films that deal with human achievements just about break even at the box office. For some reason, what we have come to expect as news is colored by shock, tragedy, disappointment, or violence. And yet, the viewer has come to accept these disasters with a momentary gasp followed by the feeling of, "So what else is new?" The announcer says, "Fifty thousand people have been left homeless by a tornado that has killed hundreds and injured thousands. And now, this important message from our sponsor."

The news media have done a better job of telling us who our villains are than they have of informing us of our heroes. More should be written and said about the nice things that happen in society so that a person can get recognition without committing a crime or doing something antisocial. Notoriety has become a stepping stone to success. We look for it in the news because we expect it to be there. In their zeal for delivering the news, newsmen have given publicity to those who seek it to further selfish and antisocial causes. By giving a riot full camera coverage, the news media have encouraged the curious and thrill seekers to swell the ranks of the demonstrators. Frequently, this has resulted in injury and death to people and extensive damage to property. Few people would know of a proposed demonstration that might predictably become a riot unless it was publicized. Revolutionary leaders can command press conferences to stir up their followers as well as others who are "looking for some action." Violent demonstrations that have resulted in tragedies might have been averted if the news media had used discretion in their coverage.

When antisocial groups or revolutionary leaders become heroes or models for children, it creates problems for parents. Parents are troubled if children see that crime is tolerated, that destroying property is not punished, that arrests for violence in demonstrations do not hold up in court, that throwing rocks and bottles at police is no more punishable than throwing insults and obscenities at them. The position of the news media has seemed to be, "look, folks, we're just here to report the news. If people are killed in a 'peaceful' demonstration, or if a building is blown up, we'll cover the story so thoroughly that you'll think you were there." The occasional editorial that deplores the event or tries to place the blame on someone is not sufficient to offset the spectacular coverage that makes destructiveness exciting.

The free press in this country is essential. Without it, we become subjects in a totalitarian state. No attempt should be made to curb the freedom of the press, but the press must become more aware of its role in contributing to social problems. It must take responsibility for determining what priorities should be given to news stories. Will the coverage increase or decrease the probability of a reoccurrence?

Who pays the price for making an event a "news happening?" It would be interesting to speculate on the effects of low-key coverage for crimes and violence. How many fewer sky-jacking incidents might there have been had not the details of the successful ones been so well publicized? Is it really important for the public to know how the police tricked the sky-jackers into getting captured? How many campus riots would there have been had not the first riot received so much attention in the news? How many people get dangerous ideas that are later put into action because of what they see and read about? Would it be better for all concerned if assassins and would-be assassins did not get so much attention in the news? Would it help the accused to get a fair trial if the news did not reveal so much? Justice is delayed and even prevented when it can be shown that publicity has resulted in biasing the jury, preventing a fair trial. Exploiting the criminal or the criminal act does not protect society, but encourages more crime.

The news media are charged with the responsibility of reporting the news and of keeping the public informed. They must consider how the news is reported and how it can be dangerous to the public. Because we have come to expect the shocking headline, we are anxious when a television program is interrupted to bring a news bulletin. We might even become angry if a television program during prime time was interrupted to bring news that a major breakthrough had occurred in the treatment of cancer. The news media have trained us to expect the worst, for much of what is offered as news is an emphasis on the negative. This trend can be reversed.

Even the entertainment media directed at children have focused on antisocial and aggressive behavior. The main theme of most "harmless" cartoons for children is violence. Older children watch ingenious crooks who are foiled by overlooking one detail, which the child has now learned, and children see plots which arouse and excite them into sleepless nights and aggressive behavior. Children identify with and emulate the behavior of the people they see on television programs. Many of the distorted views that young people have about our society began with their early impressions of what television says happens in everyday life. Many impressionable children have learned antisocial behavior from television.

Motion picture and television producers have learned that the average American enjoys seeing and reading about violence and sex. In giving the American public what it wants, instead of what would be better for them, they are saying, in effect, let the viewer beware. Television can attract the big sponsor and motion pictures can attract the big gate by capitalizing on the public's interest. However, this dangerous policy offers no protection for the many who may be harmed by the effects of an exposure to negative and unacceptable social behavior: the children, adolescents and adults whose lives and values may be seriously changed by what they see or read, and all children with a developing value system that does not differentiate fiction from reality or right from wrong.

The attractiveness of behavior that is not socially acceptable may indicate an underlying hostility or aggressiveness that is common in man. The news and entertainment media can stimulate this aspect or they can play it down. Parenting is affected by the choice of the news media, for they teach, and we are influenced by what we read, see, and listen to. It is no credit to the entertainment media when a thief says his idea came from a program or movie he saw.

Parents can only hope that the people who publish magazines and newspapers, and those people who are responsible for radio and television programming consider the importance of their positions. They are in a key position to influence and educate millions of people and to stimulate constructive thinking. The news and entertainment media can have a positive impact on society and still sell the sponsor's product. If they accept their responsibility to have a beneficial impact, they must examine the role they play in creating some of the problems which affect children and parents.

Law Enforcement

Few agencies have experienced such strong opposition and attack as law enforcement has in the past ten years. The problem is compounded because serious conflicts have developed within the law enforcement agencies. Police are frustrated when they make an on-the-scene arrest only to see the case thrown out of court on a technicality. The public is angry at this too, for it returns a criminal to the streets with the confidence to try again. Judges are frustrated because they have a large backlog of cases to be tried. The public view of our system of justice is that it is too lenient on the violent criminal and too willing to dismiss a case because of legal technicalities. When crimes are committed by persons who are free on bond pending an appeal of a conviction, or by persons who are on parole, respect for the present system of justice dwindles. Poor conditions inside prisons bring about a feeling of ambivalence; on one hand the public wants the criminal removed for the protection of society; but, knowing that our penal system angers more than rehabilitates, the public is reluctant to put someone into jail.

The increase of violent crimes in our society cannot be attributed to social factors alone. The increase must be viewed, in part, as a flaunting of our system of justice by the criminal who has reason to feel that he will be more likely to succeed than to pay a price if he gets caught. Increased crime in our cities has made parents worry about the safety of their children. Muggings and rapes that go unsolved or unpunished add to parental concerns.

As problems with law enforcement agencies affect parents, they serve to weaken parental authority and remove a source of help for both parents and children. A stronger law enforcement system could give parents help in dealing with such problems as drugs, dropouts, and disobedience.

Parents know there are laws regarding the sale, use, or possession of illegal drugs. When they cannot discourage their child from using drugs, they hope that law enforcement agencies will. Parents do not know what to do when they discover a bottle of strange pills in their child's room, or when they come across an envelope that contains something that looks like it could be marijuana. They want to report it to someone, but they don't want to get their child in trouble. They want help for their child, but they fear punishment. A closer contact with law enforcement agencies might alleviate this problem.

The most logical way to discourage the use of illegal drugs is to eliminate their source. However, for a reason that is unclear, we seem to be prepared to say that this can no longer be accomplished. The feeling on the part of some officials and leaders is that since we cannot control the use and distribution of an illegal drug, such as marijuana, we might as well make it legal. After all, they point out, there is no research that says that it is a dangerous drug. Of course, there is also no research that says that it is a beneficial drug. As a matter of fact, there is no long-term research that can make any definitive statement about the effects from frequent use of marijuana.

The logic that says, "if you can't control it, legalize it," is very hazy. It admits defeat in a situation without having made a strong effort to overcome it. Colleges and high schools are locations where much illegal drug traffic takes place. In most schools throughout the country, a student who knows the "right" person can buy almost any known illegal drug. Yet, attempts to prevent or even reduce the sale, use, or possession of illegal drugs in schools are minimal. Many schools will admit to having some drug traffic, but deny that it is a problem. Young people attend rock concerts and flagrantly get "stoned" in front of police who just watch. The police, fearful of starting a riot, make few arrests. They have been rendered helpless by ineffective law enforcement practices.

When parents, who are helpless to control their child's illegal drug usage, turn to law enforcement agencies, who seem helpless to control illegal drug usage, the child is free to continue what he has been doing. Indecisiveness and confusion as to what the laws should be perpetuate the problem. It shouldn't be too difficult to develop drug laws that are just and clearly defined. Nor should it be difficult to deal with drug problems in a consistent manner.

Juvenile authorities who tend to overlook first offenses should examine their thinking to see how overlooking an offense can prevent a reoccurrence of the offense. For many children, the first offense is the last; others develop into chronic offenders. There are predictors that can determine into which category a child will fall. Law enforcement agencies, including the police, the judges, the probation officers, and juvenile court workers have a lot of decisions to make and actions to take if they are to help parents with their problem children.

Law enforcement agencies can strengthen their stand on home and school drop-outs. Parents cannot force their children to attend school and must rely upon the schools to enforce truancy laws. If the school passes the buck to the juvenile authorities, and no one takes any action the child is free to drop out of school. He is also free to drop out of his home, for usually a runaway child is just returned to the home if he is found. Juvenile agencies should be able to exert some pressure on the child to stay home, in addition to making an attempt to understand what the home problem is and what steps can be taken to improve the parent-child relationship.

Parents of adolescents are frequently disturbed by their child's complete disobedience and refusal to accept their controls. Although juvenile law enforcement facilities cannot be expected to make a child obey his parents, they can help parents by enforcing regulations that govern curfews, loitering, sale of alcohol to minors, and illegal drug traffic. They can also help parents with the unmanageable child by initiating programs directed at specific offenses. Just as there are traffic schools for drivers who are unsafe, there could be drug schools, shoplifting schools, alcoholic schools and a variety of other types of programs for juvenile offenders. It is unfortunate when parents must wait for their child to get into serious trouble before they can get help in improving a potentially bad situation. When the prevention of a problem is not possible, there should be ways to treat the problem before it becomes untreatable. Frequently, this could involve a referral to local community mental health facilities, where the parents and child could be encouraged to work out the problem together.

Our Future Problem

There are many problems that must be resolved in society today. They will not resolve themselves, nor will the solutions come about without additional changes. The future problems could be related to our continued growth and increased numbers. Our population has more than doubled in the past 50 years. One way to describe the difference between society today and conditions fifty years ago would be to say that we have more of everything today. Because we have more people, we have more sickness, more buildings, more crime, more poverty, and in general, more problems. We cannot educate our children today the way we did when there were fewer children. We cannot operate our businesses today the way we did when there were fewer customers. And, we cannot be the kind of parents our parents were because we must cope with more changes, which have come about because there are more people.

Changes in society can be expected as our population increases. Whether they will improve conditions or add to the troubles in society remains to be seen. One thing is certain, regardless of what the changes are, they will have an impact on parenting.

- 3 -

Why Things Go Wrong

Parents from any generation in the past have had problems with their children, although the specific concerns have changed with the times. At one time the parental worry about the child centered around the child's health and the fear of incurable diseases. Before medical technology reached its current level of competency, infant mortality and death of the mother at childbirth were common problems. In 1915 there were 728 maternal deaths for every 100,000 live births. This figure decreased to 207 deaths per 100,000 live births in 1945, and in 1968 the number of maternal deaths due to childbirth was 24.5 per 100,000[1]. The death rate from measles was 6 for every 100,000 people in 1933, and less than 1 per 100,000 people in 1962[2]. Little attention was given to the child's behavior; children were thought of as miniature adults and were both dressed and treated accordingly. Young children were required to work in "sweat shops." In 1831, seven per cent of the cotton mill workers along the Atlantic seaboard were children under the age of 12. It is estimated that in the 1830s, there were at least one million children from 6 to 15 years of age who were not attending schools.

---

[1]Vital Statistics of the United States. Vols. I and II.
[2]Vital Statistics Rates in the U.S. 1940-1960. Grove, R. and Hetzel, A., US Dept. of HEW. Washington D.C. 1968.

As cause for concern about the health and welfare of the child has diminished, concern about the child's behavior has increased.

This is not to say that behavior problems with children are anything new. Had there been child psychologists in Biblical times, we could well imagine Adam and Eve telling one, "We've just got to do something about Cain's temper! One of these days it's going to get him in real trouble." It is interesting to note that in the story of Cain and his brother Abel, there is no mention of what their parents did in rearing them which could have caused a son to become so jealous and hostile that he murdered his brother. Adam and Eve are blamed for one sin, but nothing is said of their role as negligent parents who failed to recognize or do anything about the sibling rivalry that undoubtedly existed.

It is only recently that parents have been blamed or held responsible for what their children have done. In some ways, the blame is only buck-passing, for parents could blame their parents, who in turn could blame their parents, back to Adam and Eve. And yet, there is not sufficient justification for placing the entire blame on parents for what a child does or becomes. Parents can never represent the totality of the child's contacts or influences. Neither can we exempt parents altogether from the responsibility for the outcome of their parenting. It is not an either-or situation in which you either blame parents or you don't, but one in which you decide to what degree parents are responsible for the outcome of the child.

The Explanation of Behavior

Personality theorists have sought answers to questions surrounding the development of personality. What has emerged from their research has been a number of different views concerning the nature of man and the factors that are responsible for the development of his personality. Sigmund Freud was the first to emphasize developmental stages of personality. For Freud, the behavior of an individual was explained on the basis of learning effective ways to reduce tension. He stressed the importance of early experiences without discounting the influence of heredity. *How* learning takes place has not been agreed upon by all personality theorists, nor has there been universal acceptance of the importance of heredity, the existence of an unconscious, the impact social forces exert on an individual, or whether it is best to study a single trait of a large sampling of people or a number of traits in one individual.

There is agreement that behavior can be explained as a function of heredity and environment. These two causes of behavior have been debated extensively in terms of their relative importance in explaining human actions. Proponents of heredity as the explanation for behavior argue that chromosomes and genes explain traits and temperament. Environmentalists say that behavior is learned through exposure and experience. Since neither group has been successful in producing the precise research to satisfy the other, an honorable compromise has been agreed upon; both heredity and environment are major determinants of behavior. Which force dominates, whether it is heredity or the environment which affects personality most, is a subject that is more easily debated than researched.

There is reason to feel that the infant's early behavior is influenced by his genetic endowment. Until the infant can interact with people or objects in his environment, his needs are determined by physiological drives for nourishment, sleep, and elimination of bodily wastes. And yet, long before the infant is able to interact with his environment, he is aware of it. He is born into an environment that is profoundly different from that he experienced as a fetus. The conditions inside the uterus are dark, warm, and wet. At the moment of birth the neonate experiences a lighter, colder, and dryer place. Awareness of environment is immediate; interaction with environment comes later.

Within hours after birth the newborn begins to learn. Whereas nourishment came automatically inside of the mother, now the infant has to do something to make his needs known. Schedules of feeding and bathing teach the infant that he can expect to be disturbed from time to time. Physical discomforts teach him that things are not the same as they were in utero.

Gradually, the infant becomes aware of his environment and begins to respond to the demands and pressures that are placed upon him. By the time he is 18 months old, he is walking well and can actively explore the world around him. His language is developing and, even though he cannot express himself adequately, he is beginning to comprehend the meaning of the language of others. He has heard the words, "No, No," and is prepared to test the limits within a given situation. The environment begins to exert the major influence on a child when he is required to interact with it, and when his responses can be linked to specific environmental practices.

The child is not influenced by a single environment. Although the home is the initial—and therefore the most important—environment, the child will be influenced by many factors outside the home, which can neither be predicted nor controlled with any assurance. He will react to a composite of the environments to which he is exposed. The social environment begins when he expands his world to include people and situations outside the family. It includes the initial contacts with neighbors, playmates, and other people with whom the child interacts. It expands to take in experiences in restaurants, department stores, playgrounds, or places the child visits. This early social environment is an important one, for the child starts to realize that there is another world in addition to the one that he experiences in the home. The child begins to learn about himself by comparing himself to others. He soon learns that he is not as adequate as older children, or possibly even other children his own age. He strives to overcome feelings of inadequacy. He becomes eager to test out newly acquired skills and to identify himself as an individual who is capable of doing things that others can do.

The child's early social environment is somewhat private, for it contains a minimal amount of interaction with others and is predominantely self-centered. Soon, another social environment opens up to him, and he begins to become a part of a group of children his own age. Initially through contacts with neighborhood playmates and later from attendance in pre-school classes, the child begins to engage in group experiences. His need to have one or more friends illustrates the impact of his social environment in which the child seeks to both identify and interact with others. As he gets older, he seeks an even closer identity with peers. He may show this by wanting to dress like his friends, or joining a club or team.

Each group in which the child is active, and each situation in which the child is exposed to people, offers an opportunity for social interaction and will influence the development of his personality and behavior. The reaction the child receives from these social situations and the way he views his adequacy in socialization will have an impact on the child's future behavior.

And yet, because he is a unique individual, the unpredictable can occur. All of the child's behavior cannot be traced to his parental or social environments, nor is all behavior predictable. It cannot be said that a common stimulus will bring about a similar response from all who are exposed to it. Ten people who are exposed to the same stimulus, such as a snake, may respond in several different ways. Some may run from the snake, others may faint from the sight of it, and still others may approach the snake with curiosity. The response will be determined by the person's past experience or attitude toward the stimulus. It may also come about because of the individual's uniqueness. Although *most* children who rebel against their parental environment may do so because of the parenting they have received, not *all* children who rebel do so because of the parenting. The individual must assume some responsibility for his own behavior on the basis of exclusive traits which give the person a distinct and individualized personality.

The Uniqueness Factor

One of the reasons that it is difficult to predict behavior is individual differences. An individual is the product of his heredity and environment, but he is also influenced by the unique interaction of heredity with the environment. Our personality reflects the impact of our experiences and since two people cannot have identical experiences, differences are evident even between identical twins who share the same inheritance. Parents are quick to notice personality differences between their children. They are often at a loss to explain these differences, for they make the assumption that they have reared each child in a similar manner. They look to themselves as the explanation why two of their children may be different. Birth order and sex differences could offer a partial explanation, for parents are aware that their response to the first born is not the same as it was to the second born. Likewise, they may have different feelings about little boys and little girls. A parent may have a preference for one sex, which could account for one child being very responsive to the parent while a child of the opposite sex is less responsive to the same parent.

Differences can also be explained on the basis of individual uniqueness. Uniqueness is the pattern of personality traits that are identified with an individual. The sound of a person's voice, his handwriting, his way of walking and his fingerprints are evidence of uniqueness. Uniqueness could explain why some children show less curiosity than others, why some children become active participants while others remain passive witnesses, why children have certain talents and interests, despite what they have observed in their parents or experienced in their environment. Because of individual uniqueness, or the life style of a person, people respond in different ways to the same set of circumstances. Some people worry more than others. Some people are content with what they have; others constantly seek more. Some youngsters are naturally more competitive than other youngsters. Some children can draw and others cannot. Although learning and experiences may explain these differences, individual uniqueness could also be a major determinant as to why personality traits develop as they do.

Every individual is born with different amounts of both physical (bodily) energy and psychic (mental) energy. Each individual possesses a different amount of this energy potential. A person is born with only a given amount of energy, although resting the body and physiological processes involving the endocrine system can enhance the energy system in an emergency. One of the critical variables that explains uniqueness is the way in which the individual utilizes and deploys his energy. A person could almost totally deplete his physical energy system by overexercising his body. There would then only be a small amount of energy available for any other task.

Thinking, remembering, learning, and deciding are mental tasks that utilize psychic energy. Personal problems involving conflicts, frustrations, pressures, and anxieties also require an expenditure of psychic energy. The more serious a problem is for the individual and the more problems a person has, the more psychic energy he will need. Each mental process requires some output of energy. The individual determines how much energy will be expended according to the importance he gives to the situation. For example, one person may utilize a great deal of mental energy in deciding on the color to paint the kitchen, whereas another may use very little mental energy in making the same decision. One parent may panic if his child gets a failing grade in school, another parent may react to the failing grade with indifference. The difference in responses can be due to individual uniqueness in the way psychic energy is deployed.

It is important to learn to deploy psychic energy in accordance with the realistic needs of a situation. Energy can be wasted, by expending more than is needed, and it can be held captive, as in the case of energy that is being utilized for an unsolvable problem. Prolonged mourning is an example of energy held captive. If the amount of psychic energy becomes seriously depleted, the individual finds it difficult to function and efficiency is affected. He begins to feel mentally exhausted, tense or anxious, and depressed. This can occur if all of the psychic energy is deployed into one problem, as in the case of an obsession, or when worries are excessive and no relief is in sight. Solving the problem returns the deployed energy back into the basic system and restores the person's supply of psychic energy that is available for new problems or mental tasks as they arise. Effective problem solving and successful completion of a task are two vital ways to keep the psychic energy system functioning well.

The potential power of uniqueness cannot be overlooked. Each child uses his individual blend of psychic energy in his own unique way. This can explain why some children are defeated by their environment, while others have been able to rise above their environmental influences. Some youngsters can cope with the stresses of daily living, others cannot. Many problems that a child has relate to his uniqueness and are only indirectly traceable to the parenting he has received.

Parental behaviors and training practices can encourage or discourage the development of uniqueness in their child. Parents encourage uniqueness when they allow the child the freedom to express individuality. They discourage uniqueness when they insist upon rigid and unyielding standards of conformity.

Case Illustration Number 1

An instance in which uniqueness was discouraged can be seen in the following case illustration.

Mr. and Mrs. S. were intelligent and well-educated adults who looked forward to being parents. Each had definite ideas as to how they would rear their children, and they were generally in agreement on parental practices. Their definite ideas were based on their determination to develop a child who would conform to their standards and measure up to their expectations. The first child was a boy.

They insisted on complete obedience from little Roger. Although they wanted him to eventually become independent and be able to demonstrate good judgment, their approach did not encourage early choices, decisions, or problem-solving practices. The rationale for their highly structured approach was that until Roger had learned enough from them they felt he could not be expected to know right from wrong. Consequently, the parents did most of Roger's thinking for him. The schedule he was placed on as an infant was strict and allowed for very little deviation. Mrs. S. weaned him from a bottle at ten months and initiated toilet training at one year. As the parents recalled, giving up the bottle was not difficult for Roger, but toilet training was slow and created a problem for both the parents and Roger. At the age of six Roger still had accidents at night with some frequency.

As a toddler, Roger was discouraged from expressing his needs to be autonomous and independent by parental punishments and reprimands. His parents demanded that he adjust to their ways and reasoned that since Roger showed signs of being a bright child, there was no reason why he could not learn to think things through logically and acquire early self-control.

The parents were distressed by his preschool and kindergarten performance. They were also unhappy over his behavior in the first grade. Roger was described by all of his teachers as over-controlled, inhibited, and fearful of making an error. These teachers' statements resulted in parental pressure on Roger to be more spontaneous, outgoing, and unafraid. His parents did not suggest changes but rather commanded them. They frequently referred to his brightness in order to impress upon Roger what he *could* do, and then insulted his intelligence when he did not perform according to their expectations.

When Roger attempted to test parental limits by acting in a way that was typical for children his age, the parents said, "Shame on you, you're acting like a baby!" On several occasions, Mrs. S. lost her temper and called him stupid. She then felt guilty and made Roger feel guilty, as well, for making her so upset with him.

Despite the fact that his parents were usually warm and loving to him, Roger was learning to fear their critical comments since he was trying so hard to please them. Because he worried so much about success, he usually failed. Roger was learning that acting impulsively or spontaneously resulted in being scolded, that his opinions and judgments were not considered to be important—since his parents disregarded or even ridiculed them—and that his parents' goal for him was perfection. In a final analysis, he was learning that it was safer to control individuality than to express it.

The development of uniqueness in a child should be encouraged by the parents. It does not come about if the parents simply show approval for everything the child does. It develops because the parents are aware that the child possesses the quality of uniqueness and they are careful not to stifle this quality or prevent it from expressing itself. The child must be encouraged to make decisions that involve making judgments. When these decisions do not endanger the safety or well-being of the child, they can only have positive effects on the child. Allowing a young child to make a choice between two cereals at breakfast, or a choice between two garments to wear, will give the child confidence in himself, for he is being given the freedom to act according to personal preference, and he is learning early problem solving.

Because he has been free to make decisions that concern his welfare, the child will begin to feel important and will acquire a positive image of himself. Self-confidence and self-esteem are outgrowths of good feelings about one's ability to cope with life situations.

Decisions that involve training habits, health considerations, and general welfare of the child should be made by the parents. Even so, certain parental decisions can be handled in such a way that the child feels some responsibility for having made them.

For example, the parents are the ones who decide on the bedtime for the young child. But, if special guests are coming for dinner, and the 6-year-old child wants to stay up several hours past his normal bedtime for the occasion, he could be asked to decide whether he wants to take a nap in the afternoon or go to bed at his regular time. The child is aware that his parents have determined the amount of sleep he needs, but he is also aware that he has some say about when he gets his sleep. This encourages a child to feel that he can have the opportunity to make choices according to personal feelings and momentary needs.

The Intellectual Factor

Personality can be affected by factors that are beyond the control of the individual. Neurological impairments or handicaps that have an organic or physiological cause have an influence on behavior. Intellectual ability is another explanation for personality. What is referred to as intelligence is responsible for unique responses and individual traits. Both "how much" intelligence a person has and "what kind" of intelligence a person possesses will determine what a person does. The quantitative amount of intelligence, or the "how much" factor, can be measured by standardized intelligence tests. Basically, these tests compare one child with a large number of children of similar age. The qualitative differences in intelligence are more difficult to assess.

The child who scores high on achievement or intelligence tests, or the adult who uses a high level of intelligence in his everyday work, could be lacking in what is called "common sense." Even though such a person would be able to store and utilize technical information in carrying out complex tasks, he could be lacking in the ability to make rational personal judgments. A man might be able to develop a scientific process that facilitates interplanetary travel, yet allow himself to be "taken" by an honest-looking, high-powered salesman selling stock in an nonexistent oil field. A person could be competent to argue a case in front of the Supreme Court, using great intellectual ability in organizing research and presenting logical arguments based upon a careful interpretation of the law, yet be unable to assemble a toy hobby-horse for his four-year-old son. An adolescent may be able to score at the 99th percentile on an English or math achievement test, yet be unable to follow a road map to a new beach. Qualitative intelligence does not necessarily match up with quantitative ability.

It is possible to make an assessment of certain qualitative abilities. School grades reflect this when they show that a child does better in arithmetic than history. Test scores reveal specific areas of ability if they show that a person has higher scores in mechanical reasoning than in spatial relationships. But there is no valid way of measuring common sense or the ability to make an appropriate judgment. Likewise, there is no way of assuring that a person will be able to see things realistically, or interpret things accurately. We could assume that the individual with a greater amount of intelligence would have a greater facility to cope with problems of daily living. However, this need not be the case. As a matter of fact, it can work in the opposite way. Extremely bright people can have problems in social interactions that the person with average intelligence does not experience. For one reason, there are fewer people with whom the extremely bright person can relate to on his own level. Also, the very bright person may put undue pressure on himself because he expects more from himself. And, extreme brightness does not always imply well-rounded or general brightness; it can mean brightness in a single area.

The amount and kind of intelligence a person has can be added to a list of factors which explain behavior. Although related to heredity and nurtured by environment, intellectual uniqueness cannot be fully explained.

Adaptive Behavior

There is a significant relationship between feelings of personal satisfaction, or what might be called happiness, and the ability to cope with life situations comfortably. Because we live in a culture that is socially oriented, interpersonal relationships are important. The individual who is unable to adapt to his environment or be comfortable in handling the stresses of everyday life will experience less personal satisfaction. Because we are exposed to frequent changes in routines and since things will not always go our way, it is necessary to learn appropriate adjustment techniques. Adaptive behavior is the ability to accommodate stress—what a person does when goals are thwarted or when things do not happen according to personal expectations. The goals of adaptive behavior are to reduce anxiety, resolve conflicts, and overcome frustration.

An inability to cope with the stresses of daily living can be due to physical or intellectual causes. Poor health or a physical disability can be reasons for a person to be lacking in the stamina to deal effectively with problems, and the inability to intellectually comprehend what is involved in a given situation can make it difficult to cope with stress. However, a poor self-concept combined with faulty habits and inappropriate patterns of behavior are the usual causes of social ineptness and inadequate problem-solving ability. In both the child and adult, maladaptive behavior relates to what a person does if effective means for reducing tensions have not been learned.

In their role as teachers, parents will either condemn or condone the behavior of their child. Problems arise when parents seek to condemn and end up encouraging an undesirable behavior. To illustrate this: a seven-year-old child may come home from school with an obscene word that is intended to shock his mother. If mother over-reacts and punishes the child severely, she may fail to accomplish her purpose of discouraging the child's use of obscene language. Her response may have revealed to the child that he has stumbled upon a weapon that he can use to upset her, to gain attention, or to punish her. Because of the over-reaction, which is a maladaptive behavior, the child may place the word in his repertoire of things to use in an emergency. The mother could have negated the power of the word by saying, "Yes, I've heard that word before. Do you know what it means?" Once an obscenity has been defined and openly discussed, its potency is removed.

Case Illustration Number 2

A clear illustration of how parents encourage actions they want to discourage is the case of a nine-year-old whom we will call Mark. Mark's parents were constantly trying to make his life uncomplicated, and in so doing, they overprotected him. In the first grade, Mark did not like his teacher, so his parents arranged to have him transferred to another first grade section. They blamed the teacher for his failure to learn the basic first grade skills. Mark's behavior in the classroom was not disruptive; he was withdrawn and shy. The first teacher made attempts to have Mark interact with his classmates, but Mark resisted these attempts and told his parents that the teacher was trying to make him do something he didn't want to do. Both parents felt that she was too hard on him. The second teacher was willing to let Mark do what he wanted, not forcing him to participate in class activities. Her actions were prompted by the strong urging of the parents to let Mark have more time to develop by himself. The parents were pleased with the second teacher, but blamed themselves for waiting so long to have him transferred.

Mark was promoted to the second grade, although his parents knew that he was not ready. The parents had Mark tutored during the summer in order to get him ready for the second grade. He responded well in the one-to-one relationship afforded in the tutoring, though here, too, Mark would only do what he wanted to do and the tutor could not get the parents to cooperate by expecting more from him.

Mark's problems began anew in the second grade. He was being teased by fellow pupils on the school bus and at recess time. His academic progress in the second grade was slow and his parents felt that his social problems were the cause of his poor achievement. The parents had frequent conferences with the teacher and principal. They rejected the idea that Mark was an unhappy child and resented school personnel's statements that Mark was immature and did not want to grow up. They became more and more critical of the school practices and finally decided to take Mark out of public school and put him in a private school.

Mark continued to have social and academic problems in the private school, but his parents were convinced that all the problems were caused by his early experiences in the public school. They did not discourage the behavior that contributed to their son's problems. They let Mark change teachers when he wished; they excused his behavior and blamed the school for his problems, and they did not take any action that might encourage Mark to assume some responsibility for himself. Failure to discourage a behavior is a subtle form of encouragement to continue the behavior.

The Importance of Habit

Children and adults are creatures of habit. A habit is any behavior that occurs so often that it is repeated almost automatically. Habits are learned behavior patterns that serve some purpose for an individual. Some habits fall into the category of daily routines. Others reflect unique behaviors and are termed idiosyncratic. Getting some daily exercise or practicing personal hygiene are good habits. Fingernail biting or staying up too late at night are regarded as bad habits. Because any learned behavior can become habit forming, the best time to discourage bad habits is before the behavior becomes automatic. Many bad habits that children develop which later become problems for parents might have been avoided if parents could have anticipated the outcomes of the behavior. A mother may discover that allowing her child to fall asleep in the parents' bed will encourage the child to fall asleep. However, she will probably discover that once the child gets used to falling asleep in the parents' bed, he will not fall asleep in his own bed. This habit can become a problem that could have been avoided.

Habit plays an important role in the developing behavior patterns of the child. Good habits are those that promote growth and maturity. Bad habits retard growth and may reveal maladaptive behavior. Habits can be altered, but the desire to change a habit is more often a wish than a reality. It is not easy for a child to stop sucking his thumb if he has been doing it for several years. It is difficult for a child to sleep in a dark room if he has been conditioned to sleep in a room with lights on. Adults know how difficult it is to break a habit. Sometimes the habit almost becomes an obsession, and the more we try to break it, the more difficult it is to stop. Also, the longer that the habit continues the more difficult it is to alter or remove. "It's easy to stop smoking," as one man says, "I've done it a hundred times." Overeating is also a habit difficult to break. Parents must be aware of how hard it is to break a habit and not expect their child to stop doing something just because they order him to stop.

Unfortunately, it is not as easy to learn good habits as it is to fall into bad ones. Good habits require training, practice, rewards, time, cooperation, and a willingness to sacrifice. Usually, we just fall into bad habits. They develop with less effort because they are largely pleasure-oriented or time-saving. It is easier to give in to an impulse than it is to develop self-control. It takes no effort to eat a candy bar if you like one, but it takes will power not to eat one if you are trying to lose weight. Watching television is more fun for a child than doing homework. You can change clothes faster if you throw the used clothes on the floor instead of hanging them up or putting them in a clothes hamper. The child or adult who is lazy is more prone to having habits that are disturbing to others. It is interesting to note that bad habits seldom bother the person who has them. Therefore, undesirable habits are usually a problem for other people, not the individual who practices them. Once in a while the person who has the bad habit wants to break it, but only when *he* terms the practice undesirable.

Habits that create or maintain problems should be examined and altered. However, just being aware of an undesirable practice does not remove the habit. Habits become needs. Needs become drives. Drives seek satisfaction, and a person responds to a drive according to the strength of the need. Failure to stop an undesirable habit is usually due to a need. In examining a habit, the nature of the need and the strength of the need have to be considered. The habit may offer security or it may be a way of expressing aggression. Nail-biting, which is a characteristic of children who are tense and excitable, is a habit that may be based on both security and aggressive needs. The child who bites his fingernails when he is fearful or uncomfortable may be gaining security from his habit. He may also be expressing anger or hostility through biting something. Since it is not safe to bite a sibling or show outward aggression to a parent, the child may turn his aggression inwardly and bite his own finger-nails. If it can be shown that this is why a particular child bites his fingernails, the problem will not be solved by punishing him, nor by putting bad tasting medicine on his fingers. In this example, the habit of nail-biting is the effect of felt pressures which the child cannot express safely. Treatment of the habit requires understanding more about the sources of the child's anger and providing the child with more effective methods of overcoming frustrations.

Because habits are learned behaviors, they can be unlearned. Unlearning a habit requires that a person be willing to give up something that he has become used to. Under certain conditions, a habit can become a crutch on which a person is so dependent that he strongly resists if someone attempts to remove it. The habit of overeating is an example of this. People who eat when they are upset may be using their habit to replace something they feel they are missing. Trying to resolve the personal problem can be a better approach to controlling the overeating habit than will power.

Strong motivation, a willingness to sacrifice, and a high level of maturation are needed if an undesirable habit is to be changed. The person who wants to eliminate a bad habit must be willing to postpone satisfaction of immediate needs for gratification later. Young children will not find this easy to do; even adults find it difficult.

Good modeling behavior on the part of the parents is perhaps the best protection against the development of undesirable habits in children. But parents, being very human, are not free from bad habits of their own. If parents are to be good models for their children, they must be aware of their bad habits and work to reduce or eliminate them. It is easier to break a bad habit when you have support from someone who is also trying to break a bad habit, even though it is not the same habit. A child will be more successful in altering an undesirable habit when the parent works on the removal of his own bad habits.

Why Things Go Wrong with Children: Problem Parents

The preceding discussion of the explanation of behavior has indicated that a child's emotional development should be viewed as the result of a combination of factors. When a child is having problems, whether they be social, academic, or emotional, they may be due to any of these factors. In all probability, the underlying cause will relate to some maladaptive behavior, and therefore it can be said that the problems of children are learned. This learning may come about from anything to which the child has had exposure.

The experience of being constantly ridiculed by a group of neighborhood children, or being exposed to bitter arguments between parents could contribute to maladaptive behavior and subsequent social problems. Initial learning takes place in the home, and being the models and teachers, the parents, will exert the greatest impact on the child. For this reason, when things go wrong with a child, one of the major explanations may be in the nature of the parents as individuals. To state it simply, *parents with problems will have children with problems.* In other words, the bulk of the problems that children have are the effect of parents who have problems within themselves, or with each other and carry these problems into their parenting.

Many parents, because of their personal problems, cannot be expected to do anything other than what they have done and are doing. Their mistakes are linked to what they were not able to do or what they could not have avoided doing. It is not a coincidence that the girl who screamed at her sister, her parents, or anyone who frustrated her becomes the mother who screams at her children and husband. Neither is it difficult to explain why the boy who continually threatened to run away from home when he didn't get his own way becomes the father who storms out of the house, or pouts in the basement when his wife doesn't agree with him. For such people, marriage is just a change in the setting for their outbursts.

Individuals who could not handle stress or who over-reacted emotionally before becoming parents cannot be expected to acquire effective ways of dealing with tensions and frustrations simply because they are married or have children. No insights, self-understanding or problem-solving techniques were magically transmitted to the couple when the clergyman said those words that pronounced two people husband and wife. There is nothing automatic about maturity. Marriage is not the panacea for a personality rehabilitation; it is frequently just new territory for the same old personality problems. The unrealistic expectations for marriage are very like those of the man whose hand has been crushed and who asks the doctor whether his hand will be strong enough to play the piano. To reassure his patient the doctor tells him that he will be able to play the piano beautifully and without any difficulty. "You're really great," the man tells his doctor. "And to think that before I crushed my hand I never even played a piano!"

Many people expect such miracles from their marriages. They fully expect that because they got married their old character faults such as vengefulness, an admitted bad temper, stubbornness, or a low tolerance for frustration, will now be left behind them. Love has conquered all, they feel, and marriage itself will become the salve for the old wounds and ways. Long before the first child has been born, the parents-to-be are usually aware that marriage has somehow failed to reform them. And yet, as they approach parenthood, they are again ready to deceive themselves into believing they can become the kind of ideal parents they read about in books or see in happy movies.

A realistic point of view is more pessimistic. A selfish person will act selfishly; an angry person will show aggression in some manner; a spoiled person will demand his own way; and an unhappy person will have to work hard to hide the unhappy feelings. Simply telling oneself, "now I won't act as I have always acted because now I am a parent," will rarely result in a permanent change. It is almost impossible to consistently act a role that is not truly you.

However, changes in behavior are possible. These changes can only take place when the need for change is recognized, when a commitment to change is made, when any barriers or resistance to change are removed, and when definite goals are set that are both realistic and carefully planned. The order of events which lead to change is equally important. Setting realistic goals is not possible unless the need for change has been recognized. Overcoming resistance to change is not possible until a commitment to change has been made. And, it goes without saying, unless there is a conscientious effort made to understand what personal needs and behaviors maintain the problem, the direction of the changes will be nebulous.

There are many parental behaviors that are potentially harmful to the child. Some parental actions "break the spirit" of the child, creating strong feelings of inadequacy, a poor self-concept, a defeatist attitude, and a sense of futility in the child. Parental actions can also develop hostility and the need to defend oneself by attacking others. "As the twig is bent, the tree is inclined." Overprotectiveness produces dependent and helpless children. Perfectionism usually results in failure and frustration. Negligence makes a child indifferent and unmotivated; over-permissiveness creates a child who accepts no controls and who rejects authority; and so on.

A mother was asked, "Why do you shout at your children?"

"Because that's the only way they'll listen to me," she replied.

"Does it work?" she was asked. "Is it effective?"

"No," said the mother.

"Then why do you shout?" she was asked again.

"I don't know," was her reply. "I guess I have to. It allows *me* to let off steam."

"And why do you have so much steam to let out?" she was asked.

At this point, the mother shook her head as her eyes welled up with tears. "I really don't know," she said.

When the mother does not know the reason for her behavior, her behavior will persist and ultimately affect the child. Knowing why we do something will not stop us, but this knowledge is the first step in overcoming the behavior problem. As an example, suppose a woman has had a bad relationship with her mother for most of her life. She might eventually learn that the basis for this poor relationship was her mother's jealousy of her. Simply knowing this may or may not change her feelings towards her mother, but it allows the woman to see whose problem the poor relationship really is and what she can do about it.

Dangerous Parental Behaviors

What are the potentially dangerous parental behaviors that can create problems for a child? The items on such a list would be numerous, but these are some of the more common ones. Children are prone to have difficulties when the parent, as a person, is:

— lacking self-control and quick to display temper
— overly competitive with people because of feelings of inadequacy
— overly jealous of people
— selfish, and unwilling to sacrifice or postpone personal needs for the needs of others
— negligent towards responsibilities
— rejecting of others when dissatisfied with self or with others
— overly zealous in attempts to succeed
— driven by a need for perfection
— lacking in self-confidence
— over-reactive to situations or overly sensitive to comments
— fearful of people or of unfamiliar situations
— indecisive or unsure of self
— unable to make a commitment and maintain it
— able to feel satisfaction through revenge, cruelty, or punitive measures
— overly demanding of self and others

— dominating or possessive of others
— overly controlled and inhibited when it comes to expressing feelings
— discontented with self
— unable or unwilling to be compassionate or to understand the needs and feelings of others
— ignorant of the process of child development
— impatient
— impulsive
— bitterly resentful of the past
— unable to resolve problems effectively
— too confident
— obsessed or preoccupied with things such as sex, religion, school, money, politics, prejudice, germs, safety, or work
— rejecting of the basic values held by society
— overly strict
— excessively permissive
— unable to see things realistically
— inclined to worry unnecessarily
— disrespectful and intolerant of others
— overly dependent upon others
— inconsistent in handling situations
— unable to admit mistakes or see errors in himself
— unfair in the handling of situations
— insecure with love relationships
— unable to find satisfaction in parenthood

The child's problems will depend on the degree to which any of these problems exist. Being strict or firm in handling discipline can be appropriate. Being *overly* strict can be harmful. For most of these items it should be apparent that the extremes are dangerous. Some permissiveness is essential if the child is to develop positive feelings about himself. Excessive permissiveness, though, is harmful, since it fails to prepare a child to assume responsibility. Likewise, the age of the child must be taken into consideration. A younger child may require more constructive criticism than an older one, but excessive or destructive criticism will have an adverse effect upon a child of any age. Conversely, no criticism of the child at all is a poor method of teaching. The real danger occurs when one or more of the listed behaviors stands out as the parent's outstanding characteristic.

It would not be difficult to trace the effects of each of these parental behaviors or attitudes on the child. For example, the first was the parent who is "lacking self-control and quick to display temper." Such a parent will cause the child to fear him. If the child is unable to predict when the parent will "explode," he cannot be relaxed, nor can he feel safe. He will see the parent as a threat rather than someone who can be trusted. He is likely to withdraw from the parent, since you don't seek out a person who is known to attack without warning. We might also predict that, having seen the temper tantrums of the parent, the child is likely to develop a similar control and temper problem.

Why Things Go Wrong with Children: Parental Practices

If parents with problems form the basis for an explanation into children's problems, *parental practices* are a second key factor contributing to the child's behavior and attitude. Each of the *practices* potentially detrimental to the child could be based on one or more of the *problems* that were listed above. For example, parental inconsistency will encourage a child to test parental limits to excess. The parent who is lacking in self-confidence, and is indecisive, impulsive, and excessively permissive will be inconsistent. The practices listed may be harmful when they become a regular pattern of behavior. This is only a partial listing of detrimental practices; however, it covers the more serious practices which have a negative effect on the child's behavior and attitude.

— inconsistency
— failure to understand what can be expected from children at various ages and stages
— expectations that are either too great or too little
— a home environment that is lacking in structure or one that has too much structure
— excessive shouting, scolding, punishing, or spanking
— making degrading, insulting, or threatening remarks in anger
— impatience with children
— harsh or cruel punishments, such as beatings, extreme deprivation, ridicule or embarrassment
— failure to understand or recognize the needs being expressed by the child
— neglecting the responsibility for proper and adequate parental supervision
— overprotection and pampering
— coercion by force or excessive pressure

— failure to demonstrate a sense of humor with the child
— refusal to allow the child the opportunity to express himself
— comparison of the child with other children
— failure to give verbal praise as a reward when it is appropriate
— competition with the child
— favoring another child or giving unequal attention to the children
— being too busy to give the child some private time
— frequent parental arguments, exposing the child to unpleasant situations and creating doubts and insecurities for the child
— failure of one parent to back up or support the statements and decisions of the other parent
— being poor models for the child
— being overly critical of the child or his friends
— rejection of the child, whether subtle or direct
— constantly threatening the child in order to get him to obey
— blaming the child for marital or personal unhappiness ("If it weren't for you . . .")
— unkind or cruel labeling of the child (words such as *stupid, liar, sneak, dummy*)
— open disgust expressed to the child ("You make me sick . . ." — "Get out of my sight . . ." — "I hate you!")
— spoiling the child by giving in too quickly and too often or by denying the child frustrations
— overly rigid standards or unbending rules
— lack of sensitivity for the child's problems
— open disagreement between parents on the handling of child-training practices
— denying an opportunity for the child to learn to make decisions and judgments
— encouraging dependence
— unfairness in the treatment of the child
— punishing impulsively and without a consideration for the severity of the misbehavior
— teasing beyond the limits of what the child can handle

Why Things Go Wrong: The Influence of Society

Parents are aware that things can go wrong for their child as a result of experiences that are directly related to interactions within society. Society is merely a concept and does not really exist per se, yet it can control us and its pressure can be felt. It can exert a major influence on how we act, why we do things, and what responses we can expect. Society can reward or punish. It can motivate or discourage. It can provide us with the feeling of success or leave you with the feeling of failure. Because of its power, society can be a reason why things go wrong with a child, regardless of the personal problems and practices of the parents, and the uniqueness of the individual.

Society has the capacity to create tremendous pressure on an individual. Whether by direct or subtle ways, society determines standards, values, and direction for an individual. It does so by imposing certain *restrictions* and *demands* on a person. Incest is a taboo and unacceptable in our society. Its practice is restricted. The same could be said for practices of murder, rape, and other antisocial behaviors. By imposing restrictions upon us, society also makes demands upon us. Restrictions and demands may serve the best interest of the individual through the protection they can offer. However, there are circumstances in which the protection that is offered by social restrictions is exploited by individuals for their own purposes. Under such conditions personal freedom may be available to some and denied to others.

Prejudice is the greatest restrictor of personal freedom. The child who must overcome bigotry and hatred because of his inherited skin color, the religion of his parents, or the cultural way of life into which he was born, is feeling the impact of society through being denied respect and dignity. For such a child, things can go wrong for no apparent or logical reason. Despite the attempts of parents to train their child in a socially acceptable way, a child who is a member of a minority group, or who happens to be too tall, too short, too fat, too thin, or too individually different, can be exposed to social processes that are very harmful and destructive. Cruel name-calling, social rejection, physical bullying, and other forms of discrimination can create serious problems for children that will have an effect on their total lives and can extend far beyond childhood.

There is only so much protection that a parent can give a child. Eventually, the child will have to face the world by himself. Upon his introduction to society, the child must be prepared to cope with what he finds. Through reassurance and encouragement, the parents can protect the child from hurt feelings and motivate him to accept social challenges. But they cannot always prevent harmful social interaction. When the mother watches her child walk into a school room for the first time, she knows he is on his own. Can he stand up under the pressure he will face? Can he take care of himself? Can he meet a crisis? Parenting practices and observable experiences offer some clues to the outcome of these questions, but the unpredictable pressures from the child's social world cause the mother to be anxious.

Problems Created by Conformity

Another pressure society exerts that creates problems may develop because of the demands of social conformity for the child. The individual is greatly influenced by the thinking and behavior of groups that have importance for him. Initially, the child is expected to conform to the expectations and values of his parents. He soon learns that he will be rewarded when he conforms and will be unrewarded, even punished, if he rebels. When the child begins to interact with other children, he becomes aware of social pressures which also will reward conforming behavior and penalize nonconformity. The child informs his parents of this social pressure when he announces that he wants a pair of sneakers because the other kids have them, or that he no longer wants to wear a certain pair of trousers, because his friends laughed at him and called them "sissy pants."

As the child becomes older, he is more conscious of the pressure that groups have on his behavior. As a means of protecting himself from abuse and also to be accepted by a social group, the child learns conforming behavior. The adult does the same, although he may elect to refer to conforming by other names. In our society, the idea of conforming has the undesirable connotations of surrendering personal freedom and suggests a lack of creativeness and a willingness to passively submit to others. It also implies overdependence on others and overreliance on those who are in authority. Yet, it is socially desirable to be "in style." It is permissible to "keep up with what is going on." And people go to great lengths to avoid being called "old-fashioned." Because of social pressures people adopt the new clothing and hair styles, they buy the new fads, and try to be seen in the "right" places.

The degree to which a person is quick to do what others are doing is an indication of his needs to conform. For this reason, conformity is defined in a relative way. When conforming behavior represents the person's usual response in most situations, his need to conform is excessive and detrimental to the development of reasoning, problem-solving skills, and ability to make decisions independent of others.

A certain amount of conforming behavior is necessary for harmonious social interactions. We are penalized by society if we elect to violate the acceptable code of conduct. The punishment is rejection, isolation, and whisper campaigns that are intended to make the guilty person feel inferior and unequal. It is not so much a question of being a conformist or a nonconformist, as it is deciding what behavior is beneficial to oneself, respectful of others, rational, and realistic.

A lot of confusion surrounds conforming behavior today. Despite encouragement for individuals to think for themselves, society rewards conforming behavior by acceptance and positive regard. Yet, many people are uncertain as to how to react to nonconforming behavior. They are not sure whether to condemn or condone acts that were once regarded as forbidden, unpopular, or even perverse. They avoid having to formulate a judgment with the rationalization, "If people want to do those things, it's up to them." Some people even resent their needs to conform, feeling that the nonconformist is getting more enjoyment out of life than they are. Many people are trying hard not to see or react to what is going on, for it is not fashionable to criticize others on social or moral issues. They are afraid to voice their objections to practices they cannot accept.

Conformity creates problems when the pressure exerted by the group demands that the individual engage in behavior that is potentially harmful and destructive. The high school sophomore may feel the need to conform to peers who are smoking or taking drugs. College students may feel pressure to conform and begin to "sleep with dates" or come back to the dorm drunk. Resisting the pressure can result in a feeling of being different and subsequent loneliness.

The child and adolescent are aware that they are members of their parents' society and also a sub-society of their own. Their society penalizes the nonconformist by labeling him "out of it," "not with it," "square," and the odd-ball of his generation. Because of the different values in some sub-societies, the youngster who is *not* in conflict with parents, or the one who *accepts* parental authority, may be the one who is rejected and ridiculed by peers.

Things can also go wrong when *parents* begin to conform to practices that are not beneficial to themselves or their child. Some parents have yielded to pressures from their social groups and have abandoned their traditional values of family security and stable relationships. They have begun to conform to peers who may be indulging in questionable practices that offer excitement through elements of danger and the forbidden. A number of parents are attending "pot" parties. "Wife-swapping," which used to be socially unacceptable is becoming condoned openly as an indication of free thinking. Their justification is seldom more impressive than, "I do it because I like it." It is the same justification they could not accept if it were used by their children who were doing similar things. The child will not respect parents who do things they labeled harmful or wrong.

The Effect of Competition

We live in a highly competitive society. The pressure of competition is felt socially, academically, financially, and vocationally. Power, prestige, and status have become important in this society, and the child learns early that "it isn't what you know, it's who you know" that counts. The child who will not compete or who is not taught how to compete will have social problems. The social demand for competition ignores any individual uniqueness and requires each person to compete or suffer the consequences. The noncompetitive member of our society is frequently exploited and frustrated and may end up feeling that he is a failure.

Competition does not have to mean "dog eat dog." Similar to other behaviors, it is the degree of competition that determines whether it is healthy and productive for a person or unhealthy and destructive. Competition can be a reason for an outstanding performance. Because of it, goals can be set that encourage a great amount of effort, for competition can enhance motivation. On the other hand, competition can destroy incentives if the fear of failure is greater than the needs to seek some measure of success. Every student cannot have an A average; every applicant for a job will not be successful; every football team cannot be number one.

Ideally, a person should be encouraged to compete with himself, not others. Self-competition develops an individual's potential, for the goal is to improve on a previous performance or to maintain the performance that represents a high level of satisfaction for that person. Self-competition is fair and can be challenging. It develops an awareness of self-improvement and allows the setting of realistic goals. The businessman who plays golf once a week in good weather should not compare his performance to the professional golfer's, or even to that of the businessman who plays twice a week in most weather. The child with average ability should not feel it necessary to achieve the grades that a brighter child can earn. Competition with those of superior ability can lead to frustration and a poor self-image.

An overemphasis on competition creates problems because it makes unfair demands on the individual. Excess competition may require an unrealistic output of energy in one area that takes away energy from other areas that need it. It may also create the need for success at any price, including socially unacceptable methods. Competition is unhealthy if it means an all-out war in order to succeed. It is also unhealthy if the person loses sight of the true objective and concentrates on the reward. The youngster working for an A in school who is so intent on getting the high grade that he loses sight of the need for learning and retaining the material is an example of this.

Competition can also create hostility, even when the competition is fair. Whenever there is a winner, there must be a loser. Problems develop when the effects of losing are out of proportion to the reality of the total situation. Losing the big game is terribly upsetting on the day of the loss. However, time heals the wound and soon the athlete is looking forward to the next game, or the next season. If the individual remains depressed or becomes hostile and vindictive, he has allowed the loss to get out of proportion.

Even the young child is aware of social competition. He learns that other children are stronger, taller, and more able. He may see a sibling getting better grades, receiving more compliments, and having more friends. If the competition is unfair, he may become jealous. Even when it is fair competition, the child may be unhappy. The older child realizes that he must compete socially if he is to have friends. He becomes conscious of his appearance, his ability to carry on a conversation, his intelligence, and the image he projects to others. Because of competition, the youngster develops doubts about himself, but if the competition is healthy, it serves as an incentive for the child to develop social skills.

Things go wrong for a child if competition is so great that the child abandons the effort to succeed. If we continue to place emphasis on excellence and being number one, more children will have to fail and will withdraw from the competition. Competition creates pressure and some children do not function effectively under pressure. Parents can help their child by not emphasizing competition. It is not necessary to compare one child with another, whether it be a sibling or a friend. It is unrealistic to expect an outstanding performance from a child who does not have outstanding ability. If parents encourage their child to compete with himself then the child will try to improve on his own performance. However, there is a limit to improvement, and the parents must recognize when the ceiling has been reached.

Some parents compete with their children. This is neither healthy nor fair. A mother may compete with her child for her husband's attention, a father may compete with his child at every game or event. Parents may openly compare themselves with their children, and usually, the parents are biased in their own favor. There are parents who are threatened by the child's success. A reluctance to praise the child's achievements may reveal this form of competition. Some parents compete with their children by building themselves up and tearing the child down. A mother may say to her daughter, "When I was your age I could run a house, and you can't even clean up your room."

Finally, parents can help ease the pain of social competition by offering their child reassurance when he has not been successful in competing. Unfortunately, they can also increase the effects of social competition by hitting the child when he is down. If the daughter has not been selected to be a cheerleader, the parent may offer some reassurance by saying, "I know you are upset. You worked hard and I thought you did a very good job. Maybe you'll be successful next year." This says to the girl, I sympathize with you, recognize why you are upset, and have confidence that you may be more successful next time. It also communicates a loving and caring feeling. A less thoughtful parent might handle this in a different way by saying, "No wonder you didn't make it, you practiced too much and worried yourself sick. I told you not to build up your hopes." This is hitting the child when she is down and discourages competition. It makes failure more bitter than it has to be.

Early Indication of Trouble

A characteristic of the growing child is the emergence of stages or phases of behavior. The toddler must test his autonomy and can be negative to suggestions, the-five-year-old may go through a period of clinging to his mother, the seven-and eight-year-old is concerned with fairness, and the ten-year-old wants privacy. These are normal conditions, indicating that growth is proceeding along expected lines. They are not problems unless they appear to be excessive. For instance, while some negativism is anticipated, complete negativism or rejection of controls is a danger sign.

Early recognition of a problem is important, for it is easier to stop a new habit than an old one. Things go wrong for a child if a problem is developing and his parents wait too long to intervene. It may be that the parents do not recognize the early warnings of a problem, or they may feel the problem will go away by itself. Many times this does happen, through maturation alone, but a safe rule would be: when in doubt, inquire. Behavior is learned and habits get reinforcement. Parental practices usually explain the behavior of the child, for the child's behavior is largely a product of what has been learned and reinforced.

Parental practices will affect the child according to the stage or phase of growth he is in. We can establish a simple scheme calling infancy to age six *early childhood*; the years from six through twelve *late childhood; adolescence* the years from thirteen through sixteen or seventeen; and *late adolescence* a fourth stage of pre-adulthood up to age twenty or twenty-one.

In developing a list of behaviors that signify trouble, two cautions must be given. First, the degree of the symptomatic behavior must be significant in order for it to be a problem, and second, the child who is having a problem will generally exhibit several of the symptoms that are outlined.

In the stage that has been designated *early childhood*, these are some behaviors that indicate parental practices harmful to the emotional development of the child:
— a constant need for security objects
— sleeping problems
— excessive negativism
— reluctance to please
— frequent crying, whining, or clinging
— thumb sucking (beyond the age of 3)
— nail biting
— nightmares
— frequent temper outbursts
— excessive fears and an over-reaction to fear
— problems with toilet training (beyond the age of 4)
— speech problems (when diagnosed by a speech therapist)
— restlessness or hyperactivity
— verbal abuse of parents
— excessive stubbornness
— inappropriate and aggressive behavior
— a constant need to test parental limits
— excessive jealousy or hatred expressed to a sibling, peer, or adult
— frequent screaming and crying, with or without tears
— withdrawing or self-isolating behavior
— refusal to separate from mother
— putting nonedible objects in the mouth (beyond the age of 2)
— a martyr-like attitude towards discipline or punishment
— destructiveness of personal property or property of other people
— constipation or very irregular bowel habits
— cruelty to animals or helpless objects
— willful disobedience or refusal to take suggestions
In *late childhood* another set of behaviors emerges that may be

the forerunner of trouble. Some of the earlier behavior may persist into late childhood, but because of increased experiences and expectations, new behaviors develop that can cause concern. They will include:

— a poor self-image (self-concept)
— lack of motivation to suceed academically
— a need to punish parents or gain revenge on others
— conflict with authority figures, such as teachers or adults
— open defiance of parents, or
— subtle defiance of parents
— social and interpersonal problems with peers
— regression to more juvenile or immature ways, such as, bed-wetting, need for security objects
— avoidance of people and situations
— lying, stealing, and other antisocial acts
— inability to function in a group
— deliberately upsetting parents, teachers, or siblings
— a ''you can't make me'' attitude
— rebellion against punishment or discipline
— watching television as major source of enjoyment
— boredom with leisure time
— highly impulsive behavior
— argumentative to parents
— secretive and guarded with parents
— overdependence upon others
— easily embarrassed
— fearful in everyday situations
— using physical complaints to avoid responsibility
— blaming others excessively
— refusing to cooperate with parents or to assume responsibility for household chores
— rebelling against things that are required, such as, homework, school assignments, or respect for others
— excessive teasing or bullying of others
— frequent threats to run away from home

Behaviors that warn of trouble in the *adolescent* stage are inclined to be more serious and place the welfare of the child in jeopardy. The adolescent is prepared to experiment more and seeks excitement and adventure in order to enhance an adult-like image he wants for himself. In an almost total rejection of childhood and childish mannerisms, the adolescent tries to disengage himself from the vestiges of earlier behavior. For the adolescent, the adult world is synonymous with personal freedom. He can easily distort the implications of freedom and make adolescence a license for irresponsibility.

The adolescent is inclined to select ways of behaving that make this dissatisfaction apparent. Whereas a young child's hostile behavior could conceivably go undetected, the adolescent does not always put up a facade that enables him to gloss over problems. His behavior is usually deliberate, purposeful, and directed at immediate needs for tension reduction. The adolescent is willing to place himself in danger in order to prove a point. Adolescent behaviors that reveal problems include:

— rejection of parental controls
— rejection of parental values
— removal of verbal communication with parents
— threats to run away or actual running away from home
— loss of respect for authority figures
— misuse of freedom (getting into trouble)
— sexual promiscuity
— a very defensive attitude
— a belligerent and extremely negative attitude towards parental suggestions
— unrealistic concern or attitudes towards the future
— school dissatisfaction which has led to poor grades, apathy, or dropping out of school
— the more serious antisocial behaviors, such as robbery, shoplifting or attacking others
— withdrawal from the family unit
— inability to make appropriate decisions and the tendency to make decisions for the immediate pleasure of oneself regardless of outcomes
— frequent and quick loss of self-control
— vulgar and obscene language to parents
— abuse of alcohol
— abuse of drugs or use of illegal drugs
— careless and impulsive behavior that could jeopardize life
— pleasure obtained by displeasing and rebelling against parents
— threats or attempts to commit suicide
— conflict with police or law enforcement agencies
— hasty marriages
— refusal to assume responsibility for oneself or to acknowledge mistakes

— indifference to the feelings of others
— social withdrawal and social inadequacies
— frequent depression
— inability to cope with the stress and tensions of daily living
— extreme moodiness
— inability to compete or succeed
— tendency to be too easily led by others, regardless of the direction
— over-emphasis on needs for material things
— feelings of inadequacy and helplessness
— lack of direction or goals
— inability to profit or learn from mistakes
— excessive self-pity

Behavior that develops in *late adolescence* is not too unlike that seen in the adult. The ability to function independently and the readiness to assume responsibility are the primary ways the adult differs from the adolescent. But, as the adolescent is soon to become the adult, what can occur is a repeat of an unfortunate cycle in which the adolescent with problems becomes the adult with problems which he carries into marriage and parenthood.

Attempts at Combating Problems: Child Guidance Clinics

Recognizing that parents are increasingly concerned over the behavior and attitudes of their children, hundreds of child and adolescent mental health clinics have been established. Thousands of children are taken to such clinics or to private offices. They may be seen for individual therapy, group therapy, or total-family therapy. Countless diagnostic tests have been administered to children, and more parents know the I.Q. of their child than know his blood type. Descriptive labels are tossed at parents with such frequency and rapidity that the parents become frustrated and look upon therapy as an almost futile effort. Parents are resentful at being blamed for creating the child's problem.

Mental health personnel have a list of labels to throw at parents. They speak of the unloved child, the punishing child, the child who needs more success, more fathering, or the child who fears his parents. They label children aggressive, hostile, indifferent, and uncooperative. They refer to the child who is over-criticized by parents, the jealous and rivalrous child, and the dependent or spoiled child.

When their attention is focused on the parents, they may tell the parents that they are not consistent, that they are too harsh or too lenient in punishing, poor models to copy, or hostile towards their own children.

Families who are seen together in counseling may be given a different category of labels. They are told to be sensitive to each other's feelings. They may be called selfish, immature, and stubborn. They can be accused of maintaining dual standards, and they are expected to change their behavior *because they know they have to* and *because they want to*.

When progress in treatment is slow or not evident, more labels are employed. The person may be called resistant, hostile, unmotivated to change, or unwilling to develop insights into problems. Again, the assumption appears to be that changes will occur because the person wants to change, regardless of how much self-understanding he has and despite barriers that might preclude success.

Diagnostic labels can be helpful in understanding the nature of a problem and are useful in planning a program of treatment. But, it is not reasonable to expect to be able to actuate change by calling behavior a name. Temporary changes may occur through labeling, but the basic personality is unchanged. Telling a person that he is very jealous does not make him less jealous. He may act less jealous, or try to convince himself that now he is less jealous, but inside he has the same feelings of jealousy. Unless he can understand why he has to be jealous and can learn to feel better about himself, there will be only superficial change.

Child guidance clinics are most effective when both parents are prepared to become involved in the treatment. It is unlikely that a child can be helped without some input from each parent. Things go wrong when the parents expect change to be the child's responsibility and are unwilling to examine their own role in creating or maintaining the problem. Things also go wrong if the child guidance clinic does nothing more than label the child's behavior.

Frequently, labeling only makes the parents angry and defensive. One of the major complaints parents have with child guidance clinics is that they learn little more about their child than they previously knew. After an extensive battery of psychological tests and consultations, they are told things they could have told the staff. The parent agrees with the conclusions and says, "All right, your description is accurate. I agree that my child is angry and hostile to me and wants to punish me. I could have told you those things. What I want to know is what can I do about it?'' Often the parent wants to focus on the problem of the child but the clinic seems to direct attention at the behavior of the parent. Parents are frustrated when they are told they must accept the child's undesirable behavior and let the child solve his own problems. Their feeling is, "That's easy for you to say, but we're the parents, and we want to do something for our child." Parents often get more helpful advice and concrete suggestions from their pediatrician or family physician than they do from the mental health facilities.

Another complaint of parents is the decrease of individual attention available in child guidance clinics. The trend is away from a personal and private relationship with a clinician and towards group counseling or group psychotherapy.

The Group Movement

Groups are a fad in mental health treatment today. There are sensitivity groups, encounter groups, self-understanding groups, self-fulfillment groups, and marathon groups. There are groups that touch each other, explore each other's bodies, and interact in the nude. There are groups for married couples and singles, groups for troubled parents and problem children, groups for breaking habits, and groups for people who are bored and want to join a group.

Group leaders and group psychotherapists assume that group interaction will facilitate self-understanding. To be able to share intimate feelings in a group is deemed an important freedom, and hence, a virtue. One of the objectives of a group is to let a person realize that his problems are not really unique—that others suffer from the same problem. Members of the group are expected to help one another by offering support and constructive criticism. The labels that are applied to the person by members of the group are supposed to motivate him to change his behavior.

However, many people are reluctant to share their private feelings with nonprofessional people who are not sworn to confidentiality or an ethical code. They fail to see the virtue in being free to share personal thoughts with people who are similarly troubled, and question the expectation that this will be therapeutic. They find that the line between constructive and destructive criticism is thin, and that labeling behavior does not point the way to needed changes in behavior. Many have found group therapy too impersonal, lacking in professional direction, nonspecific to the unique problems a person may have, destructive to the ego, and of little value. Others respond well to a group approach. They feel it meets their needs and is what they want.

What should be apparent is that no single approach to mental health problems will be effective for every person who seeks help. Individual differences must be considered. Some people find individual psychotherapy, or one-to-one counseling most beneficial, others are pleased with groups, and still others may do best with a combination of individual and group methods. Research that could indicate which method is preferred is not conclusive and tends to reflect the bias of the researcher; consequently, any method can be justified by the clinician who is using it. However, the practice of putting everyone who seeks professional help into a therapy group is not defensible for it does not regard personality differences in people and fails to respect the dignity of the person who finds it unattractive.

Case Illustration: Number 3

Although many families have benefited greatly from treatment facilities in community mental health clinics, others have found the system to be frustrating and disappointing. Mental health units can improve on their methods. This is an example of how one family felt defeated by the system.

Worried and frustrated parents of a seven-year-old girl who was masturbating excessively consulted a private therapist for help. He saw the parents together for the initial interview, then each parent privately for one interview. After this, he saw the child twice privately, and then asked the parents to return for a consultation, at which time the therapist indicated that he would see the child on a weekly basis. But he insisted that both parents become involved in psychotherapy and referred them to another clinician. The second therapist agreed to see the mother, but referred the father to yet a third clinician, feeling that the mother's problems were largely unrelated to the problems the child was having. The cost of three members of the family in treatment was more than they could afford, so they were forced to discontinue treatment before it began.

They were still faced with their initial problem, so they went to a community mental health clinic. There was a long waiting list for services, but they were surprised to be called within three weeks. (Often people on such lists will change their minds about following through with a consultation.) First the parents were interviewed by a social worker. Then the child was seen briefly by a psychiatrist, who referred her for psychological testing. It was another two weeks before the testing was completed, and two more weeks before the parents were asked to come in for a report from the staff. In preparation for this meeting with the parents, the social workers, psychologist, and psychiatrist had met and formulated a treatment program for the family. The parents were informed that the child could be seen by one of the clinic doctors on a weekly basis, and that they would be required to become part of a group of other parents whose children had problems. Realizing that their child needed help, the parents agreed.

The parents were not interested in hearing about the problems other parents were having with their children; however, in order to keep their child in treatment in that clinic, they went along with the group method for themselves. The father soon became antagonistic to the group leader for not assuming a role of leadership; the wife became upset with him for not imparting his knowledge to the group or asserting expertise on how situations could or should be handled. The parents felt forced to hide their real feelings about their participation in the group. They saw no reason to publicly air their feelings of dissatisfaction with the leader because they feared the hostility of the group.

Nearly three months elapsed between the first visit with the private doctor and first treatment session in the community clinic. The unfortunate element in this case was the effect this time lapse had on both the parents and the child. Before direct steps were taken to help the child, the parents were exhausted, disgusted, frustrated, impatient, and had wasted a great deal of time and money. The child was confused by the shuffling around from one clinician to another, suspicious of the people who were asking her questions, and tired of giving the same answers to people who were trying to help her. The complexity of the system discourages those who need help.

Attempts at Combating Problems: A Critique

The clinics, the methods, the labels, and the interpretations of behavior, have not been very successful with either the parents or the child. Too often the emphasis has been on who or what to blame rather than what decisive steps can be taken to improve conditions. Many times the intention of therapy seems to be explaining attitudes and behavior, the assumption being that knowledge alone will cause the behavior to change. A label can be a confirmation of what the person has suspected or feared, an insult, a motivation to work towards change, a cause of panic, guilty feelings, or a license to continue doing what he has been doing. Once a child is labeled a liar, he could continue to lie and feel that he is only doing what is expected from him. We can live up to, or down to a label.

Solutions to the problems of children will not be found simply by opening more child guidance clinics, or writing up more case histories, or developing more precise instruments to measure the behavior. Nor will they be solved by training more clinicians to see more children. Most clinicians who work with children have come to realize that you can't treat the child without learning about his family and working with his parents. We have been treating symptoms too long. We must address ourselves to causes, which requires long-range programs that are directed at prevention rather than identification or treatment.

Taking into consideration the growth in need for child guidance services, the increasing number of parents who express concern over their child's attitudes and behavior, and the number of parents who have already lost contact with their children, it is safe to assume that we are confronted with a very serious and very dangerous situation that seems to be perpetuating itself. Either we make an effort to understand what is happening and what can be done to alleviate the problems, or we allow ourselves to watch the snowball gain momentum, knowing that some day we will have to fear its size. From all appearances, we are dangerously close to a point of no return.

Conclusion

In somewhat of an oversimplification, we can understand and explain why things go wrong with a child if we know enough about the personality of each of the parents, and about their parental practices. Add to this the factors of uniqueness, the specific kinds of habits, and the adaptive behaviors that are used to cope with stress. Then, examine the pressures that are brought about from social forces and it makes growing up sound difficult.

Many children resist growing up, and many adults are still resisting it. However, to resist growth is to view growth in a negative way. This need not be so, for it should be recognized that *things do not have to go wrong*. They do so largely because of human errors, not human intentions. Since errors can frequently be corrected, the outlook can be optimistic. The answer is knowledge, and no one is ever too old to learn something.

- 4 -

Guidelines for Early Child Training

The day that the parents bring the baby home from the hospital certain problems begin. Some are basically management problems involving setting up schedules and learning how to feed, bathe, and care for the baby. Some are adjustment problems, involving the changes the parents have to make in their daily lives, for having a new baby in the house will alter the normal daily routines significantly. Everything in the home will be different, and both parents will need time to adapt to the new conditions. For the first born, these management problems are frequently complicated because of parental fears, doubts, and feelings of inadequacy.

The pediatrician or family physician is an available resource person for answering questions, offering reassurances, and making recommendations that will reduce parental anxiety. He is not the one who must assume the primary responsibility for the emotional, social, and intellectual development of the child. Neither are the grandparents going to be held accountable for how the child develops. Although parents may be bombarded with advice from many well-meaning sources, the commitment and responsibility for the child is theirs. For some parents recognition of this responsibility is the first problem that has to be solved. Inexperienced parents should be willing to listen to suggestions, seek information, and ask questions, but they should be the ones who make the final decisions.

Models of Parenting Practices: A Historical Review

Because parents have reason to be concerned about their children today, and have no reason to be encouraged by the prospects for the future, some thought should be given to the model that has created the conditions that have become so upsetting to parents. Models give the standard for behavior that others copy. They reflect the practices that are engaged in by a large number of people at a given time. In retrospect, the model that may have been responsible for the present generation of children, teenagers, and young adults seems to leave much to be desired. The first problem to arise in trying to analyze this present model is finding one to analyze. Over the past three generations, methods of child training have run the gamut from authoritarianism to permissiveness. The pendulum has shifted somewhat with each generation, for child-rearing practices have been a combination of both the acceptance or rejection of what the parent liked or disliked from his own upbringing, and the influence of social conditions.

The chances are that if you were born prior to 1910, you were raised in a father-oriented family in which the father's word was law, even for his wife. If you were born in the 1920s, the father was still master of the home, but the mother was assuming more responsibility in child rearing. If you were born in the 1930s, the mother's role was beginning to change, as she was moving towards being the person who was fully responsible for the handling of the child.

In the 1940s, with many fathers away in the military service and many mothers working in defense plants, child care took on new forms. Children were frequently placed in all-day nurseries, and the working mothers were becoming more impatient with the ways of babies. Available advice on how to rear children promised parents that children are really good natured, and if allowed to develop without too much parental interference, they would naturally unfold and become what parents would want them to be. They were advised, too, that since children outgrow many things, it wasn't necessary to make many demands on youngsters under the age of 3, or thereabouts. The advice was not to worry the two-year-old about what consequences his behavior might have and not to expect the two-and-a-half-year old to pay any price for his destructive acts. Mothers were told that they could not spoil the month-old infant, and that a pacifier would calm both the baby and the mother.

In the 1950s, the practice of child rearing was a mixture of either a very permissive structure or a very authoritarian approach. Many of the children exposed to either of these models were to become part of the adolescent generation who chose to reject parental controls and to rebel against the "establishment." In either instance the child did not grow up with respect for his parents. The parents who were too strict were labeled unfair and unreasonable by the child, who grew to resent his parents when he saw his friends from permissive homes given more freedom that he was allowed. Children from the permissive home could not respect their parents because their parents had failed to make much of an impact on them. Permissiveness was eventually interpreted by the child as being a composite of neglect, indifference, and weakness on the part of the parents.

It would be difficult to classify any trend in child rearing in the 1960s. Parental concerns and fears had already begun to set in and possibly the word cautious would be the best way to describe the feelings about child-rearing practices in the 1960s. The reasons for the caution could be attributed to social changes that were having an impact on parenting. People were talking about the population explosion, cities were becoming larger, and crime rates were beginning to rise. Sputnik had made its presence felt and educational systems that were unprepared for the onslaught of public pressure began to feel the demands that were being placed on outdated educational machinery to turn out scholars.

Parenting was affected by the social discontent that was developing. Civil liberties were demanded with sit-ins, civil disobedience and demonstrations focusing on social injustices. As the "Negro" was becoming the "black," white middle-class families were becoming uneasy and with fear and violence dominating the headlines, even those parents who had tried to remain detached from things were finding it difficult not to get involved.

Parenting was also affected by the war in Viet Nam which brought increased draft calls and created confusion between loyalty and responsibility in some minds. Drugs and drop-outs were becoming a problem for parents, and when a President of the United States and a powerful civil rights leader were assassinated, parents echoed an alarm. "What has happened to this country?" was their helpless and frustrated question.

The model of child rearing in the 1960s reflected these social problems and became a combination of liberal parents who believed the child should be free to grow in a manner that satisfied the child, and more conservative parents who either resisted the changes they could not accept, or who disapproved of the product being developed by parents who abused the liberal approach with children. The emergence of the "hip" generation made it easy for some parents to hold to their more traditional views.

One interesting change in the 1960s that could be observed was that parents no longer represented the social views of the family. In the past, it was assumed that parents would represent the family values. Although the adolescent might not agree with what the parents were saying, he was not free to voice his objections, or when he did, he was careful to do it tactfully. In the 1960s, the young child's voice was heard—for the adolescent had already begun to outwardly express opposing views. The already weakened family unit was experiencing another split, this time at the value level. Things that parents felt were important were no longer important to their children. Schooling and the idea of work in general were not appealing to the teenaged population and the child began to push for more and more freedom. Worried parents felt helpless to prevent the child from slipping away from them. The term "generation gap" was coined and adults were often viewed as being the youngster's enemy.

Although many parents tried to make "deals" with their children, more and more youngsters were telling their parents that they didn't need them. Dismayed parents were saying, "I can't understand it. I was never allowed to talk to my parents the way my kid talks to me." But, few parents took decisive action to discourage the kind of talk they objected to. Their occasional threats were not carried out, and outbursts of temper were ineffective.

The model for child rearing in the 1970s seems to be a reversion to earlier parental concern for the welfare of the child. Despite the reduction of structure in society and liberalized views towards morality, parents are worried about the possibility that today's young child will become what many of today's adolescent's are: discontented, restless, and involved with drugs. To prevent this, parents are prepared to assert themselves and many have gone to extremes to teach discipline. Parents have seen what can happen when children are given too much freedom and when there is no respect for parental authority. They have learned what can happen when there are serious differences between the parents and children in values and morals. The abuse of liberal child-training methods and permissive views have brought about demanding children who reject more than they respect, who expect more than they earn, and who are trying to bring about changes by methods that appear selfish, destructive, and incompatible with a society whose goals are built around security and freedom for all.

There are many things parents with young children can do to prevent problems and develop a child who has positive feelings about himself. An examination of the parenting practices which have contributed to many parent-child problems would suggest a need for a model that emphasizes parental involvement and more attention to the emotional needs of a child. Methods are needed to re-establish the family as the basic unit of society. For this to happen, child training is needed that will strengthen the family unit by focusing on positive and constructive practices.

Guidelines for Child Training

The months between the time a woman learns she is pregnant and the actual delivery of the baby are long and busy. Many details must be attended to and, if this is the first baby, there is considerable emotional preparation for the event. There is speculation on whether the baby will be a girl or a boy, about the kind of person the baby will become and the kind of world he will have to cope with during the growing years. For many married couples, this is a time for fantasy goals and wishing. It is also a time to consider the practices that will become parenting, and the type of home the baby will find. Thought should be given to early child training and the parental actions that turn their good intentions into reality. The wise parent is one who can profit from the mistakes of others and utilize the most effective methods from a variety of approaches.

It is not sufficient to just recommend another swing of the pendulum, for reversing permissiveness to an authoritarian approach is not the answer. Both systems have been used and neither has produced a stable generation of young people. Even the so-called democratic method leaves much to be desired, for parents who have used democratic principles have been reluctant to assert themselves since the method requires the family to share in all major decisions. Children have liked this system as long as they are on the side of the majority.

There are strengths and weaknesses in any system of child training. Permissiveness encourages the child to develop independence, but it also can result in an abuse of freedom and a lack of self-discipline. Authoritarian methods teach the child to do what is right, according to the parents' values, but an authoritarian approach is usually based on fear of the parents and does not encourage the child to think for himself. Democratic parents provide the child with a feeling of importance, since they seek the child's input, but decision making is difficult with a system in which no authority emerges. Some families are governed by a laissez-faire philosophy in which the children are left alone and there is no observable structure in the home. If there is any merit to this method, it could be that it produces a pressure-free atmosphere.

The guidelines that are being recommended could be considered liberal in that they encourage the child to develop independent ways and ask the parents to respect the individual uniqueness and abilities of the child. They could also be called conservative in that they expect the parents to assume responsibility as the most significant influence on the child and to provide the child with early structure in the form of controls. They could be seen as being based on democratic principles, for they emphasize the dignity of the child and seek his contributions to family decisions. But, since emphasis is placed on developing a positive relationship between people, these guidelines could more correctly be termed *interactionary*. Throughout our lives we are called upon to interact with others. Most of our local, national, and world problems reflect the difficulty people have in interacting with one another. The ability to interact positively with others is an acquired, rather than inherited, trait, and it is well to begin teaching it early.

Characteristics of the Normal Child

Before proceeding with the training guidelines, it is important to consider some of the fundamental characteristics of children. The child has long been the recipient of considerable attention and research. Growth is a fascinating process and the many variables which can effect growth continue to make the child a source of tremendous interest. If the parents are to train the child, it is important for them to have an understanding of the characteristics of children upon which the guidelines have been developed.

The normal child, regardless of age, has some capacity to think, or reason, or respond. It goes without saying that as the child gets older, this capacity is expected to increase. The very young infant cannot reason, and it is doubtful that he can think, but he can respond. He can be conditioned; he can learn to anticipate a response from his environment. He can show pleasure or displeasure. Even a month-old baby can be responsive to certain conditioning techniques. The theoretical basis for conditioning is that a person will respond to a given stimulus in a particular way, the specific response given being determined by the nature of the stimulus. As an illustration, a child cries and the parents pick him up. Crying is the stimulus for the parents. It makes them respond in a particular way; namely, by picking up the child. When the child cries and is picked up, the child has conditioned the parents. On the other hand, when the child cries and is not picked up, conditioning has occurred again. This time the child is being conditioned not to cry, for there is no reward for crying behavior. Conditioning is a way of training the very young child.

The child, regardless of age, has something that can be called personality. It can be expected that every child will show some uniqueness. His early personality will be a combination of his heredity, environment, and his uniqueness. In his early years, the child is basically self-centered or self-oriented and he thinks only of what he wants, what will please him, and what others can do for him. Parents who have spoiled their child will have reinforced this egocentric period of life and in some instances will have prevented the child from ever wanting to give up his autonomy and self-centeredness.

Children have the need to maintain things as they like them to be. They seek sameness as long as they are pleased with what they have. If a child is pleased with his mother, he is reluctant to give her up. The same is true for a toy boat, a nightly bedtime ritual, or any situation he enjoys. The child must be taught to give and to share. The child does not want to share his mother with his father, his sibling, or even the telephone. Because he is self-centered, he is reluctant to part with anything he thinks is his. Possessiveness in the young child is security for him. Ultimately, he must be taught that his security does not lie in what he can hold onto, but that he can be secure within himself. When he learns this, the child can be said to have a positive image of himself.

A child is prepared to test any and all limits that he sees as barriers to what he wants. The child's creed could be stated as, "Even if I don't get what I want, it is worth a try." When the limits are not firmly established and the child succeeds in controlling a situation because of a tantrum, his creed changes to, "If at first you don't succeed, cry, cry, cry some more." Indeed, the child cannot be blamed when limits are not established or when the limits are extended; the parents have either failed to set limits or failed to enforce them consistently.

A child seeks structure and is most comfortable when the parents develop it for him. With structure comes additional security, for the child knows when he is out of bounds with his environment and when he is safe. The young child soon learns that it is more comfortable to feel safe, and, therefore, he will attempt to stay within the limits that have been established most of the time. At other times, a child has the need to push the limits in order to assert individuality and to test his power over his environment. But, since the child does not want to be in conflict with his environment, he will be willing to accept the structure set by parents. For the child this is security; for the parent this is control. The fact that the child and adolescent seem to resist controls or structure does not mean that they do not want them. They want them even though they may grumble or complain. Most people would like to have life on their own terms, but this does not mean they expect it will ever be that way. Structure is a part of everyone's life in varying degrees.

A child is a natural imitator. This is the reason for the strong emphasis being placed upon the parents to be good models. However, the child does not differentiate the appropriate from the inappropriate behavior that he copies. The child will pick up both the strengths and weaknesses of those people who are important to him. In his determination to grow up and be like big people, he copies everything he can grasp and often much of what he cannot understand.

Basically, a child wants to please those people who are important to him. The opposite of this is also true; namely, a child will not please those people whom he desires to punish or who are of no importance to him. The frequency with which a child seeks to please his parents is an indication of the strength of the relationship as well as the comfort the child has with his parents. It should be noted, however, that pleasing behavior can also indicate an over-dependence upon the parents. Whereas the child who pleases as an indication of his positive feelings about his parents does so because *he wants to* please them, the child who is overly dependent upon his parents will please them because he feels *he has to* please them.

A child cannot develop positive feelings about himself or have confidence in himself unless he has been able to trust his parents. Unless the child can trust those individuals who are to be his first teachers, love objects, providers, and confidants, he will have doubts about himself, some insecurity in his environmental relationships, and some feeling of isolation and rejection. If the child cannot trust his parents, whom can he trust? Without trust, the child must be on guard and defensive. Broken promises create disillusionment, and this brings about depressed feelings, self-pity, and anger. The child who cannot trust is both suspicious and tense, for he cannot be confident that he has heard truth.

The potential for self-direction and motivation is present at birth. This suggests that the child is prepared to mature, unless something in his environment prevents him, but that social, emotional, or intellectual maturation is not automatic. The assumption of natural unfoldment, whereby the child will realize his potential as long as there is no interference, must be rejected, because a child needs structure, direction, and protection. Left to unfold in a "natural way," the child will have to learn everything for himself and everything the hard way. It is not necessary for a child to touch a hot stove in order to learn it is dangerous. If a child is to derive any benefit from the experience of his parents, he will need early advice that can prevent accidents involving danger to him physically, and guidance that can prevent impulsive judgments that can create social or emotional problems. The child has the potential for self-direction and motivation, but unless this potential is developed, it will not be expressed. Although the potential for self-direction can be encouraged through training and experience, it is also related to such things as intellectual ability, biological temperament, and other uniqueness factors that are not controlled by the child.

Children are able to recognize the fairness of a given situation and will respond negatively when they perceive unfairness. Parents are fair when they are consistent, when they do not compare one child with another, when they do not show favoritism, and when they make a promise and keep it. Parents are unfair when they fail to do these things. Long before children can communicate their feelings about unfairness, one can sense that they are aware of it. The overly aggressive child and the negativistic child can be registering their perception of unfairness without saying a word; their behavior communicates their feelings.

The influence of the home environment exerts the greatest impact on the development of the child's early behavior. Because the early environment is the most influential, most of the behavior that is observed in the child beyond the age of two has probably been learned. The early learnings that have been reinforced or rewarded can be very difficult to change. In addition to the child's resistance to change, there is the problem of breaking habits that the child may not want to change. This works *for* the parents who reward acceptable behavior and *against* parents who give recognition to behavior that is potentially unacceptable.

There is a natural tendency for people of all ages to resist change. This does not mean that the child or the adult will not accept change, but that a period of adjustment is necessary before changes are accepted. Parents who are in the process of trying to change a child's habits or behavior should be prepared to ease the child into the new behavior. Suddenly exerting a great deal of pressure will make change more difficult, while a gradual change will reduce the amount of resistance. Changes are best effected by evolution, not revolution. They are more difficult for the person whose thinking is rigid, or the person who is satisfied with things the way they are. If the child's behavior is rigid or extremely stubborn, he has apparently had subtle encouragements to become this way. The child's resistance can be reduced and his rigidity relaxed through his need to please those people who are important to him. In the process of learning socialization, the child realizes that he must make a decision whether to please others or gratify his selfish drives. When the child accepts change, he communicates his desire for approval is greater than his need for autonomy.

The essential nature of the infant at birth is neutral. The infant is not born with natural goodness, nor with innate evil, as defined by a society. At the moment of birth the child possesses the potential to become "good" or "evil." These words, good and evil, are used to describe behavior that is acceptable or unacceptable to the culture or to the environment. Being equipped with only the potential to go either way, the child is largely at the mercy of his early environmental influences. The view of a neutral nature at birth implies that we will become what we have been taught and concomitantly, that we are what we have learned to be. We learn something from all influences and experiences. Such a view, however, does not preclude the possibility of a child "rising above his environment," nor does it offer a guarantee that a child who is brought up under stable conditions will necessarily be stable.

The guidelines which are proposed have been developed in accordance with the belief that certain behaviors and attitudes are healthy for the child and necessary if there is to be a good parent-child relationship. They are based upon high ideals and goals which can be attained to some degree. They are intended to:

—create an environment within the home that will motivate the child to grow emotionally, socially, and intellectually, in accordance with the child's potential for development

—encourage the child to develop a set of personal values that will give meaning and purpose to his life

—encourage the child to develop a positive and realistic self-concept

—assist the child in making an acceptable adjustment to life situations

—develop in the child the ability to see things as they really exist

—enable the child to become competent to anticipate the consequences of his behavior

—facilitate a good relationship between the parents and the child as well as between the child and his friends and siblings

—teach the child to relate warmly to others through continual experiences of positively interacting with others

The recommendations are an action-oriented rather than talking-oriented approach to child training. They focus on what the child sees in the reactions and behavior of his parents more than on what he hears them say. The language that is used in the home and the dialogues that take place between the parents and the child are not being ignored, for words and the way we say them are important. However, since the actions of the parents can often betray the words they are using, the emphasis is placed on what happens, rather than on what is said. Parents can say that a person should not get angry just because he can't always have his own way. But, if the father gets angry because the mother objects to his bowling night, or if the mother loses her temper when the father refuses to discuss a problem, what is the child to think when he is called spoiled because he gets angry when he can't have an ice cream cone? "Don't do as I do, do as I say," is hypocrisy. "Monkey see, monkey do," is reality. The child will learn more from deeds than he will from words. The actions of the parents must back up the words and give them meaning; otherwise, the child will eventually regard them with contempt.

These guidelines have been developed with the strong belief that unless the child can learn to interact with his parents lovingly, he will not develop respect for them and a good parent-child relationship will not be possible. The child who cannot respect his parents will not respect other adults with whom he will be required to interact. When a youngster grows into adolescence and adulthood without a respect for people, he will be forced to develop a respect for something other than people, such as material goods, power, or selfish objectives. When there is no respect in a relationship there must be something else, frequently contempt or indifference.

These guidelines for training young children are directed at preventing such negative attitudes. Many of them are familiar, representing a common sense approach to training a child, yet the violations of these guidelines are responsible for much of the trouble parents have with their children.

Guideline 1. *The development of meaningful positive human relationships should be encouraged.* Human relationships are the interactions between two or more people. For the interaction to be meaningful it must be mutually satisfying and rewarding. The relationship that exists between the newborn and his parents is a human relationship, but it is not a meaningful one to both the infant and his parents. It is meaningful only to the parents, for the baby is unaware of who the parents are and what a relationship is. As the baby becomes the toddler and child he will learn that a relationship can be satisfying and rewarding. His first meaningful human relationship will develop with his parents whom he will grow to love and respect. But, this will not develop by chance or accident; it will only come about if the parents have encouraged experiences that promote positive interactions.

Playing with an infant can be a positive interaction, but teasing the infant is not. Showing warmth and affection can be a positive interaction, but ignoring or rejecting the child is a negative interaction. Parents interact positively with their child when they show pride in his accomplishments and become actively involved in his interests. The interactions are negative when the parents are critical, harsh, scolding, or unfair.

One of the most vital elements in the development of meaningful human relationships is something that could be called *caring*. One of the criticisms that could be leveled against our society is that there has evolved a lack of caring for one another. Thousands of people do not know their neighbors. Apartment dwellers may not know people who have shared the same floor for years. People attend meetings and sit next to strangers. They usually leave the meeting as strangers. One excuse that people give for their aloofness is that it isn't safe to talk to strangers. Others wait for the other person to say the first words. Maybe the truth is that too many people don't care.

Caring should start in the home with the very young child. The child should learn that his parents care. It would be nice to know that his teachers care. It is comforting to know that his friends care. The child who develops an "I don't care" attitude may be reflecting the disappointments and negligence in his early environment. From the child's point of view, when his parents are too busy for him, or when they are too quick to shout and punish him, they are not showing him that they care about him. When the child perceives that his parents do not care for him, the chances are he is not motivated to care for them.

The child who learns to care for someone has taken the first step in being able to develop a meaningful human relationship. The parents must show him how to take this step.

Guideline 2. *Encourage the child to regard himself as an important human being.* Confidence, self-esteem, and pride are very positive and secure feelings. They are the products of good feelings about oneself. In the adult they are facilitated through successes and the recognition that others give to accomplishments. For the child who is too young to have had many successes, self-confidence develops when the parents successfully communicate to the child that he is an important human being. A child feels important when adults spend time with him. He also feels important when he is praised, encouraged, and rewarded, and when he feels that his judgments are accepted. Giving a child an opportunity to voice his views and showing consideration for his right to an opinion also contribute to his confidence, self-esteem, and pride.

In many ways, the young child is a helpless little person who is at the mercy of his bigger and more powerful parents. Abusing the power, parents can literally destroy the child's potential for ever feeling good about himself. Negligent, critical, and harsh parents can make a child feel unimportant, worthless, and lonesome.

One of the easiest ways to help a child regard himself as an important human being is to give the child many opportunities to feel that he is loved. Telling the child that he is loved is not sufficient; actions and attitudes in parenting will convey this feeling to the child. Love is perhaps the highest compliment that one person can give another. The child who feels love will feel secure with those who love him and will feel that he is important to them. Feeling wanted and needed is also a high compliment and the child who can feel loved in addition to feeling wanted and needed will know that he is important.

Guideline 3. *Parents are the child's first models.* Parents are not the child's only models, but they are his first ones and their behavior and attitudes will be copied by the child. The child makes the assumption that if his parents can do something, it must be right. Since the child will learn the acceptable as well as the unacceptable behavior that he observes, the parents are obliged to become good models. A child can accept the fact that there are differences between what his parents, as adults, can do and what he is permitted to do. For example, he can understand that his parents can have a martini before dinner but he cannot. He can accept this just as he can accept the fact that his parents will stay up later than he can. He will understand and go along with the differences because these kinds of behavior are attributed to older people and the child comprehends age differences. But age does not give parents freedom to lie, or lose their tempers, or become violent. It is one thing to tell a child that older people can stay up later than children, but it is another matter to tell the child that older people can tell lies but children cannot. The child sees staying up late as an advantage in being older; he sees the dual standard about telling lies as hypocrisy.

The parent who punishes his child for lying about taking a cookie looks very bad when the telephone rings and the child hears the parent say, "If that's for me, tell them I'm not home." As models for the child the parents are under some pressure. They must recognize their responsibility to set a good example, otherwise they are unfair when they punish for behavior they themselves are guilty of committing. It is unfair for parents to scold the child for having a messy room if the parents' room is equally messy. What is right for the learner is right for the model.

Guideline 4. *It is the responsibility of the parents to train the child.* Parents are in trouble when the child has begun to train the parents, for this means that the child is in control of things. As the adults, the parents are certainly more mature, better informed, more experienced, and more competent to assume the child-training function than the infant, child, or adolescent. The simple message of this guideline is, don't be afraid to train your child. Many parents actually fear taking over the training function, for they doubt themselves and fear the child will not like them. The young child's first few tantrums are inevitable. If they persist, the child must have been rewarded in some way for having had the tantrums. Once the child has learned that he does not gain anything by his tantrums, he will realize that they are ineffective and discontinue having them. Being a creature of habit, the child will continue any habit or practice that provides him with pleasure or satisfaction, regardless of the danger or harmful effects of the act. A child cannot assess the rightness or wrongness of an act until he has learned right from wrong. This must be taught by parents through their training.

Given the opportunity, a three-year-old would stay up until midnight and perhaps sleep later in the morning. If the parents have said that eight o'clock is bedtime and the child is still walking around the house at eleven o'clock, the parents are being trained by the child. They have allowed the child to have a victory over them by mani- pulating their behavior. Because they have allowed the child to see that the bedtime they set can be ignored, the child will ignore other requests. The child has learned that the first "It's time for bed" will be followed by a few, "Now this is the last time" statements, a couple of "Now, I really mean it" remarks, a few "If you don't go to bed" threats, and finally the voice, gesture, or physical act that tells the child he has really achieved his purpose. It is probably three hours past his bedtime and at last the child goes to bed, but on his own terms!

Guideline 5. *A home in which there is a young child should be a child-oriented home.* This does *not* mean a child-centered home. A child-oriented home is simply one where the parents do not forget that a child lives in the house. A child-centered home is one where everything in the home is centered around the child, and allows the child to feel power over his environment. A child-oriented home would be one in which parents exert caution in having arguments in front of the child, or avoid filling a room with interesting but delicate objects that can be touched and possibly broken by the child. The parents will also be careful of the language that is used in front of the child, who or what is discussed in front of the child, and what the child can observe that might be disturbing to him. The child-oriented home concept says that it is the parents' home but a child is living with them. The child should not be ignored; neither should he be the center of attention. The concept implies certain parental restraints, but they need not adversely affect the parents.

Guideline 6. *Active parental involvement is necessary.* The word *parental* includes both the father and the mother. *Active* means that the involvement is not passive. Parents must be willing to spend time with the child, not an excessive amount, but a significant amount of time. This principle states that the *parents* should train the child, not leave the training to a maid, nurse, babysitter, or grandparent. It is unfortunate when the mother must return to full-time work before the child is old enough to be in school a full day. Perhaps the money the mother brings in is not worth the sacrifice the mother is making in absenting herself from the child. In the long run, it may be better to have less materially and work toward developing a happier child.

Active parental involvement would mean that the father has a function that is no less important than the mother's. Merely changing an occasional diaper or reading an occasional story to the child is not a sufficient commitment for the father to make. The child needs both a mother and a father. He can easily perceive paternal rejection when he becomes aware that his father prefers playing golf on Sunday to spending time with him, or when the father comes home and reads the paper or watches television instead of spending time with the child. The actions of the parents are indicative of their priorities and the child soon learns who and what comes first. Fathers who work long hours and who see very little of their families are in danger of defeating the purpose of their efforts. One function of the father is, of course, to support the family. But, being a part of that family is no less a function of the father.

Many fathers feel that they cannot relate to young children. They say that they will show an interest in the children when the children get older. Fathers who have this philosophy have often learned the hard way that when they are ready for their children, their children are no longer interested in them.

It does become a matter of priority, for we are usually able to find time for things that are highest on our priority list. Often when a parent perceives he has been neglectful, he will try to "make it up" to the child. Covering up for guilt by buying something for the child is common. Many people find it difficult to give of themselves, so giving "things" is the best they can do. The child sees it as a poor substitute, for just as you cannot buy love, neither can you offer an acceptable substitute for a missing parent. Many affluent parents have reared their children under conditions that parallel those of the underprivileged child. But, the affluent-underprivileged-child syndrome is even more tragic than the conditions of the underprivileged child, for the affluent parents are in an advantageous position to care for a child.

Guideline 7. *For parental controls to be most effective, they must be established early.* Because the newborn is quick to acquire routines, the first month of the baby's life is not too soon to begin parental controls and good habits with the child. Parents can encourage good sleeping habits by not allowing the baby's crying at night to upset them. The baby can begin to learn that there is a time and place for everything. The baby learns that in the daytime people will pick him up, play with him, and give him attention. But, the baby can also learn that night, and a darkened room, are for sleep. Once the parents put the baby to bed, knowing that he is not ill and no pins are sticking him, they should not return to his room and pick him up if he cries. The newborn will wake for a three a.m. feeding, but when this can be discontinued, the child will learn to sleep through the night. New parents either have to learn to disregard the baby's night crying or end up with months or years of bedtime problems.

When good habits are developed in a young child, parental controls develop simultaneously, since the parents are exerting their controls by what they do to either encourage or discourage a particular habit. For example, if the parents wish to discourage crying or whining behavior, they simply do not allow the unacceptable crying to manipulate them. In this way, the parents control their child's crying by showing him that they will not be influenced by such behavior. This not only discourages the development of a crying habit, but also informs the child that his parents are in control.

However, insofar as early training is concerned, it must be remembered that any behavior that is affected by maturation cannot be expected to develop until the child is physically or emotionally ready for it. A child will not develop certain skills until his maturational level allows him to. Beginning training too early wastes time and can even create a barrier to learning. Toilet training that is started too soon will frustrate a child and can lead to more serious problems later on. The same is true for other skills that require physical maturation, such as walking or talking, and emotional responses that are based on thinking, reasoning, or memory. The six-month-old baby can express the emotions of anger and fear, but not jealousy and joy, which do not make their appearance for another year.

As for parental controls, parental practices that reveal consistency, fairness, firmness, calmness and a sense of humor will do much to establish an early respectful relationship. The child, at any age, must know that his parents mean what they say. Begin this early and avoid later problems. Trite though it may sound, say what you mean; and mean what you say.

Guideline 8. *Child training should follow a law of diminishing structure.* The young child needs the greatest amount of structure and control. As the child matures and gains experience, there should be a resulting expansion of the child's judgment and ability to solve problems. With improved judgment and a greater ability to predict the outcome of his behavior, the child will have less need for parental structure or control. By late adolescence, or when the youngster is 17 or 18 years old, the amount of parental structure should be minimal. This will be the natural outcome when there has been a diminishing structure throughout the child's life and the parents have had many opportunities to assess the child's ability to handle stress, solve problems, and exert rational judgment. A child may know right from wrong, but until he can demonstrate that he is able to practice what he knows he is not ready to go without some external structure. The parents feel they can reduce their controls over the child because of the increased confidence they have in him. This parental confidence is gratifying for the child and is a big boost for his self image. Gradually, the child is made aware that his parents are more trusting of his judgments and ability to make independent decisions. His parents' respect for him adds to the respect he has for himself.

Diminishing structure enables the parents to show their child trust and thereby help him develop confidence in his ability to deal with problems and make good decisions. It can also relieve some of the parental worry since they will have observed the way the child has handled situations that require common sense and appropriate judgment.

Guideline 9. *Parents should encourage only the behavior they term acceptable.* Parents should avoid doing things that encourage the behavior they really want to discourage. Many times parents will inadvertently encourage a child's behavior, despite their desire to see it discontinued. The parents will talk as if they want to see a change, but their actions either perpetuate the problem or do nothing to alter it. The occasional punishment or scolding fails to deter the unacceptable behavior and, under some conditions, could even contribute to the problem. To illustrate this, let us assume the parents of an 8-year-old boy are upset over their son's aggressive behavior. He is constantly hitting his peers and younger sibling; they want to discourage this behavior and feel they have tried all they know to do. This has meant harsh discipline including spanking, shaming the child, taking away his privileges, sending him to his room, and scolding him severely. They have also tried reasoning with him and begging him to stop. Nothing has seemed to be effective for the child continues to hit others.

If the child is aggressive because he seeks attention and is jealous of his younger sibling, or if the child wants to punish his parents for being mean to him, their behavior could actually be encouraging the child to remain aggressive. He is getting the attention he seeks, regardless of the nature of the attention, and he can justify hurting others, for he is also being hurt. Since he cannot hit his parents, who may be the source of his frustration, he hits other, safer targets. He also sees his parents getting verbally and physically violent and, modeling after what he sees, acts in a similar way. For the child to become less aggressive, his parents will have to become less aggressive first. They will have to understand what his behavior is telling them, and do whatever is needed to reduce the problem. The child's aggressive behavior should not give him the attention he may be seeking, and only when he can respond in acceptable ways should he get positive parental attention. However, this does not mean to ignore the unacceptable behavior.

Many parents have been told that if they ignore a child's problem, it will go away. Although this may be good advice for some problems and certain children, there are many problems that are encouraged by ignoring them. Poor table manners, abusive language, temper tantrums, excessive teasing, or mischievousness will not go away if they are simply ignored. Taking no action on these kinds of practices frees the child to continue them and soon they can get out of control.

There are times, though, when a problem resolves itself through patience, understanding, and time, and when not focusing on a behavior can reduce the symptoms. Rather than ignoring the problem, the parents refrain from attention to certain behaviors, so that the child will not become self-conscious or apprehensive. Facial and body tics, early stuttering, and body rocking are examples of behaviors that may disappear when no attention is called to them. When parents are in doubt as to what to do about a specific behavior, it is best to seek professional advice.

Parents often worry about a child who feels inadequate and inferior to his friends. They may see him rejected by his peers and unhappy because he has few friends and is afraid to compete. In their attempt to encourage their child to become more confident they may put pressure on him to socialize more. But, if the child is unsuccessful because he has negative feelings about himself, the parents may add to these feelings by being critical. Saying to a child, "Why do you have to let people push you around," or, "Don't just stand around like a dunce," or, "No wonder people don't want to play with you," does not encourage the child to have more positive feelings about himself. Dwelling on his weaknesses discourages the kind of behavior the parent wants to see.

Nor does the parent discourage unacceptable behavior by reminiscing about his own childhood problems that are similar to the child's. Telling a daughter who has a negative attitude towards her sister, "I can recall how much I hated my sister when I was your age, and how I was punished when I hit her," does not discourage the negative feelings. Such a statement helps the girl to justify her attitude, since she feels just as her parent did.

Parents also inadvertently encourage an unacceptable behavior when their statements and actions are contradictory. A mother may want to discourage her children from tattling on each other. After explaining why this is an unacceptable practice, she may later become angry when one child hits another and say to the child, "From now on, don't hit your sister. If she hits you first, you tell me and I will punish her." This inconsistency is confusing to a child.

Failure to consider a child's readiness can also encourage behaviors that are unacceptable. The child who misbehaves in public is not ready to be taken to a restaurant or department store. The child who cannot play with other children without teasing them or getting into trouble is not ready to be put in a social situation. Similarly, if a child cannot handle short car trips, he is not ready for a long car trip. When experience has shown that their child will have problems in a certain situation, parents must exert caution so as not to allow the child to collect one more bad experience. It is often necessary for parents to protect the child from his own behavior.

The critical element of this guideline is to be careful that what is being done to discourage undesirable behavior is not having a reverse effect. Rewards, which can be verbal, should be given only for behavior that parents want to encourage, and the child's attempts to control his parents by threats or misbehavior must not succeed. Emphasis on positive behavior and constructive things will develop the desirable goals. Punishment is not a positive action, although it may be necessary to deter an unacceptable practice. But even when it is needed, punishment need not be harsh or cruel. It should be firm, fair, and appropriate.

Guideline 10. *Unless parents can be consistent, training will not be established.* This is one of the most fundamental, necessary, and obvious principles. Yet, it is the one that is most frequently disregarded, the one that parents knowingly neglect, and the one that parents allow themselves to believe is the hardest to practice. Consistency is a test of self-discipline. All that it requires of a parent is to do whatever the parent said he was going to do and to do so with regularity. The failure of the parent to be consistent is an invitation to the child to test parental limits, especially when the child relies on the parent to either forget what was said or to weaken and have a change of heart.

There are several reasons for parental inconsistencies. One reason is that parents make threats that are impractical to carry out. A mother may want her son to stop using obscene language. In anger, and impulsively, she could say to him, "If you don't stop saying those things, I'm going to call a policeman and he'll come and put you in jail." The nature of the statement or threat practically assures the child that the parent is bluffing. Another reason for parental inconsistency is laziness. The parent knows that he should follow through with what he said he was going to do, but for one reason or another he just never gets around to it. The excuse is usually, "Well, I forgot to do it." Sometimes parents are inconsistent because they feel sorry for their child. If a parent identifies too closely with the child's problems, he may see his own childhood being repeated and make the same mistakes his own parents made. In this case, inconsistency would relate to sympathy, and the parent would be lacking in courage to be stronger.

Probably the most common explanation for parental inconsistency is the insincerity of the parental statement, whether it be promise or threat. The parents never really considered carrying out their threat, nor can they remember what they threatened. They said what they thought would move their child to do what they wanted. Their hope is that the child will not call their bluff, and to insure this they often become dramatic, emotional, and irrational.

A favorite threat of some parents is that they will do harm to themselves. An actual threat parents have used, "You are going to cause me to have a heart attack," is a variation of the insincere threat. The parents are in trouble if the child is unmoved by unrealistic threats. They may then do or say something that diverts the child from the original threat. For example, having threatened to throw away all of his son's toys because the child did not clean up his room, the father realizes the impracticality of the threat and, for monetary reasons, might divert the child by the threat of taking away desserts for one week. This he is prepared to carry out, and the child will lose his desserts, not his toys.

Punishments that are too harsh are another form of insincerity and cause parents to be inconsistent. In anger a mother might tell her daughter that she will have to go to bed without supper for a week. After the anger subsides, she may realize the unfairness of her punishment and "make a deal" with her daughter. If parents are to be consistent in carrying out punishments, the punishments should be carefully thought out before they are given.

The usual excuses offered by parents for not being consistent are indicative of parental feelings of guilt. Because parents know they *should* be consistent, and because they know they *haven't* been consistent, they feel guilty for contributing to their child's problems. "I know I haven't been consistent," the parent says, "but it's hard to be consistent all of the time." Though it *is* hard to be consistent, the alternative is so devastating to child training that the parent has no choice but to exert a determination to become consistent. Consistency is not the same as inflexibility. Parents should also be flexible, for there are always circumstances that arise which require an exception to the rule. However, once consistency has been established, occasional flexibility is no threat to the training.

Guideline 11. *Firmness and fairness are behaviors that promote parental controls.* Firmness is not meanness. Firmness is related to consistency and will be interpreted by the child as an indication of stability. A firm approach need not be harsh. It should be a calm, confident, and convincing method in which the parent does not have to resort to verbal or physical aggression in order to establish the kind of relationship that encourages mutual respect. With fairness added to it, the relationship can become trusting. Again, there are times when flexibility is necessary. Rigidity in parental behavior fails to recognize the need for adaptations in unusual circumstances. The principles of consistency, firmness, and fairness should be practiced by parents, allowing sufficient latitude for freedom to respond to an unusual situation in an appropriate way.

Guideline 12. *The parents should prepare the child for the world of reality.* The training that parents give to their child should be consistent with what the child will face in his world. In society, people are expected to live by rules. These rules should be taught in the home. In society, people are expected to assume responsibility. This should be taught in the home. Parents do not help their child when they encourage practices in the home that will not be acceptable outside of the home. Nor do parents prepare their child to function in the world if they have overprotected or pampered him. Children who remain dependent upon their parents, even after they have married, and those who have difficulties assuming adult responsibilities, have not been trained to cope with the world.

Many adolescents have not learned to cope with the reality that work is an essential part of life. They view working as unpleasant and avoidable, and see fun and pleasure as the basic purpose of living. Some are resentful of anyone who tries to tell them otherwise. It is possible that the work-value has been over-stressed or not explained properly. They may be negative to work because they cannot understand how work can be a source of much satisfaction and an important and necessary part of life. They see only the routine and boring aspect of work, which unfortunately for many people, is reality.

The child learns reality from what he experiences in his interactions with people. It is important that parents are able to anticipate the everyday problems the child is likely to encounter and begin to discuss ways of coping with them. Parents teach reality when the child is told that things outside the home may be different from what the child is used to. People in the home do not steal from each other; outside the home some people cannot be trusted. A child may see no evidence of violence or abuse in his home, but he should know that for some people this is a common experience. It is unrealistic for a child to believe that all of his associations will be with fair and understanding people. Certainly, there is no need to frighten the young child about reality, but unless he learns how things really are, he will be helpless to deal with problems when they arise. Preparing a child for reality is teaching him about life. Because this is so very important for the child, it should come from the parents in a gradual and meaningful way.

Guideline 13. *Attention should be focused on major issues.* Some people are unable to differentiate a happening from a crisis. When parents make everything a potential disaster, the child will not learn what is important and what is less important. Parents should be careful not to alarm the child unnecessarily, but before this can happen, they must learn not to get alarmed unnecessarily themselves. A home in which everything is a potential crisis is filled with tension and pressure. The child needs to learn to put things into a proper perspective so that he can make a rational evaluation of the relative importance of an event. If he observes that his mother worries when the mailman is late, panics when the refrigerator is left open, and flies into a rage when his father is late for dinner, he will see everything as a big problem, since everything creates tension. The child will not gain perspective on what the really important issues are. Parents may be upset with a daughter who is disrespectful to them, rejects their controls, is doing poorly in school and threatens to run away from home. If her parents make a big issue over the fact that she refuses to make her own bed they are focusing on the least important issue.

In order to overcome the tendency to concentrate on minor issues, parents would have to examine the total situation and decide on those things which are most distressing. If it is discovered that everything is distressing, then it becomes a matter of determining which of the distressing issues should have priority over others. Sometimes it is best to deal with the most serious problem first, and ideally, it is best to deal with causes rather than symptoms. It is helpful if causes can be separated from effects. In the case of the girl that was just cited, her refusal to make her bed would certainly be the effect of something. Negative feelings about herself leading to hostility to parents might be the cause of her behavior. Focusing on the bed-making issue would be inappropriate and unproductive. When the major issues cannot be identified, professional help may be necessary. Parents are often too close to the problems to see the issues.

Guideline 14. *Parents should learn to react, not over-react to behavior.* A reaction is the response that is given to a stimulus. We can react by thinking and reflecting, or we can react by doing or saying something. A reaction can be evaluated by the appropriateness of the response that is given. When it is inappropriate, we are not reacting; we are over-reacting, or possibly under-reacting. Worried, tense, frustrated and unhappy parents are inclined to over-react. They make the "mountains out of molehills" by over-responding to a situation. Most temper outbursts and arguments are examples of over-reaction. The tons of tranquilizers consumed yearly attests to the fact that people do a lot of over-reacting.

When something occurs that interferes with the plans a person has made, a reaction can be expected. It can be one of expressing disappointment, showing anger, or being upset over the change of plans. This is reaction. If the person storms around the house, kicks the furniture, shouts, sets out to get revenge, or allows himself to become so upset that it interferes with the things that must be done, this is over-reaction. When a child spills a glass of milk on the table, the parents should react. They should help the child clean things up, or if the child is old enough to do it all himself, they should expect the child to clean it up. They can explain to him why it happened, or they can say nothing about it if it was an infrequent accident. If they over-react to it, they will put on a display of temper that could make the child feel he has committed a felony punishable by a prison sentence. The child whose parents over-react learns to respond in a similar way, and soon the home becomes a place where everyone over-reacts to everything.

Guideline 15. *Parents should encourage the child to solve problems for himself.* If the child is to grow emotionally and socially, he will have to move in a direction of becoming independent. If parents assume responsibility for solving their child's problems, he will not learn problem solving for himself and will be forced to cling to dependency. The young child may not know how to solve problems, or he may only know how to solve problems in one way. The responsibility of the parents is to ascertain whether or not the child can do anything to help himself. Should they find the child is helpless or frustrated by a lack of problem-solving techniques, they may have to suggest ways to the child, not telling the child what to do, but giving the child a choice of several alternative ways to solve the problem and explaining the consequences of each. Parents who assume the child knows more methods of problem solving than he really does, or parents who stand back and let the child learn everything for himself, can be negligent and even sadistic. If a three-year-old child can do nothing but cry when another child grabs a toy out of his hands, he has communicated his helplessness. If the parents do not suggest different ways for the child to react in the future, he will continue to be helpless in this situation, regardless of how many times it occurs. The parent should make suggestions, allowing the child to make a choice of a more appropriate response, so the child can feel that he has had a role in solving his own problem. For the parents to ridicule the child by calling him a sissy or a coward is simply cruel, and does not help the child to solve his problem.

One of the secrets in making appropriate adjustments in life is a person's ability to find acceptable solutions to problems. Effective problem solving does not happen suddenly. It is the result of training and experiences that have enabled a person to develop confidence in judgments and satisfaction with the usual outcomes. Parents who deny their children these experiences and opportunities for personal success are doing little to encourage the child's positive regard for himself and much to create feelings of personal inadequacy. When parents do not encourage problem solving in their child, they are encouraging dependency upon themselves, possibly as a way of showing the need for parental control in a selfish, rather than constructive way. Parents who are reluctant to see their children grow up and leave them or who want to impress their children with their importance will do problem solving *for* their children, instead of *with* them. Possessive or dominating parents will be threatened by the child's ability to be independent of them. Parents who consider the best interests of the child, however, will encourage him to solve problems for himself as soon as this is practical.

Guideline 16. *Parents should make an effort to understand the child's behavior.* Although parents are not professionally trained to be analytical, they can acquire insights into the reasons for their child's behavior. This understanding puts emphasis on *why* a child is doing something, rather than on *what* the child has done. A common mistake that parents make is to reverse this and concentrate on what the child is doing and expect the child to know why he is doing it. "Why did you do that?" the parent foolishly asks. "I don't know," answers the child. The parent assumes the child must know why he did it and does not accept the only answer the child could possibly give. If a child is six years old and is still wetting his bed at night, the parent who focuses on what the child is doing will be responding to the child in a very different way than will the parent who wants to understand *why* the child is wetting his bed. Could the child be responding to too much pressure? Does he want to displease his parents? Why have attempts to overcome this habit failed? The only time the word *what* will be important to the understanding of the child's behavior is in answer to the question: what does this behavior tell us about the child?

   This guideline asks parents to think about possible explanations for the child's behavior. Why is bedtime a problem? Why does the child cry so much? Why doesn't the child have friends? Why does he dislike school? Perhaps the parents will not be able to come up with answers to questions like these, but they are advised to think about causes before taking any actions on effects. Sometimes it helps for the parents to attempt to put themselves in the child's position, asking, "If I were a six-year-old child, why would I punch my three-year-old sister whenever no one was looking?" They will answer themselves with a variety of *maybe's*. "Maybe I'm jealous of her . . . but if so, why?'' ''Maybe my parents make too much of a fuss over her.'' It could even be, ''Maybe I just want to hit someone, and she's the safest thing I can find.''

Understanding the reasons for a child's behavior should begin with a *parental analysis* of the troubling situation. This involves a search for possible explanations and should focus on the causes of the behavior rather than the symptoms which are observable. Initially, the search is one of speculating and making inferences about what a specific behavior may be signaling. Then each of the possible explanations should be examined to determine whether it can be a contributing factor, or if it can be ruled out. The items that remain can provide some understanding into the child's behavior.

To demonstrate how a parental analysis might operate, consider the problem of a seemingly bright child doing below average work in school. We might speculate that a child's poor performance in school could be due to a variety of causes and proceed to list them.

A seemingly bright child may do below average work in school when he is:
— really not as bright as his parents think he is
— resentful of authority and sees his teacher in this role
— unwilling to please his parents, who want him to do well in school
— in conflict with his teacher
— unable or unwilling to compete
— being unfairly compared with siblings or peers
— teased by classmates when he gets high grades
— fearful of failure and therefore unwilling to exert an effort
— involved in too many extra-curricular activities
— angry with his parents and seeking to punish or upset them
— stubborn and only does what he wants to do
— not used to completing a task
— lacking knowledge of the fundamentals that are needed to do assignments
— not receiving appropriate encouragement from his parents
— in poor health, not getting a proper diet, not getting the amount of sleep his body requires
— suffering from vision or hearing difficulties that interfere with learning
— lacking good work habits
— in a classroom that is disorganized or lacking in structure
— bored by work that is below his ability level

—   pressured by parents to get higher grades
—   upset because of personal problems that interfere with learning

This would not represent a complete list of possible explanations, for more knowledge about the child would suggest other reasons for his behavior. Nevertheless, the parents would then examine the list in order to develop insights into the child's problems. A conference with the teacher or school counselor would be helpful. There may be times that additional professional assistance will be needed, but before consulting with mental health personnel, parents should have done their homework by sitting down with each other and trying to discuss the problem in an objective way.

Parents who attempt to understand their child's behavior will discover they get to know the child as a person, not just as their child. This not only encourages parents to appreciate their child, but also communicates to the child that his parents care enough to want to understand him.

Guideline 17. *Parental interactions are more effective when they are positive.* One of the most common problems parents have with each other comes about when they do not agree on child-rearing practices. The father may feel his wife is too protective of the child; the mother feels her husband is too demanding of him. Their disagreement usually results in arguments, but the child's behavior goes unchanged. When parents feel they have a problem with their child and do nothing but blame, insult, accuse or criticize each other, nothing constructive is accomplished.

If both parents are involved in the training of the child, it is inevitable that some differences of opinion will occur. But, this does not mean that differences must create bad feelings between the parents, nor does it mean that the differences cannot be resolved. Angry feelings between parents are usually the result of defensive and dogmatic attitudes in which the problem of what to do about the child becomes instead a matter of who is right and why. What frequently happens when parents disagree over training practices is that one parent removes himself from the situation with the sarcastic comment, "O. K., since you know everything, you take over and leave me out of it!" Needless to say, this only creates additional problems.

The resolution of parental differences lies in the ability of parents to be able to discuss differences without becoming defensive and negative. When parents can view a child's problem as a common concern and see the need to work things out together in a positive way, the task of problem solving is simplified. There is a fine line between constructive and destructive comments and the difference often lies in the attitudes of the people involved. If the listener is defensive and overly sensitive to criticism, he will interpret what he hears as destructive. Because a lot of what parents do in training children is based on trial and error, parents have to learn to become understanding of each other and be willing to listen to the feelings expressed by the other person. A mother may have strong views about the need for a child to go to school in the morning in a good mood. In putting her feelings to practice, she may avoid a confrontation with her child that could lead to a blow-up before the child goes off to school. By telling her child, "When you come home from school this afternoon, we have something to discuss," she is postponing an action with the hopes that the problem can be worked out after school. This is a trial effort and only experience will show whether it is an effective method. The father, who may disagree with the postponement of a parental action, should be willing to give the mother's method a chance and privately discuss her rationale with her.

Positive interactions between parents would involve open discussion and an explanation of feelings. More can be accomplished in an atmosphere that is calm and in which tempers are kept under control. Little is accomplished when parents are fighting each other and the child is witness to the disagreement. The child can know that his mother and father do not always agree on everything, but if he is to learn self-control, he should see his parents resolve their differences in a mature way.

The same positive interaction that should be possible between parents should be present between the child and his parents. No useful purpose is served by insulting, labeling, degrading, or embarrassing a child. When parents find it necessary to be critical of their child, they can do so without doing harm to his developing self-confidence. They can show that they disapprove of what he did without withdrawing their love or showing indifference to the child. Interactions that are negative will encourage negative responses and lower the individual's feelings of self-esteem. When this happens, people who have reason to love and relate to each other develop hostile and aggressive feelings towards one another.

Guideline 18. *Establish and maintain a strong family unit.* In unity there is strength, and words from the Revolutionary War still hold true: "United we stand, divided we fall." Family unity can offer support, security, and the knowledge that someone really cares about you. This is important, for without these feelings a child can experience the pain of loneliness, the despair of being isolated, and the depression that accompanies the feelings of not belonging anywhere. The family unit is the most fundamental and necessary unit in society. When it weakens, society is weakened. The family provides meaning to the child's activities through approval, encouragement, and rewards. It gives the child identity and is both a safe place to express feelings and an appropriate source of protection and trust. When it functions as a cohesive unit, the family teaches the values of cooperation, honesty, loyalty, respect, and love.

Family unity requires a commitment and an unselfish feeling towards each other. It comes about as a result of a joint effort from all the members of the family to work together and live harmoniously. It need not result in a loss of personal freedom, but it does demand the sacrificing of selfish freedom. The unified family requires active participation and certain basic agreements in terms of purpose, process, and beliefs. It is not simply a matter of doing things together, but a willingness and desire to please one another and work towards common goals.

The weak family unit encourages separatism and selfish attitudes. It teaches the child to think only of himself and to use others as a means to gratify personal pleasures. When members of a family feel free to go their separate ways and "do their own thing," they do not contribute to the welfare of others in the family. They give little or nothing, and take what they can. They cannot trust and respect others, for they are not trusted and respected by members of their family.

The breakdown of the family unit is often responsible for delinquent behavior, for the child who is not protected by his family turns to delinquent gangs for his identity and security. Lack of family protection, which is afforded in the strong family group, is seen as one of the underlying causes of juvenile delinquency. The family that can meet the needs of the child can prevent the child from seeking satisfaction from groups whose values run contrary to society.

Everyone has a function in the structure of a family unit. At times these functions are quite specific and individually prescribed; other times they are broadly defined and involve group participation. When parents can establish an atmosphere in which family members help one another and share, they communicate the idea that everyone in the family is important and needed. By teaching responsibility they are enhancing the individual's feeling of worth and value. At a time when computerization is making life so impersonal, the family must be a source for self-identity, lest the child grow up seeing the world as an indifferent mass. The presence or absence of a unified family determines whether the place the family lives should be called a house or a home. A group of strangers can live in a house; a family lives in a home.

Guideline 19. *Build on a child's abilities and emphasize positive behavior.* The best way to motivate a child is to offer encouragement in those things he can do, rather than to dwell on what he cannot do. The self-confidence gained through this encouragement will enable the child to have a better attitude towards improving himself and pleasing his parents. The child who is continually told what he cannot do and is made to feel inferior may become defeated and develop the attitude, "What's the use!" When it is necessary to be critical of the child, it is important that this criticism does not belittle or ridicule him. Nor is it sufficient to say, "We know you can do better," and expect changes to result. A child is motivated to learn only when he wants to learn and feels he can be successful.

Building on a child's abilities involves knowledge of what to expect from him. It is not realistic to expect a child to function beyond his potential, and attempts to embarrass the child into a better performance only frustrate and antagonize him. Parents have to assess what their child can do and begin at that point. A child who can play well with one or two children may have difficulty with a group of playmates. Rather than stressing his inability to interact with the group, the parents should reinforce his ability to play with one child and encourage him to develop similar behaviors with groups of children. A child who is having difficulty in learning to tie his shoes might be encouraged to learn to tie them if he can feel praise for being able to zip his zipper or dress himself. He gets the feeling of, "I can do it, and I want to." This promotes growth for it makes an accomplishment something that gives pleasure to both himself and his parents.

The home that dwells on negative behavior is usually punishment-oriented. In such a home, the child must find ways of adjusting to the punishments. He can develop an indifference to negative and punishing behavior and become a martyr, or he can rebel and become negativistic. Either way the child and his parents are in conflict and the child will not be motivated to please others.

When the child learns that his parents reward acceptable and appropriate behavior, he is encouraged to exert effort in ways that are mutually satisfying. Rewards can be verbal, for recognition or praise is frequently sufficient. Taking the time to look at his school work, commenting on his progress, and showing pleasure in his accomplishments is very gratifying for a child. Material rewards, which are more appealing to the child, are often not as effective, for the child may begin to work for the bribe, rather than for the feeling of accomplishment. Frequent gift-giving can encourage the child to expect to receive gifts for everything he does. An occasional reward of a toy, candy bar, or other object is not harmful and lets the child know his parents want to please him, too. The emphasis should not be on gifts, but rather on approval for things that are done well or behavior that indicates maturity.

Guideline 20. *Permit the child to experience some frustration.* The training the child receives in the home should be consistent with the kind of training that will help him adjust to his world. Every person experiences some frustration in his daily interactions with society. To deny the child the chance to learn to cope with these frustrations is to over-protect him. The child whose parents have gone out of their way to avoid exposing him to frustrations will not be equipped to handle them when they arise in situations over which his parents have no control. Parents who have spoiled or pampered their child have not allowed him sufficient frustration.

Because children often seek to do things beyond their ability and want to copy older children and parents, frustration in children is inevitable. The child becomes frustrated with himself when he cannot accomplish what he wants. He wants to be older, bigger, and more capable. He wants to succeed in everything he tries, and have things on his terms. Because this is not possible, he becomes frustrated. A certain amount of frustration, however, is both healthy and desirable. When frustration can motivate a child to improve on skills he is maturationally ready for, or result in determination to succeed, it can be an asset for the child.

Permitting a child to experience frustration and teaching him how to deal with it are parental tasks. Frustration, like competition and conformity, is a part of social living. Learning how to handle it is vital to a person's stability and ability to adjust to the stresses of everyday living. In order to learn to cope with frustration we must have experience with it.

Guideline 21. *Assess the child's readiness for an activity.* If a child is ready for an activity there is good reason to expect a successful performance. Putting a child in a situation before he is ready can result in failure, frustration, or a refusal to engage in the activity. The young child cannot always assess his own readiness for a situation. Because he wants to do something, he is prepared to say he is ready for it. He may feel he is ready to cross a street by himself because he wants to visit a friend. The parental assessment of his readiness for this activity might not support the child's feelings. In this case, the child thinks he is ready, the parent does not. The reverse occurs when the parent feels the child is ready for something, and the child's actions show otherwise. The musicallyminded mother who decides her four-year-old should begin to take piano lessons or the father who feels his pampered six-year-old needs an overnight trip may both believe their child is ready for these activities. Yet, they may have neglected to consider the child's feeling of readiness and consequently, the former child could end up being frustrated and resentful of piano lessons, and the latter child might become afraid of camps and avoid them in the future. The child's facility with the activity and his enjoyment of it can be indicators of his readiness.

Some children may never appear ready for certain activities. The child who wants to remain home with his mother may never indicate that he is ready to begin school. Some children who have strong dependent needs may wait a long time before they begin to take an interest in dressing or feeding themselves. There are times when a child needs some pushing, but parents must be cautious with respect to both the how and when of introducing new activities. A safe rule is: When in doubt, wait.

Guideline 22. *Reasoning with a child is more effective than authoritarianism.* Many parents think that it is necessary to shout, threaten, spank and show force in order to develop controls over their children. Such parents believe that loudness means firmness and that the child who fears his parents will obey them. How effective is shouting when parents find themselves shouting frequently? How effective is spanking when parents find themselves spanking almost daily? An effective method is one that either deters or prevents misconduct. Authoritarian demands and harsh punishments will develop fear, anger, and disrespect within the child. Reasoning with the young child is much more effective and has fewer harmful side effects.

Parents can begin to reason with a child as soon as he can comprehend the spoken word. Reasoning does not require lengthy explanations or long lectures. It should be brief and to the point and should contain the common courtesies of "please" and "thank you." "Please don't throw your spoon on the floor," a mother tells her three-year-old. "You'll need it to eat with." The child may have to test the mother, but mother's tone of voice and facial expression will convey to the child that she is not teasing or fooling. When the child holds the spoon in the air, as if to throw it on the floor, and then puts it down on the table because of the mother's request, a "thank you" from the mother communicates that she is pleased with her child's behavior. The child feels he has accomplished something that was good, and everyone is pleased. This is far better than the impatient and harsh statement, "Put that spoon down this minute or I'll give you a good spanking." Although each child may comply with his parent's wish, the former child does so out of respect, the latter out of fear.

In reasoning with a child, the parents attempt to offer an explanation for their requests. With the very young child, these reasons need not be complicated and whenever possible should offer positive suggestions. If a child is standing on a swing, the parent could say, "Please don't stand on the swing; you might slip and fall off. Why don't you sit down on it and then you can swing." As the child gets older, reasoning is easier since he is better able to see the logic in things. Reasoning is not the same as defending a position. "Because I think you will be hurt" is a valid reason. To defend this statement is something else, and although the child may want his parent to engage in a defense or debate, reasoning is based on a judgment and once the decision has been made, the parent should stay with it.

The child who is not happy with the parent's decision may ask, "Why do I have to . . ." Some parents answer this with, "Because I told you to, and I'm your mother." "Big deal," the child says under his breath, "who asked you to be?" Saying, "Because I'm your *mother*," is really not a reason that a child will accept. Whenever a parent says "No" to a child, he must have had some reason, and the child is entitled to know what the reason was. Even if the reason was based entirely on a parental judgment it is better to say, "I feel it's too cold to go outside and play" than to pull parental rank on the child.

Reasoning can also be used in seeking cooperation from the child. The authoritarian parent might say, "If you don't do your homework you won't have dinner." The bribing parent might say, "If you do your homework I'll let you go to the movies on Saturday." The reasoning parent would say, "*When* you have finished your homework, you can watch television. Homework comes before television." No bribe is being offered, no deal is being made. The child is learning a priority system that places first things first. Reasoning with a child is also training him for the many times he will have to use reasoning in his daily life.

Guideline 23. *Develop sensitivity to the feelings and needs of the child.* Becoming sensitive to the feelings of a person requires a deliberate attempt to understand how he feels. A person who is sensitive to the feelings of another person is able to pick up the cues that convey the feelings of that person. It is not difficult to know when a child is happy or when he is upset. When a child comes home and bursts into the kitchen and excitedly wants to tell his mother that his class is going to the circus, the sensitive mother is aware of what her child needs at that moment. He needs his mother to listen and share his excitement. If a child has just scraped his knee and is fearful of the blood oozing out of the wound, the sensitive parent offers reassurance, comfort, and attention. Being sensitive to a child's feelings requires the parent to attempt to see things as they must appear to the child. It is easy for an adult to forget what kinds of things are upsetting to children. Not being allowed to have a penny for a bubble gum machine, being called a sissy, or being excluded from a game of hopscotch, can be very disturbing to a young child. Being sensitive is not the same as showing pity or giving sympathy; it is based on understanding feelings and identifying with the way a person experiences something.

In order to be sensitive to a child's needs, parents have to know their child. They have to know the kinds of things that interest and excite him, what situations he feels comfortable and uncomfortable in, what his needs for privacy are, how self-directed he is, how dependent or independent he is, and how he reacts to winning or losing. They also have to know when and how to encourage their child and how much pressure to put on him. Knowledge of the child enables the parents to predict feelings in order to understand how the child may be reacting.

Insensitive parents are oblivious or indifferent to the feelings of their child. They expect the child to react as they do and have difficulty in sharing his joys, excitements, sorrows or frustrations. They reason that what is not important to them should not be important to the child, and being insensitive, these parents judge things according to their attitudes about things. For this reason, insensitive parents are usually selfish, despite the things they may give to their child.

The sensitive parent knows when his child is frustrated and

needs help, when he is asking for private time with his parent, when he is ready to make certain decisions for himself, and when rules can be relaxed. He also knows if the child has had an upsetting experience in school, such as doing the wrong homework, he doesn't need another bad experience at home by being insulted and reminded of his mistake.

The importance of developing sensitivity lies in the support it can give a child. There will be many times when parents are helpless to give anything more than support, understanding, or reassurance. Parents are not always going to be the child's panacea, but they can always be his source of comfort and security. Relating to the child in a way that communicates, "Yes, I understand how you must feel," can be a source of comfort, even though the parents are helpless to do or say more. Similarly, sensitive parents will react with delight when they perceive their child is pleased with himself and proud of a performance. Their actions communicate "We are happy for you and share your satisfaction."

Guideline 24. *Create an environment that is relatively free from pressures and tensions.* No environment can be completely free from pressures and tensions. A home is relatively free from them if pressure and tension are the exception, not the rule of the house. Although some people say that they function well under pressure, they cannot say that constant pressure is comfortable or desirable. Growing up is filled with numerous inevitable built-in pressures. The very young child feels the pressure of striving to walk and to talk, learning what to do and what not to do. The older child feels the pressures of school achievement, adherence to rules at home, social relationships, and learning to control impulsive behavior. The adolescent feels the pressures of competition and need to succeed in social and academic situations. With pressure will come tension, expressed in worry, fear, and feelings of inadequacy.

Since the child cannot always escape these feelings, it stands to reason that he needs a safe place where he will not have to worry about pressure. His home should be this place. One way the parents can help create the safety the child needs is to hold demands to a minimum and keep them appropriate to his ability. The child will then not feel pressure to produce beyond his means, even though he may need some pressure to insure that he produces according to his potential. Respecting the child as an individual who possesses uniqueness and not expecting him to live up to unreasonable goals are ways of accomplishing this. Another way to create an environment that is relatively free from pressure and tension is to attempt to put things in a proper perspective. When parents over-react to stress, they are not developing a calm or relaxed environment.

A third way to reduce pressure in the home is to become aware of those things that bring about pressure and try to avoid them when possible. Arguments create pressure; can they be avoided, or at least significantly curbed? Busy schedules create pressure; can they be reduced or organized more efficiently? Differences in opinion create pressure; can they be put in perspective or resolved?

Most young children have a low tolerance for pressure and tension and many of their problems can be traced to home pressures. Frequently they are expressed in observable and physical symptoms. Nail biting, bed wetting, stuttering, facial tics, sleep problems and restless behavior may indicate that the child is feeling pressure. Keeping pressure at a minimum is advantageous for the entire family.

Guideline 25. *Mutual respect is necessary for a good family relationship.* One of the best predictors of a good family relationship is the respect shown between members of the family. Parents show respect for their child when their attitudes and behavior convey a feeling of trust, confidence, and positive regard. A child will feel he is respected by his parents when he is included in their discussions, when his opinions are encouraged, and when he is able to realize that he is an important person in their lives. Conversely, a child will not feel respected by his parents when they intimidate, insult, or abuse him.

The child communicates his respect for parents when he willingly and spontaneously seeks to please them and accepts their controls. He also shows respect when he incorporates the parental values as his own and can be comfortable with his parents. The child who fears his parents may not respect them, nor will the child who is in frequent conflict with his parents show respect to them.

Mutual respect does not mean complete agreement with or submission to others. Parents and children who respect each other may disagree on many things and, at times, become angry with each other. But, mutual respect gives the members of a family the right to disagree without fear of threat, loss of love, or unpleasant arguments. Parents show their respect for their child as a human being when they allow him to have an opinion that differs from theirs, even though their judgment may prevail in matters that involve parental decisions.

They are respecting the child's right to express his views as well as his right to understand the reasons for their decisions.

As parents take pride in their child's accomplishments they develop respect for the child's ability. When the child can sense parental pride, he can feel good about what he is doing and soon will begin to respect himself. Respect of oneself is important, for it leads to respect for others.

The lack of respect between members of a family is one of most common features in a poor family relationship. A home in which respect is lacking is one in which children willfully disobey and torment parents by verbal abuse, show open rebellion to parental authority and an insensitivity to the feelings and needs of others. The correlation between family problems and mutual disrespect is high and the reasons that have brought about the disrespect are not easy to forget.

Respect must be earned; it is not automatic. Nor does it come about by parental legislation. The parent who repeatedly finds himself telling his child, "You should respect your parents," should realize that if the basis for respect were there the statement would not be needed. Just as parents respect the positive qualities they see in their child, the child learns to respect the positive qualities he sees in his parents. Mutual respect will develop when members of the family have a meaningful and positive relationship with each other.

Guideline 26. *Smiles and a sense of humor are indispensable in child training.* One of the most satisfying and pleasant experiences that parents of the newborn baby have is when they see their infant smile. Smiling signifies satisfaction, contentment, and happiness, and conveys the feelings of friendliness and acceptance. Unhappy people seldom smile.

Having a good sense of humor is not the same as being able to tell a funny joke or being successful in getting others to laugh. It is the ability to recognize the imperfection of a situation and identify with the consequences in a non-threatening way. A parent who can see the humor of the situation when the three-year-old decides to wear his bowl of cereal upside down as a hat is showing an awareness that the three-year-old is not a perfectly mature child and an appreciation of the slap-stick comedy of the event. Of course it takes time and energy for the parent to clean up the child's mess, but it would take the same time and energy whether the parent is angry or amused by the child's behavior. A repeat performance of the act can be discouraged by a firm "no," and to avoid the child having the notion that what he did was entertaining to his parent, an audible laugh would not be appropriate.

In the training of the child, a sense of humor enables the parent to relate to the antics of the child, aware that he too was once a child. The parent without a sense of humor will be inclined to take everything very seriously and play up issues that should be played down. The child is responsive to what he sees, and seeing the parent smile is a signal of approving behavior and is also rewarding.

A sense of humor should not be confused with sarcasm or ridiculing remarks. The parent who laughs at his child's mistakes or awkwardness is not revealing a sense of humor, but insensitivity or a sadistic need. Many things that a child says and does are funny, but sometimes it is best not to laugh in front of the child, especially if the child senses you are laughing at him. Humor can release aggression and hostile feelings. It can also break the tension in a situation and help put someone at ease. When used effectively by parents, it can soften the impact of an otherwise grim set of circumstances.

The young child becomes frustrated easily because many things are not easy for him to do. He likes to play with toys but does not have the same enthusiasm for putting toys away. Cajoling the child who is frustrated because he must put away his things is a more effective method than one that is demanding or angry. "Let's pretend you are a big vacuum cleaner, and swoop up all these blocks and put them on the shelf," says the parent. A child would rather hear this than some angry threat and harsh voice.

A sense of humor requires patience and a willingness to look at the lighter side of things. The child who acquires a sense of humor can be more objective about his shortcomings, for he will have learned that he is not perfect and that it is silly to expect perfection. The child who can say, "Boy, did I mess up this room," is one who will be more likely to see the humor in the situation and cheerfully go about the task of cleaning it up.

Guideline 27. *Encourage social behavior. Discourage antisocial behavior.* Because social interaction is so important in our society, the child should be taught the social behaviors that are acceptable and rewarded by society. A list of social behaviors would include common courtesies such as "please" and "thank you," learning to take turns in play, not teasing or bullying others, respect for other people's property, honesty, fair play, cooperation, appropriate table manners, personal hygiene, and consideration for others. Parents do not usually teach antisocial behavior, but neither do some parents discourage it. The parent who looks up from his newspaper and casually says, "Now you know you shouldn't have hit Billy, you're much bigger than he is," is not really doing much to discourage his child from aggressive behavior. Likewise, parents who buy their child toys that are replicas of machine guns, flame throwers, hand grenades, bayonets, or pistols, are not encouraging social play. Toys that simulate violence will stimulate violent play. It is unfortunate that our crime rate has made it necessary for parents to give their children lessons in self-defense, for teaching a child karate and other ways of protecting himself is not developing social behaviors. Because a child has learned to hurt someone, the likelihood he will practice what he has been taught is good.

That little boys have always been given guns to play with and that we have always been involved in wars are not unrelated facts. Toy knives do not encourage a child to play in a nonviolent way; toy soldiers do not depict a peace-loving society; toy battleships do not stress the fun of boating. Cartoons that show violence are not relaxing for a child; western movies with "bad guys" and killings do not present an attractive view of early America; and clever plots to steal or murder do not teach a child to trust and relate to his peers.

A certain amount of antisocial behavior can be expected in all children and is considered "normal." It is expressed in negative and antagonistic actions and is related to a lack of maturation. It reaches its peak during puberty when the greatest number of changes in the child's self-concept occur. The child who engages in antisocial behavior usually does so intentionally, for he is old enough to know the differences between acceptable and unacceptable behavior. By choosing the unacceptable, he may be revealing his needs for self-gratification, revenge, power, or a scapegoat for feelings of hostility and frustration. It is usually not accidental when a child constantly hits and abuses his younger brother, knowing he will be punished for it. He must feel that it is worth any punishment he will receive, and lectures about right and wrong are usually ineffective. Somehow, his antisocial behavior has been encouraged. Harsh punishment can encourage it by making the child angry and vindictive. Lack of parental consistency, or giving too much attention to negative behavior can also encourage it.

The best way to discourage antisocial behavior is by giving no reward to unacceptable behavior. Shouting may be a reward for the child who wants to see his parents get upset, and who gets the attention he seeks. Spanking may be a reward if the child gets satisfaction in being a martyr. Once a child's actions are unsuccessful in getting him what he wants, and he realizes what he is losing by being antisocial, he may begin to be motivated to alter his ways.

Guideline 28. *Encourage conversation in the home that includes the child.* Parents become excited when their baby says his first words and reward his early speaking efforts. They encourage speech because it indicates the child is maturing and, through language, communication is facilitated. It also helps to establish the relationship between the child and his parents. When parents encourage their young child to talk about his daily experiences, they communicate their interest in his world. This motivates the child to become more aware of his activities and provides him with a practice situation in relating to others on a verbal level.

By listening to what the child has to say, parents allow him to feel that his contributions are important and this helps to establish positive feelings towards himself. In the later years of a child's life it will be important that he feel free to talk with his parents, for unless this feeling is established in the early years, it will be difficult for the child to relate with his parents when his doubts, concerns, or problems are troubling.

Many parents talk *to* their children, rather than *with* them. Stating rules, giving advice, criticism or praise is not necessarily talking with a person. Talking with a person implies a two-way conversation and is more of a discussion than a lecture or monologue. Saying to a child, "That was a nice project you made," or "don't eat with your fingers" does not encourage conversation. It is verbal communication, but it is limited insofar as a response is concerned. "That was a nice project you made. Tell me how you went about doing it," is an invitation to the child to talk about himself and his achievements. It also conveys interest and curiosity which affords the child an opportunity to instruct his parents for a change. Parents who believe "children should be seen, not heard" discourage dialogue and shouldn't be surprised if the child eventually shuts them out of his life.

Many mothers complain that their husbands don't talk with them. They are frustrated when their husbands come home from work, eat dinner, and spend the evening watching TV or sleeping in a chair. To add to their frustration, they may be aware that their husbands converse with other people, yet, have nothing to say to their wives. The complaint of many husbands is the opposite. They are critical of the "small talk" and gossip they hear and attempt to discourage it by removing themselves as a potential audience. Obviously, environments like these are not conducive for children to learn to converse with their parents. The child should hear conversation that is congenial, informative, and concerned with the welfare of others.

The lack of conversation in a family signals problems which should be explored. The reasons why members of a family are not conversant with each other could be based on fear of criticism, disinterest in the activities of family members, personal discontentment, or an inability or unwillingness to relate to others. Regardless of the reason, the lack of conversation in a home is an important symptom of family problems. Where there is a pleasant interchange of ideas and opinions, there is a greater potential for family cohesiveness and mutual respect.

Guideline 29. *Nobody is perfect.* Perfection implies the highest degree of excellence and a faultless performance. It is an unrealistic expectation in child training. The perfect parent does not exist, nor does the perfect child. There are good parents, effective parents, and parents who rear their child intelligently. Similarly, there are good children, competent children, and children who approximate their full potential. Even the most effective parent recognizes that he is going to make some mistakes and hopes they are few and not damaging to his child. He is also aware that by the very nature of what children are, namely immature in comparison to adult standards, they will also make mistakes. The mistakes committed by the child in the process of growing and maturing can be regarded as growing pains and are unavoidable in the trial-and-error learning the child undergoes in the accumulation of experience and knowledge.

Despite the fact that parents readily admit that to expect perfection is unrealistic, many would like to see their child come close to it. They reveal this by attitudes that put pressure on the child to always succeed, be the best, and do everything the right way. Such parents respond to their child's mistakes as punishable behavior. Although they say that all they want from their child is the best he can do, they are critical of an imperfect performance. Parents who do not know their child's potential are more likely to have unrealistic expectations. Also, parents who have over-assessed their child's potential will be inclined to push him beyond his limits.

Mistakes can become a catalyst for growth, for some learning may result from most experiences. The child must see that his parents, as models, are not perfect and that they will make occasional mistakes, as he does. When parents communicate to their child that they are not perfect, the child does not have to worry about copying a model that is beyond his ability. When all is said and done, parents are human, and, as Shakespeare phrased it, "To err is human."

Guideline 30. *Remember that a child is not an adult.* There are significant differences between the behavior of the young child and adolescent, and between the adolescent and adult. These differences are both qualitative and quantitative. The unknowing or impatient parent views the ideal young child as an adolescent and expects him to act accordingly. Sometimes, he may even expect the "good" child to act like an adult. If his child is fussing in a restaurant, the unthinking parent might ask the seven-year-old, "Why can't you sit still like a grown up?" and be unaware of what he is asking.

The parent does not have to talk down to a child, but he should try to approach him at his own level. This is important both in speaking with a child and in expectation for his performance. It is easy to forget that a child acquires common sense through learned experiences and the ability to predict outcomes. His judgment is not the same as his parents', nor are his priorities, interests, goals, or feelings the same.

Parents often find themselves arguing with their child as if he were an adult. They use the reasoning they have acquired in their lifetime to try to offset the logic of their child. They expect their child to see things their way since it is logical to them, as adults, that their way is best. These parents have not learned that arguing with a child does not teach a child, it simply frustrates him. When parents allow themselves to get into an argument with their child they have elevated him to an adult status, or have allowed their child to lower them to his level. Either way, when parents argue with their child they temporarily forget their child is not an adult. Verbal exchanges that explain, clarify, inform, or discuss issues are more effective than arguments.

Parents should not expect more from a child than he is capable of producing. A common complaint of children is that their parents treat them as if they were children, but expect them to act as if they were older. The parent who does not know what to expect from a child is urged to talk with his local librarian who can recommend readings that discuss the chronological development of the child. Adult education programs that deal with child development are another source for parents who need knowledge of what children can be expected to do at various ages. There is a difference between the maturity of a child and maturity in the adult. This difference is based on the expectations for both, and more is expected from the adult.

Supporting Hints

These guidelines could be regarded as "do's" in that they recommend specific actions. To balance them, here are a few "don'ts." Again, many of the "don'ts" represent common sense items, but they are principles that are frequently neglected.

— Don't expect changes in behavior to occur suddenly.
— Don't forget that a child's emotions are explosive and brief. A child can say he hates you and want to kiss you sixty seconds later.
— Don't allow the child to break down your resistance. When the parent feels that he is about to explode, it is best to leave the room and become involved in something else for awhile. Then return to the child with calmness and determination, instead of rage and desperation.
— Don't be afraid that a child will withdraw love from you because you have been firm and fair. Love is not that fragile.
— Don't allow one bad day or experience to discourage you. The occasional set-back or disappointment is to be expected, especially in the early years.
— Don't become upset or defensive when others are critical of your methods. Remember, as parents you must live with your child and it is easy for those who aren't responsible to criticize.

In all probability, most parents are using some of these guidelines in their current parenting practices. But the use of some without the use of others could negate or offset the gains. For example, parents may be careful not to argue in front of their children. They may also be consistent as well as firm and fair. But, if they are not good models for the child to copy, the child may acquire a negative set of behaviors despite some of the appropriate practices of the parents. The parent who loses his temper teaches his child very little about self-control. Even if the parent apologizes or tries to excuse himself the experience cannot be erased.

Many of the mistakes that parents make are the result of fear of doing the wrong thing or fear they have already done the wrong thing. Parents who feel they have made mistakes in child rearing have regrets and experience guilt. But, the important consideration is what is happening in the present and what will occur in the future. The past can neither be forgotten nor erased, but the future can correct some of the mistakes from the past. Feeling guilty is not constructive unless it stimulates the determination to alter the present, when this is possible.

Perhaps the most efficient way for parents to examine what they are doing in their parenting is to put their actions to the test of outcomes. Once the parents have learned to predict outcomes, they are in a better position to evaluate their actions. If a mother is upset because her four-year-old son will not eat, she may be inclined to force him to eat by making him sit at the table until he is finished. However, if she considers the predictable outcome of this behavior, she will see that it may make him despise mealtime or develop a nervous stomach. Giving the child smaller portions of food and setting a time limit without showing anger could give a child an attainable goal with a good chance for success.

If a child is afraid of a dark room, the parents could force him to overcome his fear by demanding that he go into a dark room and see for himself that nothing is going to happen to him. But again, the predicted outcome of this behavior is that the child will begin to fear the parents as well as the dark room. Helping the child overcome his fear of dark rooms by offering reassurances and gradually moving the child into a darkened room will produce more lasting results. If the child trusts his parents, he knows that they will not let him be harmed. Shaming the child into doing something by ridicule or insults will have the predictable outcome of shaking the child's confidence in himself.

Child training requires common sense, knowledge of effective methods, a willingness to assume responsibility, and the flexibility to discontinue practices that do not seem to be working. And yet, one of the most essential requirements and virtues of a parent is the patience an adult can have with a child.

- 5 -

The Trouble With Parents

Case Illustration Number 4

The scene is the office of a child psychotherapist. The parents of a six-year-old boy have come in to talk about their child. The dialogue is as follows:

Therapist: Tell me what your concern is.

Mother: Well, I really don't know where to begin. *(She looks at her husband.)* Why don't you start?

Husband: No, you're the one who thinks there's something wrong with Bobby. You tell him.

Mother: Well, I'm worried about the way Bobby gets along with people. He's always starting some sort of trouble. And he comes home and tells me that no one wants to play with him. I'm afraid that he's going to be a very unhappy child. *(Long pause.)* He's not doing well in school. I've brought his report card. You can see what the teacher writes about him. *(She hands the report card to the therapist who glances at it. There are some checkmarks indicating satisfactory progress and Ns which means needs improvement. The report card indicates Ns in self-control, cooperation, and completing assignments. There are Ss in all of his academic subjects.)*

Therapist: (After a quick examination of the card.) It looks like the teacher's concern is more about his behavior than his ability.

Mother: Yes, and that's why I'm worried. He's not paying attention in school, and he won't listen to his teacher. If he's doing this now, what's going to happen later?

Therapist: How consistent is this behavior? Do you see the same things in Bobby at home?

Mother: Pretty much. He doesn't always listen to me. And lately he's becoming much harder to handle. He talks back, and . . . well, he's never been an easy child to raise.

Therapist: (Looking towards the father.) Does he listen to you any better?

Father: He knows he has to. I won't take the stuff from him that his mother does. I just have to look at him and he knows he'd better listen.

Mother: That's not true. He talks back to him, too. I *will* say that he listens better to his father than he does to me, but *(looking at her husband)* you know that you've really got to holler at him before he'll do anything. *(Pause.)* He also knows that his father hits harder than I do.

Therapist: (To the father.) Are you as concerned about him as your wife?

Father: No, I'm really not. I remember when I was in school I did the same things. *(Smiling.)* I remember spending more time sitting in the principal's office than I spent in class.

Mother: (To the therapist.) See? That's what I get when I try to tell him that Bobby's not doing well in school.

Father: O.K. What do you want me to do? I tell him to listen to his teacher. I can't go to school with him. *(Long pause.)*

Therapist: Do you have other children?

Mother: We have a little girl who is five.

Therapist: And how does Bobby get along with his sister?

Mother: Not much better. Everything has to be his way. He'll take her things, and if we get her something and don't get him something, well, you won't believe the fuss he can make. *(Pause.)* But, I'll say one thing, he doesn't hit his sister. We've told him that if we ever catch him hitting her, he's really going to be sorry. *(Long pause.)* And, of course, I worry that Barbara will become the same way Bobby is. Lately, she's becoming hard to handle.

Father: Look, Doc, there's not a thing wrong with Barbara. You've just got to know how to let her know who's boss.

Therapist: It sounds like you two don't see eye-to-eye on rearing children.

Mother: That's probably the only thing we fight about. We always have. *(Pause.)* I'm with them all day, and frankly, by five o'clock, I've had it! I just dread the summer when they'll both be home.

Therapist: How *do* you try to control them? Or, more particularly, how do you handle Bobby?

Mother: I've become a screamer. I know it's wrong, but I can't help it. He just wears me down until I just blow up.

Father: That's the problem. I tell her that if she'd stop screaming and let them know who's boss, she wouldn't have to get so upset.

Mother: *(Turning to her husband.)* Now, wait a minute. You shout at them, too. Especially Bobby. What do you think you do when you can't get him to eat? I'm not the only one who screams.

Father: *(Smiling.)* Yeh, but I scream once. You do it all day.

Therapist: What about other times, like bedtime, or when you call him to come for dinner?

Mother: No different. He never comes when I call him. I have to call him ten times before he'll come in, or I have to go out and get him and bring him in the house. And bedtime is enough to drive you up a wall. He'll make excuses and get out of bed a dozen times. You know, he wants water, then he has to go to the toilet, then he's hungry . . ."

Father: You see? He'll go to bed for me.

Mother: No wonder. You let him stay up and watch television with you.

Therapist: *(Addressing both parents.)* Why do you think you have this problem with Bobby?

Mother: I know we've both not been consistent with him. But he can push and push until you have to give in to him, or else he'll keep on pushing you. I suppose we've let him get away with too many things, and now he knows that he can. He's making me a nervous wreck. I'm just worried sick that he's going to do poorly in school. He's only in the first grade and already he says he hates school. And I don't know what to do.

This interview presents a story that is heard with alarming frequency. The details may change, the parental attitudes may be different, but the behavior of the child is substantially the same. What are these parents seeking? What is the problem? Or, more accurately, who has the problem? The mother would say that Bobby has problems. Bobby would deny this. He would say that his parents don't let him alone, that his teacher is mean, and that there would be no trouble at home if his parents would let him do what he wants. Bobby might agree that he is in conflict with his environment, but he would say that it isn't his fault. How should such a problem be analyzed?

To begin with, we see the obvious differences in attitudes between the mother and the father. The mother is worried; the father is not. When there are differences in parental concerns, one danger that arises is the effect they will have on the child. The father's lack of concern will encourage Bobby to see his mother as the villain, while his father, who is less concerned and involved, appears to be the easy-going nice guy, when things are going well. Bobby is in conflict with the two adult females who represent authority to him; namely, his mother and his teacher. Bobby has little desire to please his mother since their relationship is mutually dissatisfying. He responds to his father more out of fear than from respect or a desire to please him.

Another danger resulting from the differences in parental attitudes is the resentment that the mother is developing towards the father. She feels alone in her concern and concludes that her husband's failure to understand her feelings and the severity of the problem are indications of his lack of support. The disagreement in child-rearing methods has become a serious threat to the marital relationship.

The mother is willing to admit her shortcomings. She has some insights as to why Bobby feels safe in disobeying her. Intellectually, she knows that she should be consistent. She is aware that she is unable to control his behavior. However, from her actions we can see that even though she can verbalize what she should and should not be doing, her behavior betrays her intellectual awareness. She would like to stop screaming, but she cannot. She blames herself for her lack of self-control, her husband for not asserting himself either to control Bobby or support her, and Bobby for what she sees as deliberate defiance of her authority.

What the mother fears and would be reluctant to admit is that her feelings towards Bobby are changing. Although she loves him, she is beginning to dislike him. Bobby is not a comfortable child for her. She cannot relax and enjoy the mother-son relationship. Bobby is becoming a source of agitation, mental strain, worry and marital conflict. To make matters worse, since she feels that she has created much of the problem and is helpless to correct it, she is developing guilt feelings about her role as a mother and has begun to question everything that she tries to do for her children.

She believes, and with justification, that Bobby's present behavior is a preview of things to come. She sees him becoming a very unhappy child and moving further away from her controls. The hopes that she may have once had for her son are slowly beginning to fade. She really wants a different type of son, and although she hopes that change is possible, she is doubtful that professional help can accomplish the necessary change. If she can develop a good relationship with her daughter, she fears she will turn away from her son altogether. Bobby's jealousy of his sister upsets her; she knows she must protect her daughter, but each time she does the separation from her son widens.

The father feels that he can control his son. He uses himself as a reference and is confident that Bobby will turn out all right, just as he did. He sometimes sees Bobby's antics as amusing. He is pleased that his wife has little control over her son, for this increases his own feeling of power. He is willing to make deals with Bobby, such as letting him stay up to watch television, in return for Bobby's promise that after the television program he will go to bed. He is content to spend a minimum amount of time with his son. He wants his son to do well in school and to get along with people, but he is convinced that in time everything will turn out all right.

The mother may not see that she is involved in a power struggle with her son, and that Bobby is winning most of the battles. He wins because she gives in or gives up. The mother does not see how she is encouraging many behaviors she wants to discourage. When Bobby talks back to her, or calls her an ugly name, she drops down to his level. She shouts at him, and soon he is shouting back. Bobby reasons that if she can shout at him, he can shout at her. Nothing is really done to stop or discourage his aggressive behavior. When his mother has reached her boiling point, she becomes violent and hits him. Her aggressive behavior does not help Bobby learn more appropriate ways of coping with stress. Instead, it makes him more angry, more aggressive, and more spiteful. He has no desire to please a mother who would hurt him. He even tells her that she doesn't love him and, when the mother is mad enough, she agrees with him. The way that the mother handles a situation does not make her a more effective mother with her son but adds to his already negative attitude. Bobby can even claim a partial victory, for he has succeeded in getting her upset, and she has not succeeded in controlling him.

When Bobby asks for something and is told he cannot have it, he continues to ask for it. This goes on until his mother breaks down and says, "Oh, all right, anything to keep you quiet." Bobby claims the victory and knows what to do the next time he wants something. He has learned how much pressure his mother can stand and is prepared to push her limits.

What do Bobby's parents want from the therapist? Each parent wants something different. The father wants the therapist to tell the mother that she is worrying for nothing. He wants to hear the therapist tell his wife that his son is acting like a typical boy, and that what happened to him will happen to his son—he will outgrow his problem. But the therapist could point out that the father may not have outgrown his early negative and aggressive behavior. The father, as a child, showed indifference, negativism, and aggressiveness. He is still displaying these characteristics, even though he is twenty-five years older than he was in the first grade. He is indifferent to the problem that his wife sees; he is negative in his attitude towards his wife; he is aggressive in bullying his child.

What the wife wants from the therapist is a solution. She wants a magical formula that will turn chaos into order overnight. She also wants the therapist to confirm her reasons for alarm and for her husband to hear that she is justified in being worried about Bobby. She hopes she can get reassurance that things can improve and that it is not too late for her son to change.

The therapist can help the mother learn more about herself and the reasons she becomes upset so easily. If she can learn better self-control, she can be more consistent, more self-reliant, and a better model for Bobby. Above all, she will not feel helpless to deal with her problems.

The therapist can help the father by encouraging him to recognize that a problem does exist. If the father can be shown that some of his childhood problems have persisted and remain problems for him now, he may realize that time did not solve all of his problems and that definite steps should be taken now to retrain Bobby. The father also can learn more about himself and the impact his behavior is having on his son. If the therapist can help the father show more understanding and respect to his wife, there is also a good chance that the marital relationship will improve.

The problem Bobby's parents have brought to the therapist is not just one person's problem. It is a *family problem*, as are most problems with children. Only by dealing with the problems of the entire family can the therapist make a change in Bobby's behavior.

Most of the problems that parents have with their children are due largely to incorrect assumptions and unrealistic expectations. Parents want to assume their child will react logically and rationally and that he will respond according to their expectations. When, for many reasons, the child does not or cannot respond in a manner that pleases his parents, they become frustrated, disappointed, and angry with the child. Intellectually, parents know that a child will not function as an adult, but if they expect adult behavior and punish for childish ways, trouble is inevitable. The uninterrupted attention span of an eight-year-old is about five minutes. Therefore, to expect an eight-year-old to sit in church for one hour without becoming restless and fidgety is unrealistic. If the child is punished because he was squirming and looking around during the service, the parents are, in essence, punishing a child for acting like a child.

When a therapist listens to the complaints of parents about their child, he is mindful that he is hearing only their interpretations and that the child may feel justified in behaving as he does. If the parents expect too much from their child, there is no way that he can please them and misbehavior could be the child's way of expressing his own frustration, disappointment, and anger. Because parents do not always have a reference or standard for comparison, it is easy for them to lose sight of what is expected of children at various ages. It is easier for an adult to remember his adolescent years than to recall his early childhood behavior. Yet, if parents are to be fair, they must have some understanding of what to expect from children and how to evaluate maturity. One of the reasons that parents are encouraged to read about children is to gain knowledge as to what assumptions can be made about children and what would be realistic expectations for them.

Case Illustration Number 5

Tom was a ten-year-old boy whose mother called him a "television addict." He was an average student in school and, although he did not seek friendships with peers, he was not an unpopular child. His usual routine consisted of watching television from seven o'clock in the morning, when he got up, until he left for school. After school he resumed his place in front of the television set until bedtime. He ate his breakfast and dinner while watching television, for there was a TV set in the kitchen. On Saturdays and Sundays he watched television almost all day.

The mother was asked what she had done to help Tom "kick the TV habit." She said she encouraged him to go outside and play or to have friends come in to play with him. The latter idea would frequently backfire, for Tom and his friends ended up watching television together. Sometimes she would order Tom away from the TV set and for punishment she would refuse to let him watch one of his favorite programs. She had tried limiting him to so many programs, or so many hours of television a day, but nothing worked. She also admitted that she was lax in following through with her threats and was not very consistent in enforcing limits.

Television had become Tom's only companion. It was a safe friend, for it could not tease Tom or require him to compete. Through it, Tom was able to forget any frustrations and escape into a world of fantasy. However, it should be pointed out that Tom came by this TV habit in a very natural way.

Tom's parents were television addicts. They were not aware of this, nor did they want to be made aware of it. They differentiated their habit from Tom's on the basis of the quality of the programs they watched and their needs to relax. Like Tom, his parents had a very limited social life. They rarely went out and spent most of their evenings watching television. They were not discriminating watchers either, for they would watch whatever seemed best of anything that was on. In admitting that she and her husband watched too much television, the mother thought that the biggest problem it caused was overeating, for they usually ate while they were watching.

Tom's parents were advised to decide upon a firm policy regarding the amount of television Tom would be permitted to watch. They were asked first to determine the priority that television would receive in their home. Thinking about the things that they wanted to emphasize, they agreed that school work was most important for Tom, then his social relationships, then the development of his interests, and finally, his recreation, including television. The parents then put these priorities into effect.

They agreed that there would be no television on school nights. Tom would not have to be distracted by hopes of watching television or by efforts to bargain, manipulate, and fuss. On special occasions when a program was educational, the rule was relaxed, but the parents decided what was educational. On nights in which there was no school the next day, he could watch up to two hours of television, but he was discouraged from watching two hours consecutively. The rules also applied on Saturdays and Sundays.

The parents also saw their need to become better models for Tom. They embarked on new social interests and began to talk more to each other. Tom's mother renewed old friendships and made some new ones. Assessing their own television viewing, they realized that they had nothing to show for the hundreds of hours they had spent watching it.

Tom's parents, realizing that Tom would not take the initiative to correct anything in himself, assumed responsibility for making the change. If they had said, ''Well, he's old enough to know what's best for himself, so if he wants no friends and is willing to let his school work slip, that's his problem,'' they would have been negligent parents. As it was, they made no deals or promises, and set no time limit on their new rule. When Tom's television viewing was restricted, he was forced to develop new interests; he even found time for his school work. Had his parents made a deal with him, asking that he finish his homework first and then watch television, he would have done the homework hastily, and there might have been a surprising number of nights on which he would claim that he had no homework.

Tom's parents were following a number of the guidelines for training young children given in the last chapter. They were becoming good models; they were being firm and fair; they were consistent; and most important, they were not encouraging a behavior that they wanted to discourage. They saw Tom's problem as their own as well. By doing something to help themselves, they were able to understand Tom's feelings more easily. Tom's parents encouraged him to make friends, and applied the amount of pressure that Tom needed to alter a pattern of behavior that was not in his best interest. In this way, they were anticipating the consequences of both his and their behavior.

Prevention is still the best antidote for problems. Although parents cannot prevent all problems, they can deter many. They cannot control in their child what they cannot control in themselves, nor can they deter what they have subtly encouraged, even though they feel their actions are justifiable.

Children have a tendency to uncover their parents' weaknesses. Having found them, they proceed to attack these vulnerable spots in ways they have learned can be successful. The child soon learns which parent to approach for certain favors; he also learns which parent is inclined to be lenient and which one can be manipulated more easily. He is not above playing one parent against the other in order to get his own way and will frequently use the argument, ''Well, mother said I could do it,'' when trying to convince his father that he should be allowed to do something.

The child can also sense when the parents are having difficulty in making decisions and when they doubt their judgment and vacillate from a yes to a no response. When parents are hesitant and delay training the child because of their fears, doubts, or negligent attitudes, the child begins to train them.

It is not easy for weak parents to overcome their weakness, for parents who love their children want to please them and insecure parents fear withdrawal of the child's love. For this reason, insecure parents tend to spoil their children. They do so in an attempt to make the child's life easier and free from frustration; but, in so doing they also allow the child to feel power over his parents and frustration when he cannot manipulate people and situations outside the home. Giving in to a child in order to avoid a tantrum or unpleasant scene may serve to reduce a symptom, but it will create problems rather than resolve them. The good intentions of parents to reduce their child's frustration by solving the child's problems for him usually fosters dependency and decreases the child's confidence in his ability to cope with stress.

An example of parents who tried to pacify their child and make her life uncomplicated is illustrated in the case of Jane. Not only did Jane's parents fail to help her overcome her basic problem of fear, but also they encouraged a series of related problems that served to complicate her life.

Case Illustration Number 6

Jane was a nine-year-old child who had many fears. She was afraid of riding on the school bus, talking in class, coping with her teachers, and making friends. She had fears at home, too. She could not walk into a dark room and was frightened of loud noises.

Bedtime had developed into an involved ritual. All of her dolls had to be facing in a certain direction, all windows had to be closed, every drawer and closet had to be closed, and a glass of juice had to be on the night table. Even though she slept with a night light in her room, she also had to have a flashlight on the night table, as well as a box of Kleenex.

Although her school fears only developed when she was in the second grade, her other fears began when Jane was two. The bedtime ritual, according to the parents, became necessary because Jane would never fall asleep. When she was two, they would put her to bed at eight o'clock and at eleven o'clock find her still wide awake playing in her crib. They read to her, gave her warm milk, told her stories, and said goodnight to her a dozen times, but still Jane would not sleep.

When she outgrew her crib, she became fearful that she would fall out of her bed, so they tucked the blankets in on both sides. They also kept a light on so that she could see what was in the room. So that she would not have to get out of bed for a drink, they began to put a glass of juice next to her, and Kleenex, in case she needed that.

These parents were encouraging undesirable habits because they felt sorry for Jane. The mother was, in her own words, "a very nervous person," and could identify with all of her daughter's feelings. Like Jane, she was very superstitious and shared many of her daughter's fears. Both were afraid of insects, cried easily, and kept lights on all over the house to avoid having to enter a dark room.

Jane's father was a warm, affectionate, and sympathetic person, who had none of the fears that his wife and daughter had and was described by his wife as being the "calm one." He acknowledged that both his wife and daughter were sensitive and emotional, and tried to reassure them. It bothered him to see either of them cry, and he worried a great deal about what would happen to Jane as she grew older. What discipline Jane received came from him. (It was seldom necessary to punish Jane for she never did anything that her parents felt required punishment.) The parent's search for help was precipitated because for about two weeks prior to their seeking help, Jane had refused to go to school. One Monday morning, without any warning, Jane complained of a stomach ache and said that she could not go to school. By ten o'clock that morning she seemed all right, but when her mother offered to drive her to school, Jane began to cry "hysterically." She then told her mother that she couldn't go back to school and that she would *never* go back to school. Jane would not relate any particular events that caused such a reaction. Although she had balked at going to school at times, her mother viewed this morbid fear of school as a new behavior. All forms of pleading, begging, and bribery failed. When Jane did not go to school the next day, the father became angry with her and, for the first time since she was a very young child, spanked her. Jane still refused to go to school and spent most of the day crying in her room. At this point, the parents were forced to admit that they were helpless to cope with Jane's behavior.

Although in many ways Jane's parents could be called good parents, in other ways it would have to be said that Jane's parents had failed her. They had failed to discourage early habits they both knew were potentially harmful for her. By yielding to her fears instead of helping her to understand and control them, they had failed to give her confidence in herself. By allowing Jane to control their parenting, they failed to teach her to cope with the world. In addition, her mother failed Jane by being a poor model to copy.

Although Jane began training her parents at the age of two, it was not too late for her parents to begin to train her. It would have been much easier to start earlier, for the retraining methods used for a child of Jane's age are different from those that would be used with either a younger child or a child whose problems are not so deep-seated. Nevertheless, both Jane and her parents could be helped.

Treating this as a family problem, the therapist encouraged Jane's mother to become a better model by gaining insights into her own fears and feelings of inadequacy. She learned that she could not help her daughter until she had overcome her own problems, and since she was motivated to help Jane, she was willing to expose herself to situations that had heretofore been considered unsafe. As she experienced more things that she had previously avoided, she gained confidence in herself and was further motivated by her successes. She saw how her past behavior was detrimental to both herself and her daughter and how she had used Jane's weakness as a protection for herself. For example, as long as Jane could not cope with stress, her mother did not have to feel inadequate. An emotionally stronger and more adequate daughter would have been a threat to the mother, for her own weaknesses would have been exposed. Although she did not deliberately keep her daughter weak, she was able to realize what prevented her from seeking help sooner and why it was difficult for her to separate from her daughter.

The father was encouraged to become more assertive and less protective of both his wife and daughter. He had not utilized his potential to be effective by having adopted a peace-at-any-price philosophy to replace his better judgment. He had to allow both his wife and daughter to grow up and become more self-reliant. This meant doing less for them when he felt they could do things for themselves. By not putting pressure on his wife or daughter, he had reinforced their weaknesses.

In working with Jane, because her habits were so long-standing, a gradual approach was used in which slow progress was rewarded. She had to develop confidence through small successes that grew into major accomplishments for her. She had to learn to trust herself and ultimately rely on her own judgment. For this to happen, Jane had to be willing to let go of her mother, just as her mother had to let go of her. She also had to be willing to experience some frustration, which she had avoided doing in the past. Once she discovered that she did not have to feel helpless and could do some problem solving, she was willing to expose herself to situations without dreading the outcomes.

This change of attitude helped Jane face her problems in school. It was no longer necessary to strive for perfection for she could react to a failure or poor performance without feeling inadequate or being devastated by it. Formerly, she had felt trapped and helpless. She could not have the safety in school that she experienced in her home, nor was her mother there to protect her. Once she no longer needed her mother's protection, and when she gained confidence in her own problem-solving skills, school was no longer a threat.

The Effect of Parental Self-Doubts

Parents who lack confidence in themselves tend to make mistakes in parenting because they are indecisive and do not trust their judgment. They are aware of their responsibility and power over their child and want very much to do and say the right thing. But, needing reassurance themselves, such parents do not know when they have made the appropriate decision. Many decisions must be made when the situation arises and cannot be postponed for contemplation or discussion. Self-doubting parents find these decisions particularly difficult to make.

The best predictor of parental self–confidence is the assessment the parent makes of previous decisions he has made and their outcomes. A parent whose personality pattern reveals a history of having made poor judgments, who feels that other people have made the important decisions in his life, who is overly fearful that he may be saying or doing the wrong thing, will be filled with self-doubts and will need reassurances from others to know that what he is doing is appropriate.

There are, of course, parents who make one blunder after another but fail to see how their actions are inappropriate. They are able to rationalize or deny their mistakes and are somewhat oblivious to what they are doing. They may, in fact, justify their actions and defend their decisions, believing, or at least saying, that what they are doing is the best thing for their child.

Case Illustration Number 7

An example of defensive behavior is the father who decided that he would assume responsibility for solving the toilet training problem of his six-year-old son, Howard. The child had never been dry during the night and had frequent "accidents" in the daytime. Physical causes had been ruled out, and the pediatrician's interpretation was that the child was experiencing pressures that needed to be reduced. The father had let the mother handle the problem but was critical of her methods. She was concerned about the child's bed-wetting but, following the advice she received from her pediatrician, was not creating pressures for him or punishing him because of it. She tried to be relaxed about the problem and to hide her discouragement. She tried pleading, promises of new pajamas, and "star charts." Nothing was successful for more than a day or two. The father was impatient with these methods and occasionally attempted to embarrass Howard into staying dry by comparing him to other six-year-olds and making reference to his lack of bladder control as an indication that the child was a baby. He was unable to hide his disappointment in his only son and, through facial expressions and sarcastic remarks, communicated to his son the disgust he felt over the fact that a six-year-old was still "making in his pants."

The father became directly involved in the child's toilet training when the family went to visit friends overnight and the child's bed was wet in the morning. The father had convinced himself that Howard's bed-wetting could be stopped as soon as his son decided to stop it. Several days prior to the visit, the father warned his son that he expected him to be dry. "You don't want them to think you're a baby?" the father cautioned him. To insure dryness and to protect the father's image in the eyes of the hosts, on the night of the visit, the father took Howard to the toilet about two hours after Howard went to sleep and again before the father went to bed. Despite the preparation and cautions, the child's bed was wet the next morning.

The mother apologized to her hosts, who seemed to understand and were not at all upset, but the father was embarrassed and ashamed of his son. Despite the mother's efforts to calm him, he spanked the child and announced that "From now on, I'll handle his toilet problem!"

The father began by initiating a set of punishments for a wet bed or any daily "accident." These included depriving the child of all privileges, having him attempt to wash his own sheets and pajamas and, if the "accident" occurred in the daytime, forcing the child to walk around wet without being allowed to change into dry clothing. He threatened to "tell everyone what a baby" his son was and, in short, made the child understand that he would be isolated and rejected until he learned to stay dry. The mother was instructed to report all "accidents" and told not to interfere.

The outcome of this approach was not surprising. The child did not stop wetting his bed, although his daytime "accidents" became very rare. He began to fear his father intensely, and turned to the mother for emotional support and reassurances of love. He had trouble sleeping and cried much more than usual. The relationship between the husband and wife deteriorated, placing an additional strain on the child. Only when Howard began to develop a facial tic did the father decide to discontinue his regimen, but by that time the process of toileting had become a preoccupation for the child.

Howard's father is an example of how a parent who should have questions and doubts over the appropriateness of his behavior can justify blundering and inappropriate behavior on the pretext of doing something to help the child. Even when the facial tic developed, the father did not attribute it to his handling of the situation. He was convinced that the tic would go away and that it was nothing more than the child's way of getting attention.

What would have been more effective for the father to do would have been to regard Howard's toilet problem as a symptom of a problem, instead of the problem itself. The pediatrician, having ruled out any physical causes, told the parents that Howard must be responding to pressures. The father might have looked to his own behavior as a possible source of pressure. Giving more support to his wife's initial attempts would have been helpful, and reacting calmly could have enabled Howard to feel that both of his parents were understanding. Taking him to the bathroom about two hours after he had been asleep might have been helpful, providing Howard was awakened and that he felt it was done to help him, not to avoid disgrace.

The tic did go away, but Howard's father had to first examine his own reactions, realize that his expectations for his son exceeded what his son could do, and become more realistic and sensitive to his son's feelings. By the time he was seven, Howard's bedwetting stopped. Maturation, both physical and emotional, brought this about. Once Howard began to feel that he could relate to his father, he was encouraged to exert greater efforts to discipline himself. The external pressure was responsible for creating the problem; the internal pressure on himself eliminated it.

Parental Protection of Images

The parents' need to protect their image is another reason why they continue to permit behavior in the child that they really want to discourage. Many parents have a strong need to protect their image to friends, neighbors, acquaintances, and even strangers. A parent might appease the child in a restaurant, or spoil and bribe the child in public, because he wants to look good, and the child represents a constant threat of exposure and embarrassment. The parent who tells the fussing child, "What will those people think of you for acting this way?" is really saying, "What will those people think of *me* for having a child who acts this way?" The parental image is in jeopardy.

It is not always possible for parents to remove a fussing child from a situation, or take the necessary steps to prevent the child from having a tantrum, but these occasions should be the exception rather than the rule. If a crying child must be carried out of a public place, perhaps people *will* look at the source of the noise. What they will see is a parent who is not going to be controlled by a child's attempts to manipulate a situation. In most instances, they will sympathize with the parent. Knowing that babies and young children characteristically cry, how critical can they be? And even if they are critical, as long as what is being done to the child is not cruel or inhumane, why worry about the occasional critical eye? Fifteen seconds after the crying child has been removed from the public place, the people who witnessed the scene will have forgotten about it. If the parents try to avoid the unpleasant scene in order to protect their image with these strangers, their giving in will encourage future outbursts. In the attempt to maintain an image to people who really don't care what is happening, some parents are willing to jeopardize the training of the child. Buying the child the candy he wants in the drugstore may avoid the stares of people who might glance over if the child howls, but buying it in order to have these strangers think that you have a self-controlled child is tantamount to sacrificing the training of the child in order to protect and maintain an image to people who do not have to live with the child's problems and do not really care about them.

Fear of Consequences

Perhaps the most common fear the parent who cannot discourage a child's bad habit has is the dread of the consequences of attempting to change the child's behavior. "He'll scream for an hour if I do that," or "She'll nag and whine and fuss until you just *have* to let her have her own way," are excuses for inaction based on fear of consequences. As long as the child feels that he has more to gain than lose by nagging or fussing, he will be encouraged to try to obtain what he wants. Only when the behavior of the parents shows the child that his nagging, whining and threats are futile will he come to terms with them.

There are many reasons why parents do not succeed in training their child. Most could be explained under one of three headings: (1) over-parenting, (2) under-parenting, and (3) lack of parental self-control. Training problems can be due to a combination of these three factors but will usually include the lack of self-control to some degree. By the same token, training can fail when parents vacillate, going back and forth from one to the other (i.e. from under-parenting to over-parenting) or through inconsistencies within any one factor (i.e., over-parenting sometimes but not always).

Over-Parenting

Over-parenting, as the term suggests, is similar to what is called over-protecting, over-indulging, or an over-concern for the welfare of the child. But over-parenting adds another dimension. The parents do not merely do too much for a child, but also fail to do enough to help the child mature emotionally. Over-parenting can be regarded as selfishness, for the parents' need for satisfaction is placed before the child's need for maturation. The overly possessive mother, who has to know where the child is every minute of the day is not just expressing concern, but fear that the child might find someone else who is more interesting to be with, or that he will need her less than he once did. Her need for reassurance that the child will never leave her is more important to her than the child's need to become progressively independent of her controls. The mother is protecting herself, not her child. If the mother wants to know where her child is because he has established a history of getting into trouble, of course, her concern is protective of the child.

The child who is a product of over-parenting will have trouble with problem solving, decision making, and guilt. Since the parents have been quick to solve problems for the child, he will lack this experience. He will also doubt his own ability to make judgments and feel guilty if he makes a mistake. Over-parenting makes the child helpless, unable to cope with his world, over-dependent on others, and lacking spontaneous behavior. Such a child does not have a good feeling about himself as a person.

Over-parenting maintains control over a child and prevents rebellion by instilling a heightened awareness of conscience and strong feelings of guilt. The child is told repeatedly how much his parents do for him and why he should be grateful. The parents remind him of the sacrifices they are making for him and when he refuses to cooperate, they go into an act of feeling hurt in a martyred way. The over-parenting parents are dramatic and appeal to the child's sense of fair play. Although they willingly give to their child, each gift has a string attached. The parents are saying, "We won't let you forget what we do for you, for someday we will expect you to return the favor." When the child does not, the parents are quick to remind him of their generosity and hope the child will feel enough guilt to comply with their requests. Frequently, the need to avoid guilt feelings causes the child to acquiesce. When it extends into adolescence and adulthood, over-parenting may produce feelings of inadequacy, dependency, and an inability to cope with daily problems. The following case illustration demonstrates the effect over-parenting can have.

Case Illustration Number 8

Mrs. D. was a mother of three children. She openly admitted that she could not cope with the responsibilities of rearing them, stating "I don't know why I ever let myself have the second one." The first child had been difficult from the beginning of her pregnancy, in which she was sick enough to be in and out of bed the entire nine months. She had dreaded the delivery. Had she not been terrified of having surgery, she would have preferred to deliver by Caesarean section. As it turned out, her delivery was induced.

The child, a boy, was colicky, had an allergy to whole milk, and became asthmatic. The mother somewhat proudly recalled that she didn't have one night of uninterrupted sleep until her son was almost three years old. During this time, her own mother was her daily companion, consultant, and amateur psychotherapist. The grand-mother never referred to the little boy as "your" baby; it was always "our" baby.

Mrs. D. had been reared as an only child. She and her mother were inseparable, while contacts with her father were minimal. He was too busy to be a devoted father and couldn't relate well to little girls. The relationship between Mrs. D.'s parents was not a good one and she had no recollection of the family doing things together.

The first real traumatic experience Mrs. D. recalled was being sent to kindergarten. She cried so much that her mother had to first stay in the room and later in the building. Mrs. D. recalled that she developed fainting spells and had to be removed from kindergarten. The same separation problem took place when she entered the first grade and for much of that year a home-bound teacher came to her house twice a week. Although she was able to go into the second grade, she always found school a difficult situation from emotional and social standpoints. Her growing-up years were largely without friends; her mother remained her constant companion.

Dating was difficult for her. She was an attractive girl and was early faced with the problem of whether or not she should date. Although in terms of opportunity she could have dated when she was fourteen, she did not have her first date until she was seventeen and a senior in high school. This date, and many of her dates in succeeding years, was uncomfortable for her. She attended a college in her hometown and after a three-year courtship and engagement was married to a man she had met in her senior year.

The first year of marriage was very difficult for Mrs. D. She had not been allowed to cook when she was living at home. She had very little experience in shopping by herself; most of her purchases had been approved by her mother. Once, while she was in college, she bought a coat that her mother did not like. She experienced so much anxiety over it that she wore the coat only a few times. After she married, Mrs. D.'s mother still went shopping with her and selected most of her furniture. (Her husband did not know who actually selected his home furnishings and just assumed it was his wife.)

Mr. D., wanting his wife to become more independent, encouraged her to do a number of things on her own. He suggested that she open up her own checking account; however, this resulted in frequent arguments when her checkbook would not balance. Although she drove her own car, she was reluctant to drive alone and cooking remained an unpleasant chore.

Mrs. D. spoke with her mother every day by telephone, some days two or three times. Her mother usually initiated the calls, but she was careful not to call when Mr. D. was home. Mr. D. resented the time his wife spent with her mother, adding to Mrs. D.'s problems that of keeping her husband and her mother apart.

The sexual adjustment in the marriage was outstandingly poor. Mrs. D. was uncomfortable with sex and, feeling guilty over this, began to mistrust her husband.

She began to have obsessional fears about her son's safety. Every fall he took became a crisis, every little fever a catastrophe. She panicked when he had an asthmatic attack, and slept almost as much in her son's room as she did with her husband.

She felt that as a mother she was a failure. She saw herself as a failure as an adolescent and now as a wife, and had doubts she could be adequate in anything. Her biggest conflict, however, was her mixed feelings about her mother. Her feelings towards her mother ranged from contempt and disgust and guilt to love. She could feel sorry for her mother and be furious at her simultaneously. One of her biggest fears was that she would do to her children what her mother had done to her. She got very upset with herself when she did things that she recalled her mother doing.

Insights into her problem did not eliminate it. Mrs. D.'s improved feelings about herself began when she was able to set a series of goals for herself. One such goal was to initiate a gradual separation from her mother. The separation made her mother unhappy, but Mrs. D. decided that her own welfare, and that of her husband and child, had to take priority over pleasing her mother. Another goal was giving her son more freedom to function independently of her. It was not easy for her to do this, for she feared that something would happen to him. She was both pleased and surprised when her son was delighted with his new freedom and was able to function well without her. A third goal was directed at her relationship with her husband. She began to put his needs over her desires for safety and made him a more important person in her life. Other goals focused on her interests, her direction in life, and her relationships with people.

Over-parenting results in training failures because "smothering" the child does not equip him with the knowledge and skills he will need to become a productive member of society. It also fails to promote emotional maturity and the development of the individual's potential.

Under-Parenting

Training failures due to under-parenting are largely the sins of omission. The parent fails to assume the necessary responsibility for the welfare of the child. Under-parenting takes the form of neglect, indifference, and deprivation of parental influence. Under-parenting is not necessarily a problem of low socio-economic levels or under-privileged sub-cultural groups. Like over-parenting, under-parenting knows no class or cultural lines. The child who is raised in extreme poverty and the child who is raised in extreme affluence can both become victims of under-parenting, and although the conditions are different, the effects on the personality are strikingly similar. Just as the symptoms of measles are the same in the poor child as the wealthy one, so are the feelings of loneliness and isolation. The lonely wealthy child may have more opportunities for pleasure than the poor child, but isolation for one child is no less painful than it is for the other.

Whereas in over-parenting the child may be unaware of what is happening, the child is usually aware of under-parenting and either suffers, feels sorry for himself, or tries to avoid and deny the whole situation. Many children choose denial of the problem as the least painful way of living in an unpleasant environment. The child realizes that he is helpless to change negative and neglectful parental attitudes. In under-parenting, the child is more aware that he is missing something.

The under-parented child may want to see more of his mother or father, or he may want them to respond to him in a different way. He might want them to accept him more and criticize him less. He will want love, help, reassurances, and respect. The child from the underparented home will come to feel that he has been cheated, to envy others and to reject himself.

Case Illustration Number 9

Arlene, ten years old and an only child, had an under-parenting home. Her father was a professional man and her mother was a college graduate. Arlene had many toys, dolls, and books, and she enjoyed the things she had. She knew she could have everything she asked for, but her demands were not great. In general, her parents were very pleased with her and proud of her few accomplishments. They offered her encouragement and showed a polite interest in things she did.

Arlene's father was a successful man financially and put in many hours in his office. He left the house at eight o'clock in the morning and returned about seven o'clock in the evening. When he got home he liked to unwind with one or two cocktails, and his wife joined him. Arlene ate earlier herself and stayed up to spend a few minutes with her father. While Arlene was watching television or doing homework, her parents had their dinner. She was usually in bed before they finished.

Arlene's parents took frequent trips together. Once, they spent a month in Europe. They went away for a week once or twice a year and for long weekends quite often. Arlene never went with them because they felt that she shouldn't miss school. In the summer, Arlene went to a camp for eight weeks and spent one week with her parents at a resort.

Arlene attended a private school and none of her classmates lived near her. She got along with both of her parents, but saw little of them. Her mother was very active socially and did weekly volunteer work at a hospital. Both parents enjoyed playing golf, tennis, and bridge. They entertained a lot, and ate at their country club frequently. Arlene rarely accompanied them to dinner. The reason they gave her was that they got home too late. Their weekend social calendar was filled weeks ahead, and Arlene didn't seem to be part of their plans.

Arlene was lonely and unhappy. Her parents would buy her anything she needed, but what she needed from them couldn't be bought. They felt they were good parents because they were providing her with the best of everything. They made plans for her future, but they were ignoring her present.

The family had a full-time maid whom Arlene liked. The maid, Karla, was probably Arlene's closest friend. One day Karla told Arlene's mother that Arlene had been talking about suicide. Although Arlene later explained she was just kidding, her parents were able to realize that, even in jest, this kind of talk signals danger.

Fortunately, Arlene's parents were willing to make adjustments in their style of living and to include Arlene in their plans. Arlene's plea for help was heard and her need for parenting was met. Nevertheless, until her parents were awakened to their inadvertent negligence, Arlene had an under-parenting environment.

Children frequently interpret parental neglect as a personal rejection. They feel that something must be wrong with them, otherwise why would the parents avoid them? They may also interpret neglect as a punishment for something they have done. A child can tell how high he is on the parents' priority list. When the father puts his poker night, daily newspaper or television viewing ahead of the child's need for private time, or when the mother is too busy to spend time with the child because she has telephone calls to make, a hair appointment to keep, or a book to read, the child clearly sees his lack of importance to the parent.

A defense that some parents use for under-parenting is that it teaches the child to be responsible and independent. The fallacy of this rationalization is that the child is required to become independent and self-sufficient long before he is ready. Characteristically, the parents make their lives easier by requiring the child to become independent; it is not a matter of what is best for the child but what is easiest for the parents.

Although a lack of parental information could cause under-parenting, this is not usually the case. More typically, it is a parent who cannot be bothered with the child, or a parent who is too busy doing things for himself, and who places his own needs over those of his child. It can be a parent who regrets having a child. It was said earlier that over-parenting is a selfish behavior; under-parenting is a different kind of selfishness. Over-parenting gratifies parental needs *through* the child; under-parenting gratifies parental needs *regardless* of the child.

The major effects of under-parenting are the child's feelings of insecurity, isolation, depression, and eventually, indifference. Parents who only find fault and never praise; parents who give the excuse that they can't relate to young children; or parents who say they don't have the time to spend with their children are all under-parenting.

Lack of Parental Self-Control

The third general factor which can explain why parents have troubles with their children, lack of self-control, is a universal weakness in man. Self-control is an ideal that most people seek but few people attain. It has become synonymous with maturity, social acceptability, and adaptability. The individual who possesses self-control is in control of his emotions and can respond in appropriate ways.

Self-control is acquired, not innate. The early seeds of self-control take root during the first six years of life because of what the child experiences and observes in his environment. When it fails to develop, it is usually because the child has been exposed to poor models or because his training did not encourage it. The importance of the parent as the model for the child cannot be emphasized enough when it comes to acquiring self-control. When both parents are lacking in self-control, the child has practically no chance to develop it.

There is a relationship between what is termed a bad temper and a lack of self-control. Everyone is expected to lose control of his temper occasionally, for it is unhealthy to always suppress anger and a build up of pressure or tension can trigger a sudden explosion. But, it is not better to vent anger at the slightest provocation and end up in an uncontrolled rage. The problems involving temper are largely a matter of *control*. Does the temper control the person, or can the person control the temper? Proper self-control means tolerating frustration and reacting reasonably to disappointments. The adult who lacks self-control may have failed to acquire adequate problem–solving skills, or be regressing to less mature behavior. He may also have had success with his bad temper and learned to get his own way with it.

The parent who is lacking self-control ends up frustrating both himself and his child. The child learns nothing that is positive or constructive from the exposure, and the parent experiences regret and subsequent guilt that can last a long time.

The behavior of the child whose parents are lacking in self-control may be expressed in opposite ways. Some children appear passive, indecisive, and beaten down, while others become aggressive, hostile, defensive, and negative. The withdrawn and passive child is expressing fear, a lack of trust in his environment, and anxiety over what might happen if the parents release their tempers. The effect of explosive and unpredictable parents is a child who never feels safe, since he does not know when parental wrath will be turned towards him. The tense, worried, and unhappy child finds that withdrawing and defenselessness are his best protection. He does not fight back because he cannot fight back. He cannot fight back because he knows he will not win.

In the case of the child who becomes aggressive as a result of poor parental self-control, his actions are indicative of his constant need to actively protect himself. Such a child regards the parental temper tantrum as a lesson to be learned. He battles because he has witnessed battles. Daily encounters with the parents serve to reinforce the child's needs to be defensive and argumentative. Parental punishments, however harsh, do not change his attitudes. A child like this is described by parents as being extremely negative to suggestions, very hard to discipline, and unbelievably stubborn.

When the mother is the parent who lacks self-control, the child is more likely to become aggressive. The mother's shouts and threats become ineffective as the child learns that he can battle her back. But to do this, he, too, must become aggressive. The mother shouts at the child, the child shouts back at the mother. He ignores her threats, for they are seldom carried out, and even when they are carried out, the child does not grow to fear the mother as he can the father. The child may grow to dislike or resent the mother, but seldom does he fear her.

On the other hand, when the father is the parent who lacks self-control, the child tends to take on a passive role. The child learns that the father can run faster, hit harder, shout louder and look meaner. This forces the child to submit, rather than provoke the father, and in submitting, the child becomes passive. He may also feel angry, revengeful, and even hateful, but out of needs for safety he will usually be passive around the father who has an explosive temper.

When both parents have a problem controlling their temper, the child is frequently a combination of passivity and aggressiveness. He may be passive in the home and aggressive outside the house, or vice versa.

Whereas parental problems due to over-parenting and under-parenting are largely a matter of what the parents do in their role as parents, the lack of parental self-control relates to the parents' role as models for the child. Parental inconsistencies, immaturities, and harsh practices can result in troubles. A case of a runaway sixteen-year-old boy will illustrate this problem.

Case Illustration Number 10

Paul lived with his mother and younger brother. His parents had been divorced when he was twelve years old. The mother had sought the divorce on the grounds of adultery and the father was very willing to break up the marriage. Paul's recollections of the marriage were vivid: he remembered seeing his father come home in a drunken state, striking his mother, verbally abusing her and bragging about his new girlfriend. These things only occurred when his father had been drinking.

The years of frustration prior to the divorce, the embarrassment of the divorce itself, and the problem of rearing two children without a father, had taken their toll on the mother. She became self-pitying and resentful of her circumstances. Her children were her only outlet for frustrations, and her temper got out of control on numerous occasions.

Paul, at sixteen, did not enjoy living with his mother. She was either extremely strict or overly lax in dealing with both children. Paul had to account for all his time spent away from the house. The mother was untrusting of him; she feared that his father, whom he saw sporadically, had a bad influence on him, and she was critical of Paul's choice of friends, the length of his hair, his clothing taste, and his indifference to school.

The mother was an admittedly nervous woman. She used tranquilizers when she felt agitated and mood elevators when she was depressed. She smoked a carton of cigarettes a week, and had to force herself to keep busy.

Paul was having school problems. He disliked going to school, although he got along with his teachers. He occasionally cut classes and skipped school. One day his mother received a call from the vice-principal telling her that Paul had been caught smoking marijuana in the boys' toilet. He was being suspended for three days and the mother would have to come to school and meet with the vice-principal and counselor.

The mother went into a rage. She berated Paul, calling him every name she had used on his father. She took away all of his privileges and forbade him use of the car. She threatened to report him to the Federal Bureau of Narcotics and she made him swear that he would never so much as talk to anyone whom he knew smoked marijuana. Paul's mother was disgusted with him, and reminded him continually of her anger for the next few weeks.

While straightening out Paul's closet, the mother found a brown bag that contained a bottle with several capsules. When confronted, Paul told her that the bottle contained two hallucinogenics, LSD and mescaline. In a sudden flare of temper, the mother slapped Paul in the face and told him to get out of her house. He did.

Paul may have been seeking a way out of his home. His views about adults and their behavior were certainly negatively colored. He knew a father who was violent, irresponsible, and impulsive, and a mother who was bitter, vindictive, and equally impulsive. He saw no direction for himself and had few pleasures to recall. When he ran away from home he fully intended to stay away, because, and this is important to note, *he did not feel that he was losing anything by leaving.*

Helping Paul meant helping his mother as well. The mother was keenly aware of her unhappiness and her role in creating problems for Paul. She wanted to change but did not think she could. Intellectually, she knew that her mood pills were no more acceptable than Paul's hallucinogens. She had to convince herself that she could become a different kind of person.

To do this, she began to receive professional help. As she learned to solve more of her problems, she had less need to take out her hostility on her son. As she acquired more self-control, she was able to establish a more stable relationship with both of her children. Paul returned home and accepted a ten o'clock curfew on school nights and a one o'clock curfew on weekends. In return for cooperation, his mother did not question where he went and, as long as he did not get into trouble, she did not object to his friends. He was permitted to use her car and in return for this favor, he agreed not to cut classes. Both Paul and his mother also agreed to converse with each other every day and to avoid unpleasant arguments. They decided to live as a family and resolve their differences through talking things out, instead of going separate ways and avoiding each other. Once he was convinced that he could gain more by cooperating, he came to realize that his previous actions had been self-defeating. Paul had been lonesome, and so had his mother. Once they became friends they were both less lonely.

Behavior can be changed. It is not unusual for someone to become comfortable and complacent with behavior that is neither constructive nor rewarding and could be potentially self-defeating. The person rationalizes his behavior and dismisses a desire for change with statements like, "Oh well, I've been this way all my life," or, "That's me, take me or leave me!" or, "I know I should change, but I wouldn't know where to start."

There is no disgrace in making a mistake. We can learn from mistakes. But in order to fail, one must make the mistake repeatedly. A single loss of temper will not cause a parental failure. But, the parent who loses his temper repeatedly could create problems. The failure to learn something from a mistake should cause concern.

Every child can be expected to experience what can be regarded as normal problems throughout his development. These would include problems which relate to social relationships, feelings of inadequacy, and the frustration of failure. Although many of these problems cannot be avoided, parents can often do things to prevent them from getting out of control. Troubles arise when parents are unable to deal with their child's frustrations and consequently, react inappropriately. Problems are created when parents go looking for a source to blame, instead of seeking a solution to the problem; when they assume primary responsibility for solving their child's problem, instead of encouraging the child to do something for himself; and, when they wait too long to take steps to correct a situation they know is not healthy. Time can work against parents if they reinforce undesirable behaviors of the child through repeated mistakes. Most of the troubles that parents have are the result of knowing what desirable behavior should be, but not knowing how to bring it about.

- 6 -

The Task That Lies Ahead

A man from a large city was driving through a small rural town in search of the main highway that led to a friend's hunting lodge. He saw the local sheriff's car parked at the curb and stopped his car to ask for directions. Approaching the sheriff, the man said, "I seem to have gotten myself lost. Could you tell me how to get back to the main highway?" "Sure," replied the sheriff, and pointing towards the north he said, "just follow this road about a mile until you come to a schoolhouse. Then make a left turn and. . . ." But the sheriff stopped and said, "No, wait a minute, that won't get you there." Turning around, the sheriff pointed south and said, "You've got to go down that road about two miles and you'll come to a fork in the road. Follow the road on the right. . . ." And, again the sheriff stopped. He scratched his chin and looked in an eastward direction. "Mister, you've got to go east three or four miles until you pass a dairy. Then make a left turn on the dirt road. . . ." And for the third time, the sheriff stopped. This time he looked perplexed and said, with a smile, "Forget what I've told you so far. If you want to get to the highway you have to go west. Do you see where those big elm trees are?" And, pointing to the west he said, "Well, there's a road alongside those trees that will take you to. . . ." And once again the sheriff stopped. This time he shook his head, and with a look of dejection said. "Darn it, that won't get you there either." Then the sheriff paused, looked into the eyes of the man from the city, and gave a deep sigh and said, "You know what, Mister? I just realized something. You can't get there from here!"

When you stop to consider the many social, political, economic, national and international problems that we are confronted with, and if you attempt to seek solutions for each of these problems, you might find yourself repeating the words of the sheriff, "You can't get there from here!" Where is the most logical place to begin to unravel the troubles in society? Who must make the first move? Is it an exercise in futility? Would we be better off if we admitted that nothing can be done, and learned to live with things as they now are?

To bring it to the level of our young teen-aged generation, or those who have dropped out or are on the verge of dropping out of society, what becomes of them? And what about the generation of youngsters in junior high school who are showing early signs of rebellion? Can we sit back and do nothing and expect them to go away? Do we sit back and watch campus violence, school strikes, militant student protests, and simply call them a fad and wait for a change? Are we willing to admit that drugs will be a way of life for the current and upcoming generation of children? In short, do we encourage the status quo by doing nothing, or do we look for possible solutions to the problems that many adolescents present? When you come right down to it, is there really a choice?

The most logical place to begin to remedy the situation would start with an explanation and understanding of the group that is responsible for the training of the people who make up our society: this would be the family. If order is to be restored to a troubled society, the cohesiveness of the family unit must first be re-established. Relationships between people, which are at the core of our society's problems, begin within the family. Children learn respect for and sensitivity to others at home. This is also where codes for morality and social values take root. Concepts of fairness, acceptance of leadership, and the spirit of cooperation have their origins in family training.

The Danger of Lethargy

In some ways, the greatest danger we face in society today is the problem of lethargy. Another danger we face lies in the tendency of some people to wait and expect others to do their thinking and problem-solving for them. Many people have voiced concern over present social conditions and fear the possible consequences; but with a lethargic attitude, they will do nothing to alleviate the fear. Fear can cause people to yield to pressures that go against their basic concepts of right and wrong. Fear can create panic and make the weak abandon efforts to seek changes. Yet, fear can be overcome with knowledge. Lethargy is more paralyzing. The lethargic person does not seek solutions; he is immobilized by indifference. He does not seek action, for he lacks the energy to function.

Parents who are lethargic wait for others to do their job as parents. They expect the schools to provide their children with the incentive to learn, and the churches to interest them in morality. They expect colleges to enforce discipline that they, as parents, were never able to develop in their children. And if their children develop problems, they expect a military school or a psychotherapist to untangle them. For some parents, the apathy is due to a lack of knowledge or awareness. For others, it is due to their affluence which enables them to pay others to do their work.

Involvement and Blame

Involvement is another word that troubles society today. In many ways we have evolved into a society that does not want to become directly involved with someone else's problems. There are ample volunteers for charity work, fund-raising collections, or benefit luncheons. One-hundred-dollar-a-plate dinners have been very successful. But this is involvement in a nonpersonal way. When we drive past an accident and fail to stop because we don't want to get into a complicated legal mess, we are avoiding involvement on a personal level. When we observe a child who is being mistreated or obviously neglected and do nothing, we are avoiding personal involvement. We can even become witnesses to crimes, including murder, and fail to come forth to help or testify because this, too, requires a personal involvement. Not only has society said "no" to the question of "Am I my brother's keeper?" but many people in society have denied that they even have a brother.

There is also the tendency for some people to blame others for their own sins of omission and commission. The father blames the mother because the child is spoiled. The mother blames the father because the child is undisciplined. Both parents blame the child because he is not doing well in school. They blame the child for behavior that they have openly or inadvertently encouraged. How shocked should parents be when they have permitted their child to talk back to them and call them disrespectful names, when they hear that their adolescent child is calling the teacher "stupid," the police "pigs," and is showing complete disrespect for a university president, the governor of a state, and the President of the United States? Actually, the youngster who does these things is being quite consistent. He has been permitted to flaunt authority, show disrespect for leadership, place his own selfish wants above what might be best for all people concerned. When parents have reared a child in an environment in which the father, mother, and children all shout, storm and scream at each other, whose fault is it that the child shows no respect for authority? Many parents cannot accept the obvious answer. They expect the child to learn to exert self-control, even though they as parents did not. They want to believe that as parents they have the right to do anything at all, and because they are parents, the child should accept it. Reality, like charity, begins at home.

The Importance of Respect

If there is a so-called "handle" to the problem of restoring the equilibrium of the family, it lies with the question of how parents can develop or regain the respect of their children. Contrary to what some parents would like to believe, a child must have a reason to respect his parents. Respect is not inherited, nor does it develop automatically; it must be earned. Impulsive actions, negative attitudes and selfish practices will prevent respect, and may foster contempt.

Many parents who have given their child food, shelter, and clothing have failed to give him reasons to respect them as parents or as people. Material things are not all that a child needs; any person with the financial means can give a child a toy, new clothes, or an ice cream cone. Giving, by itself, will not develop respect.

Nor will giving in develop respect. Parents who have never said "no" to the child, or established limits for him, may be liked for their generosity, but the child will learn to use them rather than to respect them. When the parents find themselves in the position of having to say "no" to the child for the first time, they will undoubtedly see behavior that will communicate to them that the child does not really respect them, even though they have completely given in to him until this time.

Many people confuse popularity with respect. They feel that if they are popular, they will be respected. It is easy to become popular; just do everything that others want you to do, and agree with everything they say. Give in, submit, agree, bribe, and you are almost assured popularity. Respect is another matter. Think back to the schoolteacher or college professor whom you respected the most. He may have been popular as well, but your respect was not due to his giving high grades, or setting low standards, or submitting to student pressure. Your respect was probably based on the fact that this person stood for something; he represented qualities that you admired; he possessed individuality and uniqueness; and he wasn't afraid to express his convictions. Nor did he feel threatened by someone who questioned his thinking. Above all, he was in control of the classroom.

Just as a child needs heroes to admire and models to copy, he also needs parents he can respect. There will be many times when parents are not popular with their child, for the child will not always be allowed to do what he wants. But, this temporary unpopularity is no threat to the parent-child relationship. The ability to interact positively with others begins with the parent-child relationship and only when there is mutual respect can it develop. Many social problems would be reduced if there could be mutual respect for the rights and dignity of others.

The Loss of Controls

Some parents have lost control over their children; others never had control to start with. Either they had too little confidence in themselves as parents to be assertive, or they were permissive to the extent that they failed to present any strong values to the child. The parents may have felt that controls were unnecessary and hoped that if they were ever needed, the child would automatically accept them. The child may have been surprised when he was permitted to take control of his own destiny. He may have fully expected that his parents would strongly protest his autonomous actions and attitudes and been prepared to reluctantly accept parental standards. But, when controls were not forthcoming, the child had no opportunity to learn respect for parental values.

One of the pressures that parents have acquiesced to is the one that the child uses when he says, "But everybody else is doing it." Interestingly enough, the parents were probably more consistent with respect to this pressure than they realized. Parents who bought a color television set because the neighbors just bought one, or a big car because their friends had one, or in other ways sought to "keep up with the Joneses" were being consistent when they yielded to the child's request to buy him his own car because Freddie's parents bought him one. Many parents have allowed other people to determine their values without questioning whether the other person's values are right for them.

Few parents who have lost control over their adolescent child could say that it just happened suddenly. There was usually a history of conflict dating back to the early life of the child. The first signs may have been ignored or overlooked, but the warnings were there. Early signs may have been excessive demands on the parents, disobedience, indifference to requests, and what parents refer to as laziness. Eventually there was a rude awakening to the fact that things had been allowed to slide by too long. When this realization finally came, the parents found themselves helpless.

Regaining Control

The parent who feels that he has lost control over his child should realize that he can take back much of what he has given away. Unless the child is prepared to be completely independent from the parents, they can still exert a controlling influence. They can begin by telling the youngster what will be expected of him. This is called establishing the ground rules. Although it is a sudden and authoritarian approach, in some cases there is no gradual way to gain control. To add some teeth to their declaration, the parents should be prepared to explain the alternatives to the child and, in general, to let the child know that they are in control. This requires decisive actions on the part of the parents and the decision not to permit the child to intimidate them. By taking a unified position and by communicating to the child that they are not bluffing, parents offer him the choice of cooperating with them or facing unattractive consequences.

Case Illustration Number 11

Wilma was sixteen years old and very unhappy with her parents. She resented their attempts to police her actions and refused to abide by their curfews and regulations. Her parents disapproved of her choice of boy and girl friends and the way she dressed and acted.

Wilma disliked school and cut classes frequently. She was unconcerned over her failing grades and did not expect to return for her junior year. She had a boyfriend older than herself who had quit school. Both Wilma and her boyfriend were involved with drugs. Her parents knew this, but did not know the extent to which she had experimented with them. They also knew that Wilma had slept with her present boyfriend and suspected that she had been sexually promiscuous before that. They had called her a variety of degrading names and she had returned their insults. On several occasions, Wilma's father struck her and she had vowed to hit him back if he ever touched her again.

Wilma's parents admitted that they had no control over her, and Wilma concurred. Once, she stayed away from home several days, but this was not considered running away from home because she intended to return and she even announced that she was leaving.

Wilma's parents had to realize that they had only two choices: either to allow their relationship to continue to deteriorate, or to take a firm stand and try to rescue their child who was well on her way to destroying herself. Since they felt that they had little to lose, it was easy for them to choose the latter position. At least they would be doing what they could to protect her from herself.

They began by spelling out what they expected of her, and what the consequences would be if she chose to disregard their authority. They were willing to have her try to run away, and they told her this. They were willing to have her made a ward of the court and they told her this. They were prepared to bring suit against her boyfriend for contributing to her delinquency, and they informed her of this. And, they were willing to accept any emotion she wanted to feel towards them.

They gave her the choice of attending school or getting a job. Since she was sixteen, she could legally quit school, but they refused to allow her to do nothing. If she worked she would pay them rent. She would be subject to their curfews, their judgment on her choice of friends, and their approval of her clothes. Wilma was told that if her parents found that she was using illegal drugs, they would report her to police. In short, they made it known that things as they had been would stop immediately.

Wilma's initial reaction was predictable. She flatly refused to go along with anything they said to her. She called them every name she could think of. She threatened to run away. She screamed at them, and was about to storm out of the house when her father told her that the minute she left the house he would call the police and she would be turned over to juvenile court. Wilma knew that he meant it this time. She did not leave.

For the first time in the history of their battles, Wilma was afraid to call her parents' bluff. They had not shouted at her or resorted to idle threats. They spoke to her in a firm way and she knew that they meant what they said. For the first time in years, Wilma's parents had some control over their daughter. They were willing to gamble that Wilma did not want to get herself or her friends in trouble. Once she knew the consequences of her behavior, and realized that her parents meant what they were saying, she had no choice.

For a long time, Wilma was silent with her parents. They treated her cordially and once she became responsive to them, they were ready to receive her. Wilma decided to be patient until she was eighteen and would be able to legally leave home. She remained in school and when she turned eighteen she did get a job and eventually left home. Her parents felt that disaster had been averted, for had they not taken the decisive actions to control her, those two years until she was eighteen could have resulted in a complete breakdown of the parent-child relationship. Although she left home, it was not under circumstances that would have made it difficult for her to return. Some respect between Wilma and her parents developed, but more important, Wilma did not do irreparable harm to herself.

Rebellion Against Father

Although the adolescent is frequently in conflict with the mother, his primary thrust of rebellion seems to be directed toward the father. It is the father who is looked to for family leadership and controls. In this culture it is the father who is responsible for the standard of living. The male adult is held responsible for the political and economic problems in society, and is viewed as the person who has been in the best position to effect changes in our social process.

The image that the middle-class American father has developed for himself is that of a hard-working, hard-playing, aggressive and productive individual. Status and status symbols are important to him. He typically owns more things than he needs, wants more things than he can have, eats more than he should, demands a lot from himself and expects a lot from others. He feels that he has surpassed his own father in terms of annual income, standard of living, enjoyment of life, and level of aspiration. He feels independent, confident, self-satisfied and important. He regards his ability as a good provider to be an indication of his efficiency, his commitment to his responsibility, and his pride in being a good father. In his mind, and in his eyes, he is a success. In the eyes of his discontented adolescent child, he is often seen as a failure. He cannot comprehend this discrepancy.

He is frequently criticized by his child for having been a neglectful and selfish father who saw too little of his children in their formative years and who places material needs over emotional needs. He is viewed as a father who uses his wife and family to gratify himself, and encourages a high level of competition in his children. The adolescent sees him as a person who wants to be proud of his children for their accomplishments in much the same manner that he wants to be proud of his new, larger-than-needed car. His disenchanted teen-ager accuses him of expecting too much, criticizing too often, praising too little, and seeing his own standards as the only ones.

It is not difficult for children to develop negative feelings towards a father who is rarely in the home and who makes unfair demands on both his wife and children. The child interprets the father's absence as rejection and his negative feelings become hostile and rebellious attitudes. Now it is the child's turn to do the rejecting. Through his actions he reveals the strategy of his rebellion; he opposes the father by rejecting his value system.

The father is a symbol of society. He exemplifies the work doctrine and is very concerned about appearances and images. He seeks to protect his family and to be proud of them. He places a great value on productivity and success and has high expectations for his children. When the adolescent defies his authority, the full impact of the negative response can be seen.

Adolescent boys have broken completely away from the all-American-boy image. Long hair, sloppy clothes, unkempt beards, and open sandals have replaced the more traditional crew-cut hair, grey flannel slacks, black cashmere sweater, and white buck shoes. In becoming antisociety, the adolescent has rejected not only the 40-hour week, but productivity. Illegal drugs and sexual promiscuity further "put-down" the father's value system, revealing open contempt for the image of the father and the family. By dropping out of both school and society the adolescent was rejecting the things the father was working for.

The adolescent daughter has demonstrated her rebellion in a similar way. She has become negative to those things a father wants to see in his daughter. Her unladylike appearance and language irritate the father who wants to display a beautiful virgin daughter. As dresses give way to blue jeans and the odor of perfume becomes the smell of cigarettes, the father realizes that he has been neither a hero to his daughter nor a model for his son.

The father who defines his role as that of the financial provider and the maker of decisions learns that paying the bills, throwing an occasional baseball to his son, and deciding where the family will take a vacation falls short. Many fathers feel that since they are required to put in a long and sometimes hard day at work, they are entitled to spend their free time as they see fit. They resent demands that take away this free time, even when the demands are from a wife urging them to become more involved with the children. They say that they can't recall seeing their fathers wash a dish, change a diaper, or empty a waste basket. They want to forget their own fathers' alienation from them as children, their fathers' callous attitudes towards emotions, and the lack of understanding that created the gap in their own father-son relationships. They remember only what they want to remember and define their roles from this partial recollection of their fathers.

The rebellion of the adolescent is a rejection of the father and a protest of his authority. Although the mother is frequently the direct victim of the child's hostility and negative behavior, she is more of a scapegoat than the source of the child's aggression. The uninvolved or absent father makes it more difficult for the mother to prevent the adolescent from getting out of control. Once the adolescent realizes that he can defy his mother's authority and that his father does not mean that much to him, it is easy for him to rebel.

Father the Hero: Mother the Villain

Many fathers have played a popularity game with their children. They allowed their wives to be the villains who scolded and punished the children. Because the mother was with the child more hours than the father, she was delegated more disciplinary functions. When the father was asked to handle a problem the mother was having with the child, he would frequently resort to pacifying the child with bribes, promises, and "deals." Many of these "deals," promises, and bribes served to undermine the mother's attempts at disciplinary control.

The father was anxious to maintain his image of being the nice guy when things were calm. Even when he was pressured into becoming the disciplinarian he tried to preserve his image. Inevitably, however, his wife rebelled. She became angry at the image that her husband was building for himself at her expense. She grew tired of being the villain; resentful of his popularity, and frustrated at her role as chief disciplinarian. She was demanding help from the father, both in an honest plea to restore controls in the family and a somewhat dishonorable need to topple him from his pedestal and see him dirty his hands in an unglamorous aspect of child rearing.

Many times, the attitude that the father takes when he acknowledges the request of the mother to intercede, conveys to the child that he is really condescending to the mother. He implies, "My heart isn't really in this, but I'd better say these things to get your mother off both our backs." Even in admonishing the child, the father upholds his image. Of course, he is adding to the mother's ineffectiveness by implying that the punishing was done to only satisfy her punishing needs. This keeps the mother in an unfavorable light with her child and widens a gap between husband and wife.

The lack of paternal support on issues involving controls aggravates the conflict between the mother and the child. If the father refuses to take a position on an issue, the child is encouraged to feel that the mother is making a big to-do over nothing, or that she is old-fashioned, mean, or unyielding. Mother is seen as the sole villain because father has avoided a stand on the issue. It is easier for a child to resist one parent than it is to attack a unified parental view. When parents disagree with each other in front of the child on the importance of issues or when they fail to uphold each other's decisions, they encourage the child to lose respect for parental authority.

Case Illustration Number 12

Mr. S. had been aware for some time that his wife was not pleased with the attitude of their fifteen-year-old son, Jeff. He knew that Jeff was in frequent conflict with his wife, and on occasions he would step in to resolve an issue. The wife blamed her husband's indifference for much of the problem, but Mr. S. blamed his wife's ineffectiveness. After Jeff brought home a report card with practically all failing grades, the father decided to enter the arena that his wife had been struggling in for so many years. He did so with an attitude of, "Step aside and watch how it should be done." He exuded self-confidence, for he was certain that years of being an easygoing father would pay off for him now.

The mother could not get Jeff to do his homework, clean his room, pick up his clothes, talk less on the telephone, try harder in school, or talk back less to her. Mr. S.'s attempts to have Jeff cooperate were met with the same resistance, indifference, and disrespect. Mr. S. was shocked. After he had told Jeff what he expected of him, Jeff told his father what he thought of him: how ridiculous his values were, how foolish he was to be a slave to a job, and how he, Jeff, would be better off if he left home. Jeff was now in conflict with both of his parents.

At this point, Mr. S. completely changed his tune. He spoke to Jeff as if the Lord himself was threatening wrath upon him. No more deals or bribes were offered. Jeff would shape up or else. Mr. S. then turned to his wife and declared that "*we* have a problem."

Mr. S.'s awakening was both gratifying and saddening to Mrs. S. She was sorry that Jeff was now alienated from both of his parents, but she felt some satisfaction in seeing her husband fail where she had failed. She had endured frustration for many years; now her husband was getting a taste of it. But vengeance is not sweet when someone you love is in danger of being hurt. Jeff had become the lost son, and they wanted him back.

Getting Jeff back involved introducing him to reality. His past attitude towards his mother and his current feelings towards his father were not realistic, for he was denying his role as part of the family. Many of the things he had told his father were said in anger, when Jeff felt he had to defend himself with any ammunition he could bring up. His father had to understand this and not hold him to everything he had said.

The first discussion between Jeff and his parents on the subject of reality dealt with what his parents were in a position to do for him, and likewise what they would do if the status quo went unchanged. Jeff needed to be told that he had gone beyond the boundaries, and that his parents were prepared to take immediate action to bring him back into the family.

Although Jeff's father had waited too long to assert himself, he was still able to be effective when he began to cooperate and support his wife. Though there were occasional differences of opinion between the parents as to how specific situations would be handled, these differences were discussed between themselves so that before Jeff they presented a unified position. Jeff's father also realized that his relationship with his son was a weak one, and took steps to improve this condition. The biggest action in this direction was the development of verbal communication with his son. At first, he made a point of talking with him every day. Soon it was more automatic. Jeff came to expect dialogue with his father, and the father was prepared to listen to Jeff's feelings, opinions, and criticisms.

They didn't agree on a number of issues, but they allowed themselves the privilege of disagreeing without getting upset. Jeff was learning that he could talk with his father, and the mother was frequently included in these discussions. Jeff cooperated initially because he saw no choice. Later he cooperated because he had no reason not to.

It is easy for a child to defy parental authority when parental resistance is weak and one-sided. In the case just described, Jeff seemed to be asking for controls and forced his parents to become aware of their joint responsibility. He was also asking for his father to act like a father.

The Adolescent's Choice

For many youngsters, the decision to rebel against the parents and family structure has not been a difficult one. Some children find that they are being forced into the decision. When a relationship between two people has been tense for some time, rebellion becomes both a defense and a means of survival. The child who is subjected to constant criticism and insults has the choice of resisting in either an aggressive or a passive way. When the resistance is aggressive, the child will meet insult with insult, threat with threat, and violence with violence. If the resistance is passive, the child is uncommunicative, uncooperative, and uninvolved with family matters.

To combat unsatisfactory parental relationships, some teen-aged children have made the decision to leave home. Many more youngsters, aware of the impracticality of leaving home in the physical sense, have chosen to remain home in the literal sense but have removed themselves from the structure of the family. They have withdrawn from the parents, lost interest in the family, and have become, in effect, mere boarders.

Barriers to Problem Solving

Before solutions to a problem can be developed, the conditions that perpetuate the problem must be understood and, if possible, reduced or eliminated. It does no good to simply label a child's actions irresponsible, incompetent, irrational, or immature. Granted that many of the rebellious actions of the adolescent are impulsive acts that are potentially self-destructive, and granted that much of the child's behavior is inappropriate, yet before steps can be taken by the parents to control this behavior, they must have some insights as to not only what actions have caused the undesirable conduct but also what behavior fosters the continuance of it. If it is not identified and eliminated, it will constitute a constant contamination that will preclude progress. Determination of what these aggravating conditions might be is not always easy, unless the parents are able to be very objective about themselves. The contributing factors that can be identified most easily are those that can be observed. However, it is not always possible for an individual to be aware of his own behavior; hence there is a need for parents to observe one another.

Stubbornness is one reason that problems are perpetuated. An unyielding attitude in defense of a position will prevent solutions. Stubbornness protects an ego by resisting compromise or change. When it stands in the way of settling a problem it becomes self-defeating rigidity, since the goal is a solution or reduction of the problem. The need for victories is another reason that problems are perpetuated. In the typical power struggle both parties concentrate on the issue of who will give in. The victory provides satisfaction, rather than the solution.

A third reason problems maintain themselves is that ineffective measures are used to resolve them. Parents cannot re-establish trust in a child if they try to trap him in a lie. Knowing that a child was reported absent from classes in school, it is inappropriate to ask him, "How was school today?" If the parents are upset because their child has a negative attitude towards them, they will not improve things if they are sarcastic and insulting to him. In each instance, the approach to reduce the problem is not effective.

A fourth reason that problems are perpetuated lies in an unwillingness to seek solutions. If people are content with conditions as they are, or if they feel there is no way things can be different, no effort will be made to bring about changes. People who are apathetic or too lazy to do anything to solve problems may even rationalize that it is best to let things be as they are; for, they may point out, things could be worse. An unwillingness to seek solutions to problems indicates that the person does not care enough to change the situation and, consequently, is willing to endure conditions as they are. Such a person is not motivated enough to become actively involved.

A fifth attitude that retards progress in problem solving and helps maintain conditions that need to be changed is defensiveness, which is a form of aggressive stubbornness. People have a tendency to become defensive when they perceive that they are being attacked, criticized, insulted, or blamed. People also can become defensive when someone challenges their beliefs, values, or feelings. In other words, people become defensive when they perceive someone else as becoming offensive. Once they become defensive, they call upon all available resources to vindicate themselves, defeat their adversary, or prove something to others. The defensive person is out to redeem himself, chalk up a victory, or make a point. A differentiation should be made between explaining your views and defending your views. In explaining your views, you attempt to clarify your feelings on an issue by expanding the reasoning that underlies your thinking. You are not trying to persuade anyone to agree with you, nor are you threatened or upset if someone chooses to disagree with you. You are expressing a personal view and are asking only that the other person afford you the opportunity to express yourself. Whereas explanation can lead to discussion, defensiveness usually results in arguments.

If parents are to become observant of each other's behavior yet persist in becoming defensive when criticized, they will defeat the purpose of self-understanding and attain no insights. For example, a husband may take his wife aside after she has had an argument with the child and attempt to show her how her remarks were encouraging the argument. The husband could tell the wife that she never allowed the child to express his feelings, or that she accused him before he could explain his feelings. If she begins to attack him for his initial remarks, or leaves the room in anger, it is apparent that she is defending herself and is not trying to look at the situation objectively. Or, if the wife tells her husband that his drinking is creating a problem in the home, and the husband defends himself by justifying his drinking, it is equally apparent that the husband is being defensive and unwilling to receive constructive criticism. Defensiveness is usually a symptom of a problem rather than being a problem in itself. People become defensive in an attempt to restore an image of themselves that is in jeopardy.

The Problem of Relating

A condition that is frequently experienced between parents who are having problems with their children is an inability to talk calmly with each other. Quite often the parents are so intent on blaming each other for the problems of the child that they forget how to talk *to* each other. They talk *at* one another and argue *with* each other, but somewhere in the marriage they lost the knack of talking to each other, if they ever had it. It is common to hear a woman say she and her husband are having a problem of communication. However, this is not usually accurate. In most instances, the husband and wife do communicate and, as a matter of fact, they communicate very well. When the husband is unwilling to converse with his wife, or the wife is angry with the husband and won't talk to him for two days, what they are communicating about their respective feelings is rather obvious. We can communicate with words, gestures, facial expressions, or the lack of these.

A term more appropriate than communicating is *relating*. When two people are able to relate to each other, not only will they converse with one another but they will also become sensitive to each other's feelings. A youngster communicates his feelings towards the parents' authority when he fails to return home at a designated time. He can do this without saying a word. But, in order for the youngster to relate to his parents, there must be discussion and an understanding of each other's feelings about the issue.

Once the parents are able to relate to each other, and once they can begin to look for the conditions that might be perpetuating the problems with the youngster, they will be in a better position to define the problem more accurately. Is the problem one of a child who is spoiled and demands his own way . . . or else? Does the child have a legitimate complaint, such as parental favoritism to another sibling? Is it largely a matter of the child's impulsive nature? Does the child's behavior indicate his lack of self-confidence and strong need to follow others? Is the rebellion a protest to rules that are unfair or overprotecting? In short, what does the child's behavior tell you, as the parent?

The obvious things that a rebelling attitude conveys include dissatisfaction, unhappiness, restlessness, and anger. The task of the parents is to examine behavior that might explain or offer some insights into the attitudes. For example, suppose the child rejects the parental views on education, and that his attitude towards school is one of indifference with a lack of motivation. The observable behavior is a decrease in interest in doing assignments, with subsequent low grades. Of course, the lack of studying is responsible for the poor grades. Questions the parent might seek answers to would include: What about school is so distasteful to the child? Is the child afraid of failure? Does he resent the authority of the teacher? Is learning boring because the child does not feel it to be relevant? If relevance is the issue, what would the child regard as being more relevant? Is competition a factor?

In order to answer these questions, the parents and their child must relate to one another. The parents cannot learn the answers without the cooperation of the child, and if the parents make a sincere effort to relate, rather than berate, and can avoid sarcasm and intimidation, the chances are good that the youngster will make some effort to relate to them.

Opinions, Judgments, and Expectations

There are two sides to every grievance. The youngster may become disenchanted with the parents, but when this happens, usually the parents have also become disappointed with the child. Parents call the child ungrateful; the child calls the parents old-fashioned. Both admit that they don't understand each other. Examine the following comments and criticisms expressed by adolescents toward their parents:

— "My parents are too nosy. They want to know about everything I do, and every place I go."
— "My parents are too critical of me. They criticize how I dress, how I wear my hair, how I talk, and even how I walk."
— "My parents expect me to think and act as if I were as old as they are."
— "I want more personal freedom than they give me. They over-protect me."
— "They are too critical of my friends. They want to tell me who I should see and who I shouldn't."

— "My parents don't respect my judgment or my values. Therefore, I can't respect theirs."
— "I resent their punishments. They think they can take away the car and I'll reform."
— "All they ever talk about is school, school, school. Is that all they think is important in my life?"
— "All I want them to do is to try marijuana once."
— "My mother got married at nineteen, but she thinks I'm too young."

Before analyzing these comments, it might be interesting to look at some comments that have been made by parents who are unhappy with their adolescent children.

— "I expect him to do what I tell him."
— "All I'm asking him to do is finish school first."
— "All she does is talk on the phone. She can talk to her friends for three hours every night, and she sees them in school every day."
— "I told her she was nothing but a little tramp!" (The daughter's version was that her mother called her a "dirty whore.")
— "Look, it's my house, and he's not going to tell me what to do!"
— "As long as she is living under my roof, I expect her to be part of the family."
— "I'm not spending any more money on colleges until he can show me that he intends to study."
— "When I was a kid, I wouldn't have dared to talk to my parents that way . . ."

The single most common parental complaint about the adolescent is probably that he lacks *judgment*. The worried parent does not think that the adolescent's judgment is appropriate or mature. This may reveal some parental misconception about the stage that is called adolescence. There is a middle period between childhood and adulthood. It is the time in which the youngster is experimenting with what is appropriate for himself. It can, therefore, be expected that the adolescent's judgment will not be adultlike, nor would he be mature, whatever maturity implies. Many parents seem to forget what this in-between stage of life is all about and to expect adultlike behavior from the nonadult. As adolescents have phrased it, the parents treat them as if they were children and expect them to act as if they were adults. There is reason to feel that if parents attempted to relate to their adolescent children, they would learn how adolescent judgment differs from their own, and why the adolescent is not ready to be considered an adult.

If judgment is what the parents complain about, *expectation* is what the adolescent objects to in parental attitudes. In the mind of adolescents, the parents expect too much. Some youngsters would go further and say that their parents expect the impossible.

The adolescent complains that parents expect too much from them academically. They also complain that parents expect them to assume too much responsibility around the house. As one adolescent phrased it, "My father is always telling me that this is his house, and if I don't like the way things are run, I can get out. Then he'll come home and tell me I should have seen that the grass needed to be cut, and holler at me for not cutting it. Then he'll say it's my house, too!" Some parents expect the child to be interested in the things that they are interested in, to want the things that parents want, and to react similarly to the way parents react. This expectation is, obviously, unreal. Even when both share an interest, their motivation is not the same.

Many parental complaints are justified; adolescent behavior is often immature, even for the adolescent. Many adolescent complaints are likewise justified, and many clashes between the child and the parents are due to unfair expectations.

Youngsters are doing many things to themselves that they will regret later. In some instances, the parents made the mistakes, and their children will suffer the consequences. On the other hand, many adolescents have created problems for themselves that are not due to the parental practices or attitudes. It is not always fair to say, blame the parents for doing a bad job. Many times the guilt and responsibility for misconduct rests on the shoulders of a youngster who did not assume responsibility for himself, who made no attempt to see a situation realistically, who preferred to be a martyr rather than conform to social standards, and who insisted on learning things the hard way, rejecting the advice and experience of others.

Idealism

Adolescence is a period of idealism. Perhaps one of the distinctions that can be made to differentiate adolescence from adulthood is in the ability to bridge the gap between idealism and realism. It is ideal not to have wars. But, since at no time in the history of man has a condition of world peace ever existed, it is not realistic to assume that world peace is possible. There is no valid defense of prejudice. Yet to carry signs around a city demanding an end to prejudice and expect instant results is very unrealistic. As long as there are people, there will be prejudice. There will also be poverty, unemployment, illiteracy, and many other social ills that should be reduced and, *ideally*, removed.

Parents frequently become upset when their adolescent child is critical of the way things are. Even though the parents admit that things could be better, they become defensive and accuse the child of being naive. A more appropriate response would be to pose challenging questions or cite the obstacles that prevent the ideal from becoming real. This would stimulate the child to think and to examine his solutions in accordance with what the parent presents as reality. By showing impatience, the parent not only discourages the child from future parental interactions, but also fails to guide his thinking.

One of the explanations for the "youth rebellion" is that youth is impatient. For similar reasons, others in society have also rebelled. A person who has been abused and discriminated against is often impatient, and feels that revolution makes more sense than waiting for society to evolve. Society has failed to do much about problems that require great changes and reforms. When reality is unacceptable, people set idealistic, impossible goals. When people strive for something they can never attain, they become frustrated. Frustrated people become hostile and aggressive; and what begins as idealism ends in disruption.

Freedom with Dependency

The actions of many adolescents indicate that they are desperately seeking freedom from parental controls. Yet, there is reason to believe that they are more dependent and trusting of their parents than they could ever begin to admit, for if in the quest for freedom they go too far and hurt themselves, they expect all to be forgiven and rescued by the parents, who they know will not desert them when they call out for help. If the youngster goes too far and hurts others, or is arrested for breaking a law, he demands amnesty, a full pardon, and expects society to laugh it off with a, "Well, he's just a child—what do you expect" attitude. There is a fine line between the actions of the adolescent and those of the young adult. Although age legally separates the two, a fifteen-year-old girl can step over the line very easily when she ends up pregnant. Saying that "I'm sorry, I won't do it again," doesn't make the pregnancy go away. This is reality.

Many adolescents fail to realize *when* they are playing for fun and *when* they are playing for keeps. Experimenting with drugs may seem like fun, but it can lead to long lasting problems if the person ends up with permanent side effects, messes up his life by dropping out of school, or acquires values unacceptable to society at large. After the youngster has made his mistakes, or when he becomes frightened that he has gone too far in some way, then he wants the security of his parents. In instances when the child knows that the parents will not let him down, there must have been some trust in the relationship after all.

Of course, the youngster is the parents' responsibility. He always was. What happened was that the parents allowed the child to usurp their responsibilities. Many parents were happy to relinquish their function; others acquiesced with reluctance. Parents were confused and often divided as to what their approach to their children should be. Their failure to indicate clearly to the child what the consequences of his actions would be created the freedom to rebel. The youngster knew that if he got into trouble, his parents would forgive him, and protect him from his own mistakes. The parents thus contributed to the child's lack of awareness of reality.

Readiness for Freedom

One way to examine the question of the causes of present home problems and what maintains them is to look at one of the objections the youngster has to his parents. In a universal chorus of voices, the adolescent says that what he wants most today is what he calls freedom. He is saying: "Let me do what I want to do." He also means, "You didn't or couldn't stop me from doing what I wanted to do when I was ten years old, so don't try to stop me now that I'm sixteen." The adolescent is also saying that his parents have no right to make demands upon him, no reason to place any controls on him, and no cause to worry about him, for he can take care of himself.

Many parents interpret the need for freedom in the literal sense. They take the position that the child who is asking for freedom should no longer need them, no longer expect them to assume financial responsibility for him, and no longer expect them to feed, clothe, house, and educate him. This, of course, is not allowing a child freedom, it is abandoning the child. A few children have forced their parents to assume this position. The child who presents his parents with an ultimatum is testing them, and if he demands his complete freedom or else, there is not much that the parents can do. Making "deals" is not a good practice to follow, especially when the child is not reliable.

The parents, as well as the child, can distort the meaning of freedom. The amount of freedom a youngster needs can be measured by what it takes to make him self-directing and responsible. No person in a society has total freedom; total freedom is not even desirable. The child at any age needs certain freedoms. Parental judgment should determine how much freedom and in what areas it can be granted, based on the child's readiness to handle it. Should a two-year-old be allowed the freedom to select the story she wants to hear? Should an eight-year-old be given the freedom to invite whom he wants to his birthday party? Would you allow a twelve-year-old the freedom to decide if he wants to go to a summer camp? The child should have freedom when he is ready to assume full responsibility for whatever the consequences will be. The two-year-old, in deciding that she wants to hear the story of the three bears, can learn the consequence that the story of the three little kittens will have to wait for another time. The eight-year-old may have to face some angry children if he forgets to invite, or decides not to invite, them to his birthday party. But, if he wants the freedom to make this decision, he must understand the consequences of his actions. The twelve-year-old who decides not to go to camp may have a long and boring summer. With freedom should come responsibility. Unless the child can assume responsibility for his decisions, he is not ready for freedom.

To look at the present generation of adolescents who have demanded and taken freedoms, we see many youngsters who were not ready to have their freedom, many who could not assume responsibilities for their actions, and many who have done irreparable damage to themselves because they were either ignorant of the consequences of their behavior, or too stubborn to look at the obvious outcomes. In either case, they demonstrated poor judgment and too much power over themselves.

One of the things that maintains this condition, in which youngsters have more freedom than they can properly use, or more power than they really need, is parental fear. Parents are afraid that the child will not give up the freedom and powers that he has captured prematurely. They are afraid that the child will do something irrational, get into more serious trouble, run away, get married, or carry out some threat that he has made. They are afraid, and the youngsters know it. Though some parents have cause to fear, most probably do not.

When Is It Too Late?

Is it ever too late to begin to rehabilitate? The answer is, unfortunately, yes. So the big question is, when is it too late to take steps to restore something to a more natural state? When is it too late for children who have been out of harmony with their families to become part of the family again? Many times the damage that has been done cannot be undone. The things that have been said cannot be retracted. The memories of what has happened cannot be erased. However, rules can be modified and certain compromises can be made. We can forgive, even though we may never forget.

It is too late to rehabilitate families when either the parents or the child will not reconsider their actions in light of a recognized need for a change; when minds are so filled with hatred and bitterness that all respect and feelings for the other individual are gone; when decisions that could be revoked, attitudes that could be altered, and feelings that could be repaired are not because of selfishness, foolish pride, or stubbornness. It is too late to rehabilitate families when the people involved no longer care about the welfare and actual life of the other individuals. Even so, before rehabilitation can be ruled out, some honest efforts should be made to restore things to an equilibrium.

The conditions within many families must change for the sake of everyone involved. Even if the ideal changes cannot take place, improvements can be made. Problems that evolved over a period of years will not be resolved in a matter of hours, days, or months. The next chapter will deal with some specific approaches to reducing family tensions, or rehabilitating the family whose relationships have deteriorated. When the adolescent and his parents are in conflict, it is essential that a mutual desire for improvement exists. What must happen to bring this about is the difficult, but necessary task that lies ahead.

- 7 -

Taming the Tiger

A well-known prayer, adapted from *A Prayer*, by Reinhold Niebuhr, reads:

God grant me the serenity to accept the things I cannot change,
The courage to change the things I can change,
And the wisdom to know the difference.

The dilemma this prayer expresses is faced by all parents who are having problems with their children. Should they prepare themselves to accept conditions that are not desirable? Can they do anything to correct these conditions? How can they know whether they should accept something or try to change it?

This chapter will focus on adolescents and their characteristic behavior and problems. The adolescent years are especially difficult for both the youngster and his parents, for it is during these years the parent-child relationship is put to its greatest test. The adolescent seeks freedom from parental controls, and the parents must decide how much freedom the child can handle. Conflicts arise when the child's demands for independence exceed the parent's willingness to accept his readiness for independence. The adolescent years give the child vital preparation for adulthood. Because adolescent behaviors and attitudes form the basis of the personality that is carried into early adulthood, adolescent actions and decisions will exert a significant influence on the youngster's adult life. If he decides to drop out of school at sixteen, or becomes indifferent to responsibility, his decisions could adversely effect his future life. Mistakes during adolescence could close doors to adult opportunities, for many judgment errors are irreparable. The adolescent wants to know, "Who am I and what can I do?" He will need understanding parents who are willing to help him find the answers to his questions and adjust to himself and his world.

Although a good parent-adolescent relationship is possible, many have become so bad that changes for the better are unlikely. Some parents feel they are on the brink of trouble and want to prevent serious problems from developing. Other parents are aware of the bad relationship and want help.

Which Parents Have Problems?

Parent-adolescent problems are usually an outgrowth of earlier problems in the parent-child relationship. The young child who was out of bounds with himself and uncontrolled by his parents becomes the adolescent who is hard to manage and unhappy with himself. Parents who have allowed early control problems to extend into adolescence will discover that it is very difficult for the youngster who is beyond the age of thirteen or fourteen to accept parental controls or cooperate with parental expectations. The words of one fourteen-year-old child sum up the situation accurately: "It's too late now . . . what do they expect? I never listened to them before, and I'm not going to start to now."

Parents may create some of the problems by exaggerating the importance of their child's behavior. Parents who interpret their sixteen-year-old's desire to "go steady" as a forerunner of an early marriage may be doing this. Although going steady could lead to a serious involvement, it does not necessarily do so. Problems can develop when parents distort or fail to understand the meaning of their child's actions. An adolescent may choose to be by himself rather than go out with his peers. This could mean that he has not met any friends who share his interests; but, parents could turn this into a parent-adolescent problem if they insist that he socialize and interpret his lack of friendships to mean that he is antisocial or unpopular.

The young adolescent experiences both physiological and psychological changes in himself. The parent who is not sensitive to what is happening within the adolescent is inclined to become impatient and expect too much from him. This puts additional pressure on the youngster and can trigger off a negative response that serves to alienate him from his parents. Parents who do not understand the kinds of things that are upsetting to the adolescent will have problems in their parent-adolescent relationship. Being accepted and belonging to a group are important for an adolescent; being allowed to drive the family car and have friends over for a party are equally important.

Certain parents may be prone to have problems with their adolescent children. In general, these are parents who are inclined to:

— over-react to situations, thereby making small issues a crisis
— expect adolescents to think and respond like an adult
— deny their child adequate freedom, or,
— allow too much freedom without supervision
— insist on absolute obedience
— be unable to see things from their child's point of view
— be overly critical of them
— treat them like children
— talk down to them in insulting or sarcastic ways
— forget that they themselves, as parents, are still models for their children

Which Adolescents Have Problems?

Because the adolescent wants to believe he can show good judgment, he is reluctant to admit it when he has made judgmental errors and is embarrassed to acknowledge that he has problems. He is inclined to deny and gloss over the problems that his parents worry about. Parents worry about his negative attitude towards school and the use of illegal drugs; the adolescent tells them these are needless worries. Parents are frustrated by this indifference and in desperation will bribe, threaten, or punish the child in order to persuade him to change his attitude.

The adolescent who has a parent problem is frequently seeking more freedom than his parents are willing to give him. He is also motivated to "beat the system," which means he tries to get away with doing the forbidden. Beating the system in school may mean skipping without getting caught: at home it could mean avoiding punishment by lying about the reason he came home two hours after curfew.

Parent-adolescent problems are often the result of the adolescent's ineffective ways of coping with stress. One of the most common reasons an adolescent has problems is that his parents are unable to trust him. In an attempt to protect his image, avoid blame, or possibly to beat the system, the adolescent may lie to his parents. If, after he is caught lying, he becomes defensive or resentful, or tries to justify his reasons for lying, the parent-adolescent relationship frequently becomes one of mutual distrust. The parents wait for the child to lie again, and the child begins to feel his parents are against him. Defensively, the youngster may say, "If they don't trust me, I won't trust them." Dishonest, deceitful, and overly defensive adolescents will have problems, both with their parents and their peers.

In general, adolescent problems become parent-adolescent problems when the youngster:
— rebels against parental authority
— is negative to parental suggestions
— gives parents reasons not to trust him
— takes more personal freedom than he is permitted
— rejects parental controls
— allows peer influences to negate responsibility to parents
— places pleasure above responsibility to himself or others
— rejects the concept of a family unit
— opposes parental values
— decides he no longer needs his parents, or conversely,
— remains too dependent upon his parents
— alienates himself from parents by withdrawing, ignoring, or being abusive to them
— releases his frustrations at the parents instead of the actual source
— uses resistance or negative behavior in order to punish his parents
— has not learned effective ways of coping with personal problems

Normal Adolescence and Signs of Trouble

Much has already been said about the period of life that is the transition between childhood and adulthood. Adolescents are impatient and impulsive. They are moody and emotionally explosive, self-conscious and sensitive. Outwardly, they give the impression of knowing a lot about many things; inwardly, they are insecure and unstable. They are tired of being treated as if they were children and anxious to show everyone, including themselves, that they are almost as capable as an adult. To prove this, they brag about their ability to drive cars fast, they smoke, drink alcohol, and exploit their sex appeal. Many will defy their parents in order to announce to everyone that they can get away with rejecting parental controls, and will "turn on" with drugs to prove they are not "chicken." This type of adolescent does what he knows should not be done in order to prove he can get away with it.

Parents, on the other hand, are content to see the adolescent evolve slowly into an adult. They are neither seeking proof that their child is growing up, nor are they comfortable when their child bursts into adulthood. Most parents have some awareness of the child's need for autonomy and are willing to allow their child more freedom when it can be shown the adolescent will not abuse it. When the impatient youngster feels he can handle freedoms before the parents are willing to grant them, the result is a battle for control.

One way to view this problem of control lies in the difference between the criteria for readiness as seen by the parents and the adolescent. The parents use the chronological age as an indication of readiness; adolescents prefer to use the confidence they have in themselves. A fourteen-year-old can feel that her parents are very unfair for not allowing her to have a one o'clock curfew. Because she has confidence that she can take care of herself, she feels that the factor of chronological age is irrelevant. On the other hand, her parents look upon her confidence as being naive, unwarranted, and an indication of her immaturity. They regard their eleven o'clock curfew as protective. For adolescents to want to determine their own rules is "normal." If the adolescent disregards the rules and refuses to accept them, this is a sign of trouble.

Adolescents tend to feel inadequate and are quick to compare themselves with their peers. They are critical of themselves and others and try to emulate the best in their friends. Sometimes they end up copying undesirable traits that afford them recognition or status. They feel most adequate when they are accepted by their peers, and for this to happen they feel they must dress like, talk like, and act like their friends. Preference for certain types of music, similar attitudes towards styles, use of drugs, or fighting with parents are badges that may make some adolescents more acceptable to their peer group. Sex is also a badge for some adolescents, communicating to everyone that they are free to "do their own thing." For the adolescent to want to identify with his peer group is "normal." When the influence of the peer group is harmful and when the adolescent is prepared to engage in antisocial or detrimental behavior in order to gain membership in the group, this is a sign of trouble.

The adolescent is negative to the suggestions and advice of adults. This is due, in part, to his need to assert himself as an individual. Negativism can be a form of rebellion as well as a way to inform parents that he is too old to be told what to do. It can also be the youngster's way of punishing parents. Negativism can be used as a mechanism of denial in which the child avoids or denies blame and involvement. Parents who are upset with his attitude may say to him, "You've got problems." The negativistic response would be, "I've got no problems. You've got the problems!"

Negativism as an expression of the child's need for autonomy is "normal." Negativism that appears as defiance, spite, vindictiveness, or aggression that leads to a break in the parent-adolescent relationship is a sign of trouble.

The moods of the adolescent change quickly and so do his goals or ambitions. A seemingly small incident can allow him to feel as if he is walking on a cloud or it can topple him to anxiety or depression. He vacillates in vocational goals; from wanting to be a surgeon to doubting that he will go to college. Because he realizes that his mind changes frequently, the adolescent is reluctant to make decisions that involve a commitment. The adolescent sees his future filled with many "ifs." "What will I do *if* my college board scores are low?" "*If* I decide to become a secretary, how do I know I'll like it?" or, "I'd go into pre-med *if* I thought I could get into medical school." The "ifs" contribute to the adolescent's uncertainty and pessimism cushions disappointments. For example, the adolescent may say to his parents, "Don't be surprised if I get a low grade in math." This statement not only prepares his parents for what might happen, but also puts him in the frame of mind to accept a low grade in the event one is forthcoming. Uncertainty and indecisiveness about his future is "normal" for an adolescent. Not caring about the future is a sign of trouble.

Resistance is common in adolescence. Wanting to have things on his own terms, the adolescent will resist pressure to conform or comply. Parents often view this resistance as "selective laziness," for the adolescent will find time to do those things he is motivated to do. They resist or are too lazy to attend to things that are low on their priority list. Resistance is a form of negativism, but it is also an indication that the youngster feels he has the power to stand up to pressure and do something to determine his own destiny. Resistance, in the form of being slow to comply or wanting to be coaxed is "normal." Resistance that is based on personal satisfaction gained from defeating the parent is a sign of trouble.

Adolescence is a self-conscious and self-centered time of life. Adolescents want to look attractive to the opposite sex and are embarrassed when their skin shows blemishes or when physical features detract from their appearance. They tend to ignore the feelings of others and relate everything to themselves. They have shed many of the restrictions imposed upon the younger child, yet, they are not worried about the responsibilities that adults must cope with. They are fun-seeking, pleasure-oriented, adventurous and daring. They seek to impress others by the things they do, but they have few stable interests. The adolescent is prepared to experiment and is not always concerned with consequences. All of these attitudes and behaviors are "normal" for the adolescent. But, anti-social feelings, self-destructive acts, prolonged feelings of depression, denial of reality, and nonproductivity are signs of trouble.

What Prevents Change

When parents recognize that their adolescent is unhappy or is faced with a problem, they want to do something to help him. They may offer advice or reassurances, but the adolescent knows that he must do his own problem solving, and that it is easier to be told what to do than do what he's been told. The desire for change is not always sufficient; it is important to become aware of the obstacles that prevent changes.

Most people have heard the proverb, "You can lead a horse to water but you can't make him drink." However, think of adding the phrase, ". . . unless you give him salt." The "salt" that brings about change is the motivation—the willingness to make sacrifices and the self-discipline to persevere. There are many explanations why changes for the better do not take place. Some of the more critical ones are:

— a feeling of helplessness
— self-doubts that prevent taking decisive steps
— a sense of futility that makes any effort seem like a waste of time
— inactivity due to not knowing where or how to begin

— fear of failure or of making mistakes
— strong resentment or anger directed towards oneself or others
— insincere or half-hearted efforts
— guilt that results in embarrassment to act
— impatience
— waiting for others to initiate the first action
— a tendency to dwell on the past instead of focusing on the present and future
— discouragement because of repeated failures

The most effective way to remove these obstacles is to make change an important part of the total goal. When attention is directed at what prevents change, the barriers become excuses that can be overcome by positive actions and determination to succeed. One of the determinants of motivation is maturity, for the more mature a person is, the more sacrifices he is willing to make. Because the adolescent is not yet mature, it is not unusual to find that he is not highly motivated to make changes when personal sacrifices are involved.

Guidelines for Parents of Adolescents

Not all parents of adolescents are in conflict with them. Many parents are able to enjoy seeing their child go through the transformation into adulthood. This is a gratifying experience for parents, for they can assess their impact on the child and delight in the young adult they are helping to prepare for his or her social role. Their efforts are rewarded in their satisfaction.

The guidelines that are presented are intended to prevent serious problems between the adolescent and his parents and can also be applied when minor problems have arisen. Basically, these are suggestions that call upon parents to show understanding and sensitivity to their older children. Similar to the guidelines presented for dealing with the young child, they represent a common sense approach which parents often take for granted. Collectively, they represent a logical and human approach to the adolescent child.

Guideline 1. *Learn about the time of life that is called adolescence.* Understanding is enhanced by knowledge. This is a testing, speculating, dreaming, experimenting, idealizing, frustrating, and somewhat unstable time of life. The more parents know about it, the better they are able to put the child's behavior into perspective. The adolescent years are not the same as they were when the parents were experiencing them, because society is not the same as it was thirty years ago. Libraries and study groups are a source for more knowledge about the adolescent child.

Guideline 2. *Parents are still the models for the child, although he is a teenager.* The danger is even greater, for adolescents are prepared to try more things than they could have attempted earlier. Adolescents are quick to recognize double standards and hypocrisy. The parent who comes home drunk is in a weak position to admonish his child about drinking.

Guideline 3. *The adolescent still needs parental direction and guidance.* The direction that the young child needs from his parents differs from what the adolescent can use. Parental guidance and direction for the adolescent is largely in the area of future planning and involves occupational information. While the youngster is still in high school, parents should encourage him to explore his interests and establish short-term goals. This would result in discussions about a number of vocational fields without pressure to make final decisions. A sixteen-year-old who thinks she might want to become a nurse, and whose academic ability indicates she could complete a nursing program, could be encouraged to talk with a nurse about her work, or work a summer in a hospital as a nurse's aide. If her desire to become a nurse remains strong, her short-term goals could be to take high school chemistry and make applications to schools of nursing. Whereas parental guidance and direction with the young child takes the form of teaching socially accepted values, with the adolescent it is to provide him with a sounding board for ideas and reactions to the decisions he might make.

Guideline 4. *Parents should establish limits.* This involves letting the youngster know what rules he will be expected to adjust to. They may be determined by the judgment the child has shown in the past and could be minimal. Some adolescents do not need a curfew, others do. Some adolescents have to be advised how to spend their money, others do not. Rules and limits can be imposed for such things as use of the car, responsibility for school work, chores and dating. Limits are necessary for giving the adolescent a structure that will let him know when he is out of bounds and when he is safe. The adolescent whose parents have always maintained controls over him will expect them, and even though he may not like them, he will respect controls when they are fair and when a good relationship has been established with his parents.

Guideline 5. *Parents can anticipate some rebellious behavior.* It would be strange and even unhealthy if an adolescent did not rebel occasionally against what his parents want him to do. If he is to regard himself as an individual, he has to test his power over his environment. This does not mean that the adolescent is rejecting his parents; instead, it shows that he is willing to fight for what he feels is right. In a "healthy" rebellion, the youngster will let off a lot of steam, balk and even resist parental pressure. The "unhealthy" rebellion occurs when the youngster completely disregards parental feelings and shows contempt for his parents.

Guideline 6. *Don't allow yourself to become intimidated by threats.* Remember that an adolescent will use whatever means he can to get what he wants. Often this becomes a threat or ultimatum to his parents. Parents are cautioned against allowing the first threat to be successful, for if it is, the child realizes he has power over his parents. Parents can avoid feeling intimidated when they communicate to their child they will not permit pressure or threats to influence their decisions. Then, having stated this, they must not weaken or back down from their position. A unified parental stand makes this easier.

Guideline 7. *The adolescent should know that he is responsible for his actions.* Because the adolescent tends to be impulsive, he does not always think about possible outcomes of a situation. When adolescents say they are willing to take their chances, they should know what these chances are and be prepared to assume responsibility for whatever happens. Discussions with the adolescent can make him aware of potential outcomes and might deter him from doing something that could end up in a tragedy. Threatening or trying to scare the child is not as effective as explaining the reasons that underlie a judgment. Discussion that encourages a positive interaction allows the youngster to examine his thinking and consider alternatives. In teaching responsibility for personal actions, parents communicate to their child that they are not willing to pay the price for their child's mistakes. If the adolescent gets arrested for driving too fast, or if he gets into trouble for skipping school, he will not expect to be rescued by his parents. Parental intervention does not always discourage a repetition of behavior; it may instead teach the child it is safe to break the rules. Parents are advised to stand behind the child and offer him support, but the child must assume responsibility for his own actions. Parents who assume this position, and announce it to their child in advance, help their child to think before he acts. The adolescent must realize that all mistakes are not reversible and some judgment errors have a serious and permanent impact on the child's future life.

Guideline 8. *Encourage the adolescent to discuss his decisions and judgments.* The "normal" adolescent will make many decisions that are not carefully thought out and consequently demonstrate poor judgment at times. Parents should not be critical of every mistake that is made, for if learning is to take place, it is important that he be free to talk about his decisions. If the parents feel that a wrong decision is about to be made, they could ask, "Can we talk this over before you do it?" Or, if a wrong decision has already been made, the parent could say, "Let's see if we can figure out why things turned out the way they did." When discussion offers a minimum threat to the youngster's need for ego and autonomy, good discussion can take place. Conversely, when parents say, "See, I told you so," or "If you had listened to me . . ." the adolescent will become defensive and negative. There are times when it is best to let people learn from their own mistakes.

It is also important that the adolescent be allowed to make mistakes without fear of being laughed at or insulted. Calling a mistake "stupid" can force the child to withdraw or become defensive. It should be easy for the adolescent to change his opinion about something without feeling that his parents are going to hold him to what he initially said. Saying to a child, "Oh, so you've changed your mind; now you agree with me," discourages him from changing his mind in the future.

Guideline 9. *Be a good listener.* Adolescents have a lot to say and seek an audience. They want to relate their experiences but do not want to be lectured or criticized. They have opinions on most subjects and will express them unless they fear their comments will result in a parental sermon. It is not necessary that parents agree with everything their children say, but it is important that they allow them the freedom to talk without being interrupted. There is also a courtesy involved in being a good listener in which the adolescent can feel he has the parents full attention. It means a lot to a child when his parents sit down with him and give him their undivided attention. Not only does it tell him that his parents care about what he is saying to them, but also that they respect the child as an important person. It is not always possible to drop everything and have a lengthy discussion, but when it is convenient to do so, the child will appreciate the parental interest. Because it is important that parents relate to their children, they must encourage dialogue and listen to what the child has to say.

Guideline 10. *Keep arguments to a minimum.* In many families arguing has become a daily routine. Obviously, the best way to avoid the arguing habit is never to start it. It is impossible to always avoid an argument, especially when someone is constantly prepared to argue. But, the arguments can be occasional rather than a way of life. From the adolescent's point of view, he has nothing to lose by trying to argue for what he wants. The parent stands to lose more, for in addition to displaying a lack of self-control, the parent who argues with his child either elevates the child to his level or permits the youngster to lower him to the child's level. The youngster who badgers his parents into an argument is testing the limits of their tolerance for frustration. This can be avoided, or greatly reduced, if the parents decide that there is no need to repeat what has already been told to the child. If the parents' reasoning is based on logic, or knowledge, there is no need to defend it. Of course, if the parental reasons are illogical they should be willing to admit their error and alter their stand. This suggests a need for parents to also think before they speak. Since it does take two to argue, the number of verbal battles can be significantly reduced if the parents, being more mature than their adolescent, decide not to engage in them.

Guideline 11. *A compromise can often avert problems.* Many issues that have been allowed to get out of control could have been resolved with an acceptable compromise. Parents acknowledge that many of their problems develop over little things, like when the child will make his bed, whether the son should be home at twelve o'clock instead of twelve-thirty, or whose turn it is to take out the trash. When decisions involve values or are a matter of something being right or wrong, parents must stand behind their convictions. But, if a compromise does not endanger the child or make the parent's position untenable, coming to an acceptable agreement can teach the child a valuable lesson: that differences can be settled by mutual concessions.

Guideline 12. *The adolescent should know what to expect from his parents.* Adolescents usually know from experience what their parents will do if they come home late, or if they get a poor report card. But, they should also know what to expect for some things they have not experienced. Of course, they won't know unless their parents tell them in advance. If parents are worried about drugs, sex, or other conduct, they should remove all doubts by declaring their position on each issue and indicating what their actions will be. When youngsters know that their parents mean what they say, they will not be inclined to call their bluff. Parents do not have to threaten their children, but they should provide information that might deter an impulsive or foolish act. When parents state their position they are reinforcing their values. It goes without saying, parents must be prepared to carry out what they have said they will do, for it is always important to practice consistency.

Guideline 13. *Include, but don't force the adolescent to take part in family activities.* The adolescent may wish to decline an invitation to be with the family, but the invitation communicates that his age has not removed him from the family unit. It is unwise to pressure or force the adolescent to go with the family all of the time, but it is not inappropriate to ask the youngster to do things with the family once in a while. If parents make an effort to understand the reason their son or daughter does not want to go with the family, they will gain some insight into the needs of their child. The adolescent may be embarrassed to be seen with his family if he feels this could damage his image of being independent of his parents. Knowing this, and also that the adolescent prefers to be with his peers, parents should be sensitive to their child's feelings and not interpret his needs to avoid peer pressure as a rejection of the family. When he does not feel forced into being with his family, the youngster is more likely to be willing to participate in family functions that are deemed important occasions.

Guideline 14. *Encourage the adolescent to bring his friends home.* The adolescent knows what kinds of friends are acceptable to his parents. If the parent-adolescent relationship is good, he will not seek friends who are unacceptable to them. The child should be encouraged to introduce his friends to his parents, but he needs to know that his parents will show respect to his friends and not embarrass him by offending them. The child and his friends also need privacy. This means privacy from both parents and uninvited siblings. The adolescent wants to be proud of his parents and wants his friends to think that his parents are nice people. In keeping with the Golden Rule, parents should treat their children's friends the way they would want their children's friends to treat them.

Guideline 15. *The adolescent needs some family responsibility.* If the adolescent is to feel they are part of the family unit, he must share in the work of the home. Whether his chore is cutting the grass, helping a younger sibling with homework, occasional baby-sitting, or keeping his room neat, he must make some contribution to the cooperative spirit of the family. Many parents have permitted their adolescent child to live in the home as a boarder, using the facilities of the home and giving nothing in return. Such a child is not learning much about responsibility, and the home is where he should learn it. The adolescent should realize that he has a responsibility to himself and other members of the family.

Guideline 16. *Let the adolescent choose his own forms of leisure activities.* Some parents not only try to make occupational choices for their children, but also tell them how they should spend their leisure time. Most adolescents have an abundance of leisure time. Their parents accuse them of wasting it, and many times this is true. However, if the youngster has several hours to use for recreation, assuming that nothing that should be done has been left undone, he should feel he can use this time in a way that is personally satisfying. Problems are created when the parent, who must always be busy doing something, insists that his child always be busy doing something; or, when parents decide that reading a book is a proper use of leisure, but watching television is not. If parents feel their child is abusing leisure time, they can discuss their reason for concern with the child and suggest other activities.

Guideline 17. *Nag less.* The repetitious sounds echo throughout the house: "Clean up your room . . . do your homework . . . come home early . . . get off the telephone . . . take a bath." The adolescent response echoes back: "Don't bug me . . . stop hassling me . . . alright, already." Granted there are many things that parents feel their adolescent children should be doing, but nagging them to do these things is not the most effective way to get something done. Nagging is continually finding fault with something, and it conditions the child to expect to be nagged. Although the adolescent may need to be reminded of his responsibilities, it can be done more effectively if the parent announces what he wants one time and the child knows what the price for disobedience or procrastination will be. The punishment could be a loss of a privilege or restriction to the house. Some discussion is helpful to clarify the parental position, but when the youngster knows what the consequences will be, the pressure is on him to cooperate and be responsible.

Guideline 18. *Parents should be careful not to judge the adolescent according to the way things were when they were that age.* One of the things that adolescents get tired of hearing from parents is, "When I was your age, I . . ." It is difficult for parents of today to identify with the world their adolescent faces. There are vast differences between what the parents recall from their adolescent years and what their teenaged children experience every day. On one hand, parents say they wouldn't want to cope with the problems today's adolescent has, and, on the other hand they say their children have it easier than they did. The adolescent's world will never be like the one his parents experienced, nor is it realistic to expect society to return to the way things were many years ago. With many colleges costing more than $4,000 a year for tuition, room and board, the freshman cannot work his way through school as he once could. Nor does the father work a forty-eight hour week for $60.00. The adolescent of today has many of the same problems his parents had, plus the additional load of problems heaped upon him by our troubled and complex society. Parents who are fair will recognize that the standard for rearing an adolescent today is not the same as that of twenty-five years ago.

Guideline 19. *Respect the adolescent's need for privacy.* Unless the adolescent is in conflict with his parents, there is no reason to feel that acts of secrecy are an indication that he is up to something that is illegal or dangerous. The child who is out of bounds with himself and his parents might be secretive in order to cover behavior that is disapproved. But, when the child can be trusted, he should know that he can have privacy. His room is a private place, and so are his drawers, diary, or closet. One of the benefits of a trusting relationship is the freedom to have privacy, and the adolescent should know that this privacy is guaranteed unless there is reason to feel that he cannot be trusted. Parental curiosity should not become spying. If the parents want to know what was said on the telephone, they should ask the child, instead of listening to his conversation on an extension phone. In a good parent-adolescent relationship, parents do not have to know everything that goes on with their child, and the youngster is free to say to them, "I'd rather not talk about it."

Guideline 20. *Give the adolescent some of the freedoms he is seeking.* One of the biggest problems for parents of adolescents is letting go of them. Parents realize that there will come a time when they should no longer offer the child protection, for soon the adolescent will be old enough to leave home and begin his own life. It is inevitable that the child will seek freedom and independence and that parents will want to hold on to their children as long as they can. Parents must feel that if they have provided their child with an environment that has emphasized trust, responsibility, morality, judgment and love, they have done all they can. They must hope that their child will be able to profit from their training and offer him a chance to demonstrate what he has learned. There is no way to eliminate parental worry, but it can be reduced if the parents feel good about what they tried to accomplish with their child.

The Unmanageable Adolescent

For many parents, it is too late to talk about prevention of problems. They find themselves living with an adolescent who is unreasonable, demanding, disrespectful, or indifferent. Their greatest frustration is that the child appears to be content with a condition they consider intolerable. Because they fear his threats, many parents permit their relationship to continue to deteriorate. They feel they have failed in some way as parents, for what they are able to see in the present is disturbing and what they predict for the future is alarming. They blame themselves, outside forces, and their child.

No single factor causes the child to rebel against his parents, and parents are not entirely responsible for the misconduct of their child. Although their practices may have encouraged the adolescent's problems, peer pressure and social conditions have contributed to rebellious attitudes. Laxity in the home, school, and society have not given today's youth much to respect or provided him with a good model to copy.

Some adolescents have already done irreparable harm to themselves. Fortunately, the number who have is not large, but this offers little consolation to parents whose children are among the few. Yet, such parents are highly motivated to prevent similar problems with their other youngsters. Often these parents go to extremes in attempting to avert trouble. If they have been permissive, they tend to become overly strict; if they have been strict, they become permissive. Extreme is an invitation to trouble; the middle ground is best.

Managing the Unmanageable

The unmanageable adolescent is one who has completely rejected parental controls and, by his defiant behavior, has expressed his contempt for them. He is unmoved by threats or punishments and is negative to their suggestions and attempts to improve home conditions. He is continually testing parental limits to show his power and punish his parents.

The parents of an unmanageable adolescent do not wish their child harm, although they may dislike him. They hope he will change his ways and put pressure on the child to reform him or make him want to change. The adolescent defeats their attempts, resisting change with a "you can't make me" attitude. Many adolescents have also learned that their parents just talk and will back down or weaken under pressure. They rely on their parents not to desert them and feel they can manipulate them in an emergency. They are convinced that their parents will rescue them from having to pay a price for their mistakes. The case of Sue demonstrates this.

Case Illustration Number 13

Sue was a sixteen-year-old who had been rebellious since she was a small child. She resented the way her mother treated her and was angry at her father for his attempts to punish her in harsh ways. In addition to chronic school problems, she had social problems. She became "boy crazy" when she was thirteen. She had no girl friends but was popular with boys. By the age of fifteen she had had sexual relations and she felt she was in love with every boy who kissed her. At the age of sixteen she presented her parents with an ultimatum: "Either get me birth control pills or I'll get pregnant."

The idea of sexual promiscuity was repulsive to her parents. They had worried about it for years. On two occasions they had forced her to see a psychotherapist (both attempts failed, for Sue had refused to cooperate). Her parents felt Sue was strong-willed enough to hurt herself and they dreaded the day when sex would become an issue. After much deliberation, they decided, against their better judgment, to give in. They authorized their physician to prescribe "the pill" for her. They were trying to protect Sue from herself. Actually, they were condoning a practice they abhorred. They justified their decision on the grounds that it would save their daughter from a pregnancy or an abortion.

Sue wanted birth control pills. She presented her threat and got what she wanted. She was not looking for a better relationship with her parents, nor did she find one. By their actions, her parents contributed to morality that was unacceptable to them, for in essence they were giving her a license to become promiscuous without fear of becoming pregnant. When Sue later developed a venereal disease, they had reason to feel their action had contributed to her problem.

This is an example of parents who weakened under pressure and encouraged a behavior they wanted to discourage. They would have been more honest to themselves and protective of their daughter if they had said, "We cannot accept sexual promiscuity and we believe that to sanction the pill is to encourage promiscuity. If you feel you must have sexual relations with your boy friend, you must face the possibility of a pregnancy. If you get pregnant, we will stand beside you during your pregnancy. We will not encourage an abortion, so you will have to prepare yourself for becoming a mother. This is the price that sexual freedom requires." Such a position communicates the parents' views on morality for their teenaged daughter. If the parents took a conservative view on birth control and a liberal view on abortion they would defeat their intentions. Although such a stand might not have deterred Sue from doing what she had decided to do, it would have told her something about the strength of her parents' convictions. Sue was able to call her parents' bluff, and encouraged to do it again when the need arose.

The parents' need to protect their child can deny him a valuable learning experience. In the case of Tony, his parents were aware of this but failed to practice what they knew was right.

Case Illustration Number 14

Tony was a seventeen-year-old whose parents knew that he smoked marijuana and had experimented with LSD and other hallucinogenic drugs. They were strongly opposed to drugs and tried to discourage him by scaring, threatening, and denying him money that could be used to buy drugs. They opposed drugs on the grounds that they were potentially harmful to his physical and emotional well-being, and also because they were illegal. Tony flatly refused to accept their values on this subject and tried to persuade his parents to smoke "grass" one time. He told them they could not assess something they had never used and called them stupid and narrow-minded.

To discourage his use of drugs, Tony's parents removed his car privileges, established a curfew, and forbade him to associate with his friends who were also using drugs. None of their attempts to control Tony were successful. He was able to get along without a car and he sold drugs to earn money. He refused to accept their curfew and to show his defiance of their authority, stayed out all night after he was told he had to be home by one o'clock. Tony's father threatened to report him to the police, but Tony was not worried by what he knew to be an idle threat. He knew his father would not put himself in jeopardy or bring attention to the family.

The parents' real test came when Tony was arrested for possessing marijuana. When he called his parents from the police station, they were very upset and worried that a police record would hurt him some time in the future. The thought of Tony being inside a jail was upsetting to his mother. Tony's father immediately hired a lawyer and an arrangement was made whereby Tony would have no record and would be placed in parental custody with a warning about the consequences of a second arrest.

Within two hours after his arrest, Tony's father had him out of trouble. He was not required to face any consequences of his behavior. His parents denied him a chance to learn from an experience and did nothing to discourage future use of illegal drugs. Tony's arrest did not deter him from using drugs, it only made him more careful. Tony learned that he did not have to worry about his actions, for his parents would rescue him and pay the price for him. Ironically, he was placed in the custody of parents who had no control over him and in no way could be effective with him.

A more realistic approach for Tony's parents would have been to first agree on a unified position that would discourage his use of drugs. If reasoning with him failed, they should have been prepared to report him rather than hope things would turn out all right by themselves. They should have reasoned that Tony needed protection from himself and if they could not control him, some other source would have to. Although they did not want their son to have a police record, they should have told Tony that he would have to be responsible for his own actions and not to expect favors for deliberate law breaking. If he insisted on learning about reality the hard way, they should not have helped him to beat the system.

Some parents have made a similar mistake by financing their child's rebellion. If an adolescent threatens to leave home, it doesn't make sense for parents to buy the airplane ticket for the child's trip to a commune when they are opposed to what he is doing. Parents can rationalize buying the ticket, since hitchhiking is dangerous, and even give him spending money so he will be able to eat properly. But, they are obviously encouraging the behavior that they want to discourage. Some adolescents have *demanded* the money their parents have set aside for their education, saying that they have decided not to go to college and they intend to get their education in other ways. Needless to say, this request is unreasonable. Money that has been earmarked for education should not be used for vegetation.

In managing the unmanageable adolescent, parents must be careful to state their position on issues in clear and precise language. The adolescent should not be able to say, "You never told me that!" Parents should anticipate outcomes and tell the child, *in advance*, what they will and will not do. They should tell the child, "If you get pregnant, this is what we will do . . ." "If you are suspended from school, this is what we will do . . ." "If you decide to get married against our wishes, this is what you can expect from us . . ." The advantages of removing doubts from the adolescent by declaring the parental position are twofold: first, the youngster knows that he should be prepared to assume responsibility for his actions, and second, the parents have the opportunity to think through their position carefully and in advance of pressures from a crisis that might put them in a temporary state of shock.

As was said, some adolescents are determined to learn things for themselves and reject advice. There is no way to stop this and discussions are generally ineffective. Parents should not provoke their child into doing something he has threatened to do or attempt to intimidate him. The parent who forces the child to live up to his threats may later regret the child's actions.

Case Illustration Number 15

Larry was fourteen years old. He refused to listen to his parents and made no effort to cooperate or learn in school. He was interested in cars and wanted to become a mechanic. Larry's parents were forced to punish him frequently. One day Larry decided to "show them" and he ran away from home. He was gone two nights before he called his parents from a nearby town and asked them to "come and pick me up." Nothing changed between Larry and his parents and within a few days he was doing the same things that irritated his parents. Larry threatened to run away again, and his parents said nothing to discourage him. In fact, they both said that should he decide to run away again, they would not bother to call the police and he could stay wherever he wanted. "Don't call us up and ask us to come get you," they said. Larry did not leave home.

He continued to get into trouble with his parents and was not going to school. Larry's father had used physical force to get him to do things, but his mother couldn't push him around, so he teased and insulted her freely. There were daily fights between Larry and his parents, often ending with one parent saying to him, "Why don't you just get out of our house." Or, "Go someplace where we don't have to see your face." For awhile, Larry would tell his parents that it was his house too, and they couldn't make him get out. Then one day, Larry took some money from his mother's purse and his father told him to keep the money and live somewhere else. Larry had no intention of leaving until his father began to intimidate him with remarks like, "You're afraid to leave," and "You call yourself a big shot, let's see you do something to prove it." Larry left, and his parents, fearing he would not return, called the police the next day. He was found in the same town he went to before and later admitted that he wanted the police to find him.

Larry's parents had a problem, but they didn't do much to solve it. They contributed to it by provoking their son and making no effort to understand the reasons for his unhappiness. Larry also had a problem, but he couldn't admit it or take steps to improve his unhappy condition. Larry and his parents never had a good relationship, and neither seemed to want to improve things. His parents should have initiated positive actions much earlier, for Larry had already hurt himself academically, socially, and emotionally.

It took a long time for Larry to learn to relate to his parents. Before he could accept them as parents, he had to believe they were his friends. His parents had to work at becoming friends with their child and not focus on the past. Larry was told that it was his choice to either accept parental controls or the rules that a juvenile court would establish. He was introduced to a juvenile probation officer and afterwards decided to cooperate with his parents. Larry's strong resistance made it necessary for his parents to hold the threat of juvenile court over him as their way of establishing controls. Once he knew they were not bluffing and were prepared to turn him over to the court, he began to cooperate. He knew that if he ran away again he would lose his freedom and he was bright enough to know that he would eventually be caught. Larry was learning reality.

The adolescent who decides to leave home should know that he may return, but he should understand that returning means he is willing to resolve the issues that caused him to leave. Unless something happens to improve conditions, little is accomplished by his return. Living at home is a privilege that can be removed if it is not appreciated. There is no reason for parents to be vindictive or punitive; nor should they be willing to turn the other cheek. The adolescent who comes back home should expect some structure and be prepared to cooperate more. The intent is not to make his life unhappy or make him feel sorry he returned, but to teach him how to live with his family.

If the adolescent decides to leave home and may legally do so, it is advisable to maintain some contact with him. Although youngsters may want to punish their parents and realize that going away will worry them, it is wise to encourage them to let some person know where they can be reached in case of an emergency. If the adolescent intends to travel and will not have an address, he should be asked to keep in contact with someone in the area periodically.

It is easy for parents to be misled into thinking their child has reformed when they accept a single action or statement as proof of the child's willingness to change. Because their hope for a change is so great, they are willing to interpret any shred of evidence to mean things will be different from now on. A worried parent is constantly seeking signs that offer encouragement, and even though they may have been disappointed many times, they are optimistic each time they see or hear anything that is encouraging. In the example that follows, Jim's mother was willing to believe what she heard instead of what she saw.

Case Illustration Number 16

Jim, a nineteen-year-old, frequently hit his mother and cursed her. He had a bad temper and stormed out of the house when his mother did not meet his selfish demands. His father was aware of the situation but never followed through with threats to stop him from tormenting the mother. Jim knew that his mother loved him and felt he was doing her a favor by living with her. He knew his mother was weak and took advantage of this. His mother had threatened that the next time he struck her she would call the police. She feared the next time, for she didn't think she could bring herself to make the call. Shortly after she made her threat, Jim got angry with her because he couldn't find a pair of cuff links and struck her on the arm, bruising it noticeably. Before his mother could even think about calling the police, Jim left the house. He returned in about an hour with a box of candy and once again uttered the words that were magic to his mother's ears, "I'm sorry, mother. I didn't mean to do it."

The candy and the apology softened the mother and she forgave him again. Although she had heard the words, "I'm sorry," many times before, she had renewed confidence that things were going to be different. Jim knew her weakness was her willingness to believe what she hoped for, rather than what she knew to be reality. He was willing to throw her an occasional crumb of kindness, and she was more than willing to accept it. Jim relied on his mother's lack of follow-through and ignored her threats which he saw as a bluff. As was once said, "hope springs eternal in the human breast."

Parental Options with the Unmanageable Adolescent

The choices open to parents who have unmanageable adolescents are few and unattractive. Whereas the manageable adolescent can be controlled through a deprivation of a privilege, such as being denied use of a car or confined to the house, the unmanageable youngster will ignore restrictions. For this reason, parents should state their intentions firmly and say nothing unless they are willing to follow through. There is no reason to shout or go into a rage, for the unmanageable adolescent will shout back and return insult for insult.

One choice open to parents is to seek professional help. This means talking with a psychologist, psychiatrist, or psychiatric social worker in a community mental health clinic or private office. It could mean individual or group therapy, depending upon the clinician and method used. Success in this approach depends on the willingness of the youngster to meet with a therapist and at least discuss the problems that are taking place within the family. For treatment to be successful, the youngster will have to interact positively with the therapist and work towards constructive goals. Because the unmanageable adolescent is extremely negative, his resistance to change is great and he is not highly motivated to talk with a therapist. Parents may also pose a problem if they expect the therapist to *talk* the adolescent into cooperating with them or in some way *make* the child change. For these and other reasons, professional help is not always the answer. However, it is wise to explore this as a first choice, for there is always the chance that the rebellious adolescent might find a therapist with whom he can relate. Many health insurance plans will pay some part of the cost of therapy.

If it is decided to seek professional help, the parents should be prepared to become involved in therapy, although many times this is not required. The decision to include parents in treatment is an individual one and will depend on a number of factors. Some therapists will want to see the adolescent and parents together, others will see only the youngster. Still others will see them separately or recommend that the parents see another clinician.

Other options parents have might be less appealing. If the family can afford it, the unmanageable adolescent could be placed in a residential setting. This could be a private school, military school, a school with a psychiatric setting, or a hospital-connected school. There are many private schools that concentrate on children who have academic or behavior problems and recently some public school systems have developed special programs for children with behavior and learning problems.

However, the youngster can defeat the intentions of his parents by refusing to attend a residential school or by not cooperating with the school if he is forced to attend. It is also easy to run away from residential schools, and the adolescent who refuses parental controls frequently takes advantage of the relaxed environment that many of these schools maintain.

The residential setting is usually better for the youngster who has two or three years more of school, since the younger child has a better chance to identify with his school and possibly can make friends that he can keep for several years. If the family can afford the expense of a residential setting, it will provide them some reduction of tension and anxiety. Separation of the unmanageable adolescent and his parents can be good for both. Some public school systems provide a small amount of financial assistance for special schools when it can be shown the child's needs are beyond what the public school can provide.

Transferring the child from one high school to another in the same city rarely produces good results. What is often needed is a complete change of environment. The parents must be careful to select a residential setting that offers some structure. A loosely organized and permissive environment could reinforce and support the kinds of behavior that should be discouraged. Because unmanageable adolescents are usually not interested in a place that is structured, they are inclined to reject the idea of a residential setting.

More desperate parents, and ones who fear that their adolescent might get into serious trouble, have made their unmanageable adolescent a ward of the court. This is done through the juvenile court and, in essence, makes the court responsible for the child. The parents must stipulate that they cannot control their child. When made a ward of the court, the child continues to live at home but can be sent to a detention home if he is caught breaking a law or creating a disturbance for the parents. Needless to say, such an action on the part of the parents does not always improve the relationship that the adolescent has with them. Some juvenile courts will try to prevent the need for the legal action by placing the child on probation and requiring the youngster to see a probation officer periodically. The parents maintain custody of their child unless there is a violation of the probation.

A final option to be discussed could be termed the conclave approach. The conclave is a meeting between the unmanageable adolescent and the parents. It is predicated on the assumption that the unhappy adolescent and the unhappy parents should be willing to see if there is anything that can be done to reduce the tensions that each feels. Both the parents and the adolescent would have to agree to a number of things. They would have to be willing to:
—talk to each other without becoming insulting
—refrain from interrupting one another
—make some sacrifices
—dwell on the present and future, not the past

—try to understand the other person's thinking
—avoid putting each other on the defensive

A series of meetings is necessary, and to make it more pleasant some light refreshment could be served. Hopefully, the adolescent can be appealed to on the basis of, ''We've got a problem and it isn't getting any better. Are you willing to try something that might make things easier for both you and us?'' If the answer is a negative one, the conclave approach will not work.

One hour is enough time for a meeting, and it isn't necessary that anything be resolved in the first few meetings. Before anything constructive can happen, the parents and adolescent will have to learn to talk and listen to each other. If the parents can convince their child that nothing will be lost by giving it a try, and maybe something good can come from it, perhaps the unmanageable adolescent will extend himself a bit and participate in the conclave. In this approach, patience is the greatest virtue and restraint runs a close second.

The goals of the conclave approach are to:
—develop the atmosphere in which open discussion can take place
—enable each person to state his personal feelings and grievances
—clarify the major issues by trying to define the problems
—select one issue or problem to work on at a time
—suggest possible solutions
—seek acceptable compromises
—be willing to experiment with a solution on a trial basis
—exert a sincere effort to make the experiment successful
—assess the effects of the experiment by discussing problems that may arise
—show patience, understanding, and a determination to succeed

Meetings once or twice a week are sufficient and a specific time should be designated that is convenient. The conclave approach can succeed if changes are not expected to happen overnight and if the meeting does not turn into another argument or battleground. It is a constructive approach that encourages positive regard between the adolescent and his parents and is predicated on the mutual need for a change.

Epilogue

The adolescent is like the untamed tiger. Taming the adolescent is not just a matter of letting him know who's boss, but of developing an atmosphere in which he can begin to see a need for cooperation. For some parents this can be done by respecting the child and his right to disagree with them, making an effort to relate to the child, and allowing the adolescent to feel important. For other parents it may not be possible to accomplish. The tiger who has become vicious cannot be trusted, and trust underlies a good relationship.

It is possible to tame a tiger with a gun in one hand and a whip in the other. However, the tiger will not respond out of respect but out of fear. If the "adolescent tiger" is to be tamed, parents will have to throw away their guns and whips and replace them with understanding and respect. When you set out to tame the tiger, you don't want to destroy it.

- 8 -

School Problems:
Another Parental Concern

Next to the home, the educational system exerts the greatest impact on the child. Public or private educational facilities receive the child when he is five years old and take him through the most impressionable years of his life. Because of the value that is placed on education, school is a high priority item for most parents and many children actually believe their whole world revolves around school. Privileges are granted or denied, parents praise or scold, children worry and work, and plans for the child's future life are formulated and determined because of school.

Inasmuch as schools have become a source of discontentment for both parents and children, they can be added to the list of troubles in society. Not only have they not made the task of parents easier, they have also contributed to parental anxieties. Parents are fearful that the academic aspect of school is not having a significant impact on the child, and they are apprehensive over the non-academic influences the school exerts on their child. Schools expose children to gangs and to individual bullies and subject the child to strong social pressures. Because of the need to conform to peer pressures, many children can say that they were first "turned on" to drugs in school.

For parents, schools pose the threat that the child will acquire training that opposes the values being taught in the home. If the nonacademic influences are too distracting and over-stimulating, the child's academic interest may suffer. Likewise, if the program of study that the school offers fails to challenge the child, the parents are understandably upset. Therefore, it is important to examine educational practices and take a critical look at what our educational system is fostering.

In taking this critical look at the schools, it has been necessary to make generalizations. There are many schools that are doing a fine job of educating children. More schools are probably not. Schools are initiating many changes in order to improve on traditional methods. A big word in education is innovation. However, the overall picture is not encouraging, for more problems seem to be created by innovations than are resolved by them.

Parents need not feel they are alone in having problems with their children. Schools are faced with similar concerns relating to effectiveness and controls in the management of youth. The problems that schools are having in their struggle to educate children are a reflection of the difficulties parents are having, and appear to be the outgrowth of a permissive educational philosophy that was introduced at least twenty-five years ago. As the result of this permissiveness, many schools today are no more effective in gaining the respect of the child and controlling his behavior than the homes.

What has evolved from this condition is a mutual disenchantment between the home and the school. Parents have become discouraged by the inability of the schools to provide academic stimulation for their children. They criticize the school and blame teachers for not doing an effective job of teaching. Similarly, schools have become discouraged by the attitude of parents, which they interpret to be lacking in cooperation, patience, and understanding. They criticize the home and blame parents for not having done an effective job of parenting.

Many schools have become a potpourri of teaching methods and learning devices. They are becoming vast storehouses of audio-visual media and educational "gimmicks," many of which neither facilitate learning nor stimulate interest. They boast of the conveniences and beauty of newly built edifices which have become large monuments to an affluent educational system. They offer a curriculum that ranges from a mathematics course in differential equations to a classroom for co-educational cooking.

The educator likes to view himself as an expert on the behavior of children. He is purportedly trained to educate a child. He is a product of teacher-training institutions which teach doctrines that recognize individual differences in children, philosophical ideologies that expound on an awareness for individual needs, and a belief that a goal of education is individualized instruction. He is filled with theoretical concepts and is taught how to conduct educational research. In general, schools are proud of the job they are doing to educate the child. They feel they are effective. However, many parents from the population they serve do not share these feelings. In the minds of a number of parents and children, the schools are ineffective.

Schools have been effective for some children who are able to learn and who are willing to make an effort. They have been successful with some youngsters who are motivated by their own successes and those who have set educational goals for themselves. But many children who have been eager to learn and very able to learn have been "turned off" by school, and their motivation to learn has been seriously reduced. They have even been less effective for the child who is not motivated to learn, the child who does not learn easily, or the child who can learn but feels hampered by confusing and disorganized instructional methods or ineffective teachers.

If teaching is a process whereby specific techniques and skills are utilized in order to enhance learning and develop the intellectual potential of the individual, there are many who would question what is being done under the guise of teaching. An unhealthy dichotomy has developed—the schools feel they are producing quality educational programs, whereas parents and students are expressing a decreasing amount of confidence in the ability of the schools to provide the student with an adequate education.

There is parental concern and alarm at all levels of education. The parents of a fourth grader (who could be on an equivalent fourth level in a non-graded school) may be frustrated if their child comes home confused by new math concepts of set and base numbers, and they are unable to help him. They can also worry if their child is reading below his grade level, despite the efforts of a reading specialist who sees the child in a group once a week. Perhaps they worry most because they are told so frequently by teachers not to worry. As one parent phrased it, "We're told our son is in the lowest reading group, that he is having trouble with arithmetic concepts, that he tends to be restless and is easily distracted. But when I asked his teacher what we can do for him at home, she said, 'Don't worry. He's still a bit immature, but he'll outgrow it.' "

Parents cannot understand why they shouldn't worry. The child complains of disinterest in school, balks at doing homework assignments, brings home few papers, and openly admits his dislike for school. This attitude in the elementary years is likely to get worse in the child's subsequent years of schooling.

Parents whose children are in the upper grades of junior high school, the middle school, or high school often see their children enduring rather than enjoying education. They hear complaints about dull and incompetent teachers, academic repetition, boredom, and subjects which have no interest or appeal for them. They are aware of teachers who make irrelevant assignments, expect too much or too little, and offer weak motivation for learning.

Problems of Schools

Schools face a number of problems, many of which can only be resolved by school personnel and legislative efforts that support policy decisions. There are a few things parents can do to reduce school tensions and improve home and school relationships, but the bulk of the problems that affect parents and their children are the result of conditions within the schools that make the child's educational experience less meaningful. Troubles in American education today have resulted in a lack of public confidence in the ability of schools to be effective in teaching the child. Many parents no longer trust schools to educate their children, for no longer does the parent feel that he understands the procedures and processes of education. Communication between the school and home is inadequate and this has resulted in a parental feeling of isolation which leads to doubts and mistrust. Parents have become suspicious of what they are asked to accept as being the best education for their child. Ultimately, by being critical of what they perceive education to be, they have become critical of those people who call themselves educators.

Academic Concerns

One area of problems is largely academic and involves policies and practices which have created problems for both teachers and parents.

1. Perhaps the most basic problem of schools is the confusion over educational responsibilities. What are the goals of education and what responsibilities are assigned to the school? Should the school function exclusively as an academic institution? Are schools assuming too much responsibility for things that parents should be doing for their children? Is the school expected to function as a welfare agency?

The educator argues that you cannot teach a child in a vacuum; that education is more than knowing the three R's; and that to teach the child you must work with the entire child, demanding an awareness of his social and emotional welfare. Schools have assumed responsibility for a number of things that parents feel are not functions of public education. Many parents object to sex being discussed or taught in school. Despite the fact that many parents avoid this subject with their children, they still feel that this is a parental prerogative. Should schools provide breakfasts, and dental and health care for children who may not otherwise receive these services? The child who comes to school hungry cannot be expected to be receptive to what a teacher is saying, but are schools over-extending their responsibility by providing welfare services? Much of the confusion over educational objectives is due to a lack of an operational definition that outlines school functions and responsibilities.

And yet, each school system has probably developed some statement that defines its objectives in general terms. This document could be called the school's philosophy of education and it can be found in some file in the office of the Board of Education. How many teachers and administrators have seen such a document is questionable; the number could be embarrassingly low. A statement of the school's educational philosophy can be a blueprint that spells out the goals of the school system, how the curriculum is intended to accomplish these goals, the tasks and responsibilities of administrators and teachers, and even the role that parents are expected to play in making the system work effectively. Like any dynamic program, an educational philosophy has to be examined and revised periodically and both school personnel and parents informed of changes.

Even if the responsibility of the schools can be determined, there is the related problem of the authority that schools have to carry out their functions. Responsibility without authority is self-defeating. To create regulations and not allow for enforcement of the rules is senseless. If schools have the responsibility to educate children and protect them from harmful influences during school hours, and if they are responsible for administering certain welfare services, they must have the authority to do what is needed in order to accomplish their objectives.

As long as parents can attack the authority of the schools and win court cases, schools are forced to back down from doing their job. If a faculty feels that a dress code creates an atmosphere that is more conducive to learning, they should have the authority to create one and also the means to enforce it. However, if parents can insist their child has the right to wear anything he wants and the courts support the parents, the school is powerless to do anything. The same is true for other behavior that teachers feel is disrupting to the school and classroom. The fact is, schools have some understanding of their responsibilities; but they have less understanding of their authority.

2.   Schools are not meeting the academic needs of many students. The educational researcher has known for some time that there are differences in the way children learn. Some children rely on visual cues and learn best by seeing things, other children remember things they have written down or heard. Individual differences in learning must be taken into consideration when it comes to developing programs. Many experimental programs and approaches to learning have been tried by schools, some of which last only a year or so and then disappear. A number of these approaches are effective for a particular kind of child who may not represent the majority of children who are exposed to the system. A bright and self-directing ten-year-old would probably do well in a non-structured situation in which he was able to learn at his own pace. The same learning conditions might be disastrous for a ten-year-old who had average intelligence but was negative to doing school work. An independent study program for the high school junior who is conscientious and motivated to learn is very appropriate. But, the youngster who is seeking a chance to get by with doing little and shows an indifference to school is not going to benefit much from an independent study program. A student does not become intellectually curious and self-directing by simply being told that he is expected to be this way.

Because some children need more structure than others, and children differ in terms of ability, interest, and attitude towards school, it is not possible to create the model system that can effectively accommodate all students. Many schools adopt a single method and attempt to fit every pupil into the system. When there are no alternative approaches open to the student, he must either adapt or resist. If a particular method of instruction allows the student more freedom than he can handle, or if the program is too distracting and over-stimulating for the student, he will not adapt to it. Unless such a student can be placed in an academic setting that is appropriate for him, the educational philosophy that talks about the need to recognize individual differences in children is nothing more than empty words.

School programs and classroom methods must be flexible. If the child cannot fit within the system, the system must be able to accommodate the child. Many high school students who quit school are not really drop-outs. They have been pushed out by a system that was too rigid or unaware of their academic needs. What is relevant for one student may not be relevant for another. When so many youngsters complain about boring and irrelevant subjects, something must be wrong with the learning objectives or the method of instruction, or both. We can't always blame failure on the student.

Students who do not plan to go to college are often short-changed in their education. They are frequently looked upon as being less capable than youngsters who are taking college preparatory courses. Although vocational and industrial education programs are available, frequently these programs do not begin until the tenth grade when many students who could have taken them have already dropped out of school. Many vocational-industrial education programs are outdated and inadequate. They are limited to a few offerings and often teach skills that are no longer usable. These programs should be expanded and include more apprenticeships and on-the-job training. In an attempt to reduce the number of school drop-outs and graduate students who cannot find work, they should also be started earlier than high school. The student who does not plan to attend college or is not capable of doing post-high school work can be identified long before he reaches high school. Meeting the child's academic needs would require schools to have programs available in the seventh and eighth grades for students who will go into vocational fields upon their graduation from high school.

3. Parents are distressed by a reduction of academic standards

and lax discipline in schools today. A school determines its academic standards according to the expectations it has for achievement or performance. Academic standards for the students who want to get A's are usually high. However, the large majority of students are unable to do outstanding work, and many who could are not willing to put forth the effort. Academic standards for the student who is indifferent and negative to school are often low enough that he is able to graduate regardless of his achievement level. For many students, a high school diploma only means twelve years of attendance in school. It does not even mean twelve years of good attendance. For some students it means they have endured twelve years of going through the motions of being a student. Parents are amazed how little work their child has to do in order to get by; often the student himself is surprised by what he can get away with. Many teachers "give" a student a D so he can pass because they must defend a failing grade to the principal and go through an elaborate warning process to parents. For teachers whose personal academic standards are low, it is not worth the effort to fail a student, so they pass him.

Many high schools have liberalized attendance regulations and have made it easy for the student to miss school and cut classes. Some high schools have removed final examinations and require few written assignments. Leniency has the effect of making high school more appealing, but it also makes the high school experience less appropriate for the student who goes on to college, where he will be expected to write term papers and take final examinations.

School discipline has relaxed and parents are upset when the influence of schools poses a threat to their child. Most high schools have a drug problem that has already filtered down to the junior high schools and is beginning to threaten elementary-level pupils. Parents have reason to be concerned over this problem, especially when schools do not take decisive steps to eliminate drugs. Classroom discipline is a serious problem in some schools. Students are often disrespectful to their teachers, and some teachers retaliate by shouting and threatening their students. Some of the new programs that have been instituted in elementary schools which involve learning stations, or the school-without-walls, allow students to move about freely. Often this results in a noise level that could interfere with concentration and learning. In some instances, it seems to have resulted in a rather chaotic classroom condition that is the antithesis of the classroom of forty years ago in which you could hear a pin drop. Quite conceivably, you might not hear a chair fall.

4. A number of schools have what amounts to a policy of automatic promotion. This is especially true in the elementary years because of a philosophy that regards retention as being potentially harmful to the child's emotional and social life. Some schools reason that if the child did not learn the first time around, he probably will not learn from a second exposure. From the child's point of view, automatic promotion means he will be promoted regardless of what he does or does not do. The child who is out to beat the system succeeds, for he is promoted along with those who have earned the promotion. Therefore, he will have no incentive to develop a different attitude about school work in subsequent years and may be content to get by on attendance (which may be minimal) rather than accomplishment.

It serves no purpose to retain the child who tries hard and still cannot succeed, although such a child might belong in a special class. However, the child who has average intelligence and has not achieved because of a negative and resistant attitude towards school should not be rewarded by promotion. Advancing a student into a situation he cannot handle is being unfair to the child, and even if he is placed in a slow-moving section it is doubtful that he will be motivated to assume any more responsibility than he has in the past. The child who is working below his potential will typically not do more when less is expected of him.

It is not uncommon for parents to request the school to retain their child, knowing he is not ready for the next grade. The decision to retain a student is left to the parents in some schools where administrators feel they can only recommend that a child be asked to repeat a grade. Parents should not make the educator's decisions.

School promotion and the grading system are examples of academic standards which need to be elevated. Undoubtedly there are many high school students today with average intelligence whose reading skills are no higher than the sixth-grade level. Although they may graduate from high school, their future is limited because they were promoted without sufficient cause. A student fails when he has not achieved the passing level; a school fails when the passing level is set too low.

5. From the educator's viewpoint, many of the problems in the

classroom are related to the amount of time the teacher must spend in being a disciplinarian. The average teacher is trained to teach the child who wants to learn but finds that she must spend large amounts of time dealing with discipline problems, behavior problems, and with nonteaching and clerical activities. Having inherited the problem-child from parents who have not been successful in handling him, the teacher is faced with the student who disrupts the class and whose resistance to learning complicates the teacher's tasks. The teacher becomes critical of parental home training; the parents become critical of the teacher's classroom effectiveness.

The increase in the number of school behavior problems has created a condition that requires the successful classroom teacher to be a person who can keep order in the classroom so that some children can learn. The professional problems of teachers are rarely those of effective academic instruction or subject presentations. When a teacher requests help from a supervisor about a child's particular learning problem, it is not usually a matter of exploring why one teaching method did not work or what other way of presenting the material would be more effective. It is usually to find ways to calm the child down or to cope with an attitude that is distracting others or himself. Learning problems in children are more frequently attributed to behavior problems than to intellectual reasons.

Control Problems

There are a number of school problems that relate to the management and control of students. When students are unmanageable or uncontrolled, schools become uncomfortable and dangerous. Control problems are largely social problems. In some schools, antisocial students pose problems for both teachers and students. Control problems raise questions about responsibility and authority and what actions a school can and should take to prevent them.

6.   Schools tolerate too much unacceptable behavior from students. The lack of enforced regulations soon becomes a social problem, for the high school sophomore sees what he can get away with and emulates the upper-class students. No school encourages the use of drugs; most have rules forbidding them. Even so, although schools are aware that students are smoking dope and "popping pills," teachers and principals seem to turn their heads when they see it happening. The teachers and administrators of most high schools

could identify the more serious offenders, but perhaps they do not regard this to be a school problem. Or, more realistically, they may not feel they could get backing from the school board if they attempted to eliminate the drug problem. One high school principal put it this way. "Our drug problem is under control. We don't have nearly the number of heroin users we once did." If only heroin is deemed a problem, the school is being either naive or negligent. It is certain that parents do not feel schools have solved their drug problems.

Schools feel they have something to offer the student who wants to learn. They may even feel their only task is to make learning available to those who want it. However, schools cannot overlook the social conditions that discourage the potential learner and distract students by what goes on in the classrooms and hallways. *What is missing from most schools is an atmosphere that is conducive to learning.* It would be comforting for parents if they could walk into a school and see visible signs that learning is taking place.

Attendance in public schools should be viewed as a privilege, not something to be taken for granted or a distasteful experience that has to be endured. It should be possible to remove this privilege when youngsters are unwilling to accept the rules necessary for the efficient operation of a school. The school troublemakers, as well as those who are not in school to learn, should not be allowed to intimidate or interfere with the child who wants to learn. Schools have not been effective in dealing with the child whose actions and attitudes are a bad influence on others. Scolding does not work, detention is not the answer, and threats of suspension do not deter the youngster who welcomes a three-day vacation from school.

A more drastic yet realistic approach would be to establish a *tuition school* for students who have repeatedly shown that they are either unable or unwilling to govern themselves according to rules that have been established by the regular school. For these students, public education would no longer be free. Their families would be required to pay for their compulsory education and the cost would be based on the parents' ability to pay. Requiring parents to pay for their child's education could be an incentive for some parents to do something to prevent their child from becoming unmanageable in school. It could awaken some parents to their responsibility. No student would be denied admission to the tuition school and those who cannot pay anything might be asked to perform some service for the school. Obviously, the courts would have to support this educational change, for there are many legalities that would prevent such a school from existing now.

The tuition school should have educational objectives and methods of instruction that are specifically designed for the student who is negative and resistant to school. The faculty would have to be trained to work with unmotivated learners and children who may have emotional problems that underlie their behavior. The majority of teachers in schools today do not want to teach or work with the child who does not want to learn. Nor are they trained to teach children who are emotionally or socially disturbed. Tuition school teachers would be aware of their challenge and should be part of a mental health team whose goals are to rehabilitate those students who cannot function in a regular school.

Another way to return order to schools would be to adopt a no-nonsense policy in which the student either agrees to abide by the rules of the school or is asked to leave the school. This would have the effect of removing students who disrupt the school and allowing children to learn in comfort, not fear. Such a policy could eliminate a school's drug problem in a matter of days, although it might also result in a drastically reduced enrollment for the rest of the year. But, when students are made aware that schools will not tolerate certain behaviors and they see they could lose a year of school if they are expelled, they might think twice about violating the rules. It makes sense to provide a school for the child who is expelled from the regular school, so the tuition school, combined with the no-nonsense policy, would be a way to resolve a big educational problem.

As things stand now, schools are willing to make the concessions and do everything to keep children in school, regardless of the consequences to the total school population. The tuition school and no-nonsense ideas would require the child to make the concessions and sacrifices if he wanted the privilege of attending school. They are attempts to segregate the disrupting child from the child who wants to learn and would have a better chance under better conditions. They would also reduce parental anxiety about the dangers of schools.

7. Schools do not always offer students protection from antisocial and aggressive classmates. There is a significant amount of violence in schools today. It includes threats to teachers, bullying students,

physical harm to students, and destruction of school property. (In 1972, one school system reported that 29,700 school windows were broken at a replacement cost of $535,682.00.) Many students are afraid to go to school because of threats that they'll be beaten up. In some instances, the intimidation comes from members of the faculty.

Case Illustration Number 17

Frank was thirteen years old and in the seventh grade. He was overweight, somewhat effeminate, and a poor athlete. He had been teased throughout his school life about his weight and had been a frequent target for bullies who knew he could not defend himself. On several occasions, Frank said his teachers contributed to his harassment by insulting him in front of the class and laughing at comments made by other students.

Frank's biggest problem in school was the physical education class. He was most vulnerable in this area and subject to the greatest amount of embarrassment from both classmates and instructors. One particular physical education teacher, an ex-marine, made it especially difficult for Frank. He ran his gym class in a military manner and required his students to respond like recruits in boot camp. He forced Frank to do physical exercises that he could not do and yelled and cursed at him when he failed. Frank could not run fast, and the gym teacher constantly belittled his efforts to keep up with the group. Frank saw this instructor as a sadistic and insensitive teacher who was using him as a scapegoat. In order to avoid contact with this teacher, Frank began to skip school. He thought it would be easier to do this than to cut just the physical education class. He forged his mother's signature on excuses and claimed to be sick. Both Frank and his parents complained to the principal about this problem. The principal promised he would look into it. Actually, Frank felt that complaining to the principal turned out to be a mistake, for the gym teacher made teasing remarks in front of the class about ". . . someone who said some bad man was hurting mommy's little boy."

One day the activity for the gym class was boxing. Frank was afraid he would be hurt and refused to participate. The gym teacher went into a rage and called him many unkind things, including a coward and a disgrace to God. Frank was very upset over this abuse and vowed he would not return to gym class, even if it meant failing the year or being expelled. After a very involved and unpleasant amount of interaction between Frank's parents and the school, he was allowed to be excused from physical education class for the year on medical reasons stemming from psychological causes.

Although the issue may have been resolved as far as the school was concerned, the damage it did to Frank could not be assessed. This was a traumatic experience he would not forget for a very long time. Teachers must be aware that their impact on a child may have lasting effects and could conceivably do irreparable damage to a youngster.

Although such an incident is not common, the fact that it can happen indicates that some teachers are not able to treat a student with dignity and respect. Frank was no less an important person than the student who was athletically gifted. This illustration also points out the fact that many teachers who work with children are misfit in their jobs. It could also raise the question of the need to look into the policy of compulsory physical education for every child, or at least do something about grouping gym classes homogenously.

Case Illustration Number 18

More common antisocial problems involve students who are the bullies. Bill was unpopular with his peers and had no real friends. He caused many of his own problems by being boastful and allowing himself to become very upset when he was teased. Bill was in the sixth grade and did average scholastic work. He cried easily and would not protect himself when he was hit or became a victim of pranks. He ran to his teachers for protection, but they were so used to his behavior they told him to work it out by himself. One day Bill was sitting in class when one of his tormentors poked him in the back with a pencil. Bill swung his arm around reflexively and hit the boy who had stuck him. The tormentor got angry and slapped Bill on the head. He then told Bill that he was "going to get him" after school and threatened to do him serious harm. Bill was scared. After school, he went to his teacher and explained what had happened. The teacher seemed to be unconcerned and again told Bill this was his problem and he would have to work it out with the boy who was threatening him. She said she had not seen the boy stick Bill with the pencil and there was nothing she could do. That afternoon Bill encountered the bully who was waiting for him. He tried to run home, but he was caught and hurt badly. Because the fight took place away from school, the position of the school was that this was something Bill's parents would have to take up with the parents of the other child. In essence, they did not offer Bill protection in school and would not help solve the problem outside of school.

The bully, whether he be alone or part of a gang, should not be permitted to terrorize helpless youngsters. Survival of the fittest may be the code of the jungle, but schools should not have to be equated to jungles. The antisocial child does not belong in a regular school.

8.   In the attempt to operate a democratic school and obtain feedback from all sources, schools have created a serious problem that has grown to the point that they have hampered themselves by the need to please everybody. Professional educators have permitted the nonprofessional to have power and control over educational matters. Everybody has been allowed to become an authority on education, even the student, who is now able to sit on faculty committees and policy-making groups with equal voting privileges and authority to make decisions. Schools have acquiesced to student demands for smoking areas, uncensored school newspapers, and the right to determine their own dress code. Students can call for a school strike when a fellow student complains he has been treated unfairly, and the schools back down to them. In some colleges, students have demanded and received the right to hire and fire professors and to protest on political, rather than educational, issues. They have been permitted to use political and national security matters as an excuse for destruction of school property and an avoidance of responsibility.

The power struggle for control of schools can be destructive to the concept of public education. Public education means what it says; education for the public, financed largely through public taxes. In essence, all public school personnel are employees of the taxpayers. But this does not give the taxpayer the right to prevent the schools from carrying out their responsibilities. Because of a lack of power, some school systems cannot legally retain a child over the protest of parents; they will not discipline a child if the parents object to it; and they could find themselves in trouble if they insist on beginning each day with a pledge of allegiance to this country, or an opening nondenominational prayer.

Parents do have the right to know what is going on and should be able to voice objections when they are dissatisfied with something. Parent and student participation in the educative process should be encouraged. Decision making is facilitated when it is based on knowledge of the feelings of all interested parties. Parents and students can make a valuable contribution to understanding the problems of education today by expressing their attitudes and offering suggestions for improvement. But participation and involvement should not be confused with authority to make the decisions that must be determined for the welfare of all who are affected. Authority for educational decisions involving policy and practices should be in the hands of those people who are best trained and qualified to understand issues from an objective, not a biased point of view. Whereas the parent and student are inclined to respond to what is good for themselves, the educator should be concerned with what is best for *all* who are served in education. The reluctance of our society to place this responsibility in the hands of the educator is another instance of the mistrust and lack of confidence in educators today.

Self-governing and the ability to determine what choices are best for the individual are goals of education. But it is important to know when the individual is ready to assume the responsibility for determining his own destiny. When students are permitted to decide their own educational needs, it must be assumed that the student is fully aware of what his needs are, as well as the implications of any decision. It is easy to confuse wants with needs. The student may know what he wants yet be unaware of what he really needs. He may not want to learn a foreign language. He may not want to take chemistry because it requires a knowledge of mathematics, and he has not wanted to burden himself with math courses. To allow the adolescent to plan his program according to what his present needs are makes the assumption that his long-range goals have been carefully thought out. Allowing the student to make the decision not to take a certain course because he does not see it as being vital to his life can be self-defeating, especially when his decision does not protect him from any later changes in thinking about educational goals. Can the adolescent determine his future needs for education? Generally speaking, the answer is no, he cannot.

Educational decisions should be returned to the educator. Even the board of education should be comprised of professional educators. As a matter of fact, one of the most significant changes in education could take place by altering the composition of the board of education. Educational policies, hiring of professional personnel, and selection of textbooks are made by a board of education who may or may not have educational training.

Physicians comprise medical boards; lawyers make up legal boards. But any person who professes an interest in education, and is of legal age, is a potential member of a board of education. Many school problems might be resolved if the professional board of education consisted of people who are trained educators rather than people who are just educated. A worthwhile experiment would be to develop a two-board system. The professional board would be made up of people who had educational training—teachers, educational administrators, university professors, educational researchers, and at least one adult member of the community. The superintendent would turn to this board for help in decisions that involve educational policies, educational standards, the criteria for faculty selection, in-service training needs, educational research for programs and assessment, teaching methods, and instructional improvement.

The second board of education could be called an administrative board. Their task would be equally important and would involve financial and business matters. The members of the administrative board could be bankers, lawyers, contractors, housewives, electricians, or any interested citizens who could make a contribution to the operation of schools. It would be the responsibility of the administrative board to run the school plant, develop new facilities, establish a budget, and be in charge of school upkeep and general management. The chairman of the professional board would sit on the administrative board, and vice versa. The superintendent would also be an ex-officio member of both boards.

Small urban or rural communities may not be able to have such an elaborate arrangement, but they could consolidate for administrative purposes without changing the size of individual schools. With proper representation from these small districts, this merger need not be restrictive. The board member would be voted into office and open meetings should be encouraged. A two-board system would delegate responsibilities to the appropriate body whose training and experience best qualify them for their position. Although this is only the skeleton of the idea, it would be interesting to see it implemented.

Staff Problems

Some of the problems in education deal with professional matters of staff competency, morale, and teaching incentives. Although there is not much that parents can do about solving these kinds of problems, they can be supportive of school bond issues and cooperate with school personnel who may feel they are not appreciated.

9.   Although it may seem strange and rather unrealistic, many teachers who are responsible for teaching and working with children, and who have done so for many years, do not really like children. Nor do they like their jobs as teachers. Often their performance reflects their negative attitude towards their jobs and pupils. Their impatience and insensitivity to children suggests that there is possibly an occupational hazard in teaching: that after a while, you may become tired of working with children. This could be especially true for a teacher who is required to teach the same subject several times a day, thirty-two weeks a year, year after year.

Many teachers no longer like the kind of pupil they must teach. They have not adjusted to the changes in student's attitudes and expect the student of today to be the way students were in the past. They resent their pupils' sloppy appearance, flippant attitude, social interests, and language.

Because they are protected by tenure and need the income, teachers who dislike teaching remain trapped in the system and unhappy with their jobs. Many teachers are no more motivated to teach than some of their students are to learn. Undoubtedly, there is some sort of cause and effect relationship going on in which some students have a "don't care" attitude towards learning because their teachers have a "don't care" attitude towards teaching. Hopefully, this is not a widespread problem, but it exists to some degree in every school system.

Granting a teacher a sabbatical leave every six or seven years would help reduce this problem. It would also encourage a more professional attitude towards teaching. Rotating teachers within grades would keep teaching a challenge, for it would offer the teachers variety by exposing them to different levels of maturation and ability. And, providing teachers with an opportunity to talk with mental health personnel would improve the attitude of those who have personal problems that interfere with their teaching.

10. The low pay for teachers creates another problem for schools. No one can deny that many teachers are grossly underpaid for their

efforts and talents. Our educational system can boast of having many dedicated and capable teachers and administrators in our schools. Undoubtedly, the low pay scale for teachers has discouraged count- less numbers of bright and sensitive people from going into teaching as a career. At the same time, no one can deny that many teachers are overpaid for what they do as teachers. The task of attracting good teachers and maintaining quality instruction is a challenge for profes- sional educators, professional educational societies, teacher-training institutions, and local communities. Quality education becomes everybody's responsibility.

It is very unfortunate that teachers have been forced to take to the streets with placards to spell out inequities within our society. They have found it necessary to organize into unions, call strikes, hold walkouts, and force the closing of schools. Highly professional and conscientious teachers have been compelled to humiliate them- selves by asking for what is only fair. They question the value that society really places on education and cannot rationalize the economic penalties society imposes upon them because of their oc- cupational choice. A society that spends millions to build schools, that takes pride in the accomplishments and welfare of its children, and that has parents willing to spend so much money on their chil- dren, is apparently unwilling to spend the money needed to pay better salaries to the personnel who teach the child. This is not saying that paying higher salaries to all who are presently teaching would alter the situation significantly. Those men and women who are profes- sional in their teaching would be effective in their work regardless of a salary increase. Paying the incompetent teacher more money would not make that person more competent. But, to make the teaching field appealing to those who could contribute much to the education of children, a revision of current practices and policies is needed. If the amount of training and the responsibilities a person assumes is a criteria for determining the salary of a teacher, it is difficult to justify the salary of a trained and licensed teacher in comparison with the entertainer, for instance, who can earn more in one week than a teacher can expect to receive in five or more years, or the professional athlete whose income is up to ten times that of a teacher.

11. What to do with poor or incompetent teachers poses a serious problem for education. Once they have been tenured, it is almost impossible to remove them from teaching. They can be transferred, in which case they are still in the classroom, and they can be given remedial assistance. But if the tenured teacher wants to work as a

teacher, it is unlikely he will have problems holding his job, unless serious charges are brought against him. Ineffective teaching is not usually considered a serious charge, nor is it easy to prove.

Both the educational system and the teacher's unions have created this problem. In some school systems, tenure is automatically granted after a certain number of years, sometimes two or three, unless there is reason not to grant it. After the teacher is tenured, he cannot be removed from his position unless he is incompetent or immoral. Incompetency and immorality have become very difficult to define.

Because it is not easy to remove the educator once he has been hired, more care should be given to selecting the teacher or administrator. State certification requirements should not be the sole criteria for hiring school personnel, for the philosophy and views on education of every school employee should be known in order to determine whether the employee's views are compatible with those of the school system. There is no way to accurately assess the influence a teacher can have on students. Undoubtedly, much of the unrest in schools today can be traced to faculty members who are working against, rather than with, the system. More careful screening and hiring procedures would give parents greater confidence that their children will not be exposed to antisocial teachers.

Related to hiring procedures, but not to the problem of the incompetent teacher, is the need for more male teachers at elementary school levels. This is especially important for children who have no father. It would also be good for the young child who is in conflict with his mother and perceives the female teacher as an extension of his own mother.

12. Morale has become a problem in schools today. Teachers complain of not getting cooperation from administrators and are intimidated by parents who blame them for not giving their child private instruction. Administrators complain they are not backed up by the superintendent's office, and feel threatened when their authority can be challenged. School personnel have been asked to do more, and they have not been compensated accordingly. Innovations in the curriculum require many hours of preparation and numerous meetings. Lesson plans are very involved because many different things happen each day. The conscientious teacher is truly overworked, underpaid, and often unappreciated. Teachers need more recognition and help in doing their job. Parents can sometimes be helpful. They

can ask if there are things they can do that would make the teacher's task easier.

Communication Problems

Many school problems have developed because the home and school are not in contact with each other enough. In the early years, parent-teacher conferences are common, but in the upper grades, contacts are usually initiated by the parents and only when there are problems with their child. Communication problems keep parents uninformed and deny the school helpful feedback.

13. Parents are confused and worried because they do not understand what a lot of the new words and concepts mean. They hear terms like learning stations, team teaching, ungraded classes, open schools, behavioral objectives, modules, pods, core, contractual agreements, and new math. They see teaching machines and other expensive gimmicks and wonder what was wrong with the old ways of teaching. When they try to get answers, they are not always satisfied with what they hear. The parent who wants to see or hear about the research supporting the innovations may even become frustrated.

Parents want the best education for their children. They are confused when they know that one school is using one approach and other schools use different methods. They are particularly distressed at the possibility that their child may be an academic guinea pig for an untested way of teaching such important skills as reading or arithmetic. Much of their confusion could be prevented if schools realized that parents were worried and made efforts to tell them what is being done and why. Parent meetings, newsletters, prepared statements, newspaper coverage, and an effective PTA would help parents understand what is happening in schools.

Many experimental programs have been initiated without the benefit of the necessary research that would support the change. Pilot programs are not always evaluated in objective or scientific ways. Experimental and control groups are necessary if the value of an innovation is to be properly assessed. If the results of educational research are made known to parents, schools might get more cooperation.

14. One of the traditional ways that schools have communicated the progress of the child to parents is by a periodic report card. Although schools still use this method, many parents do not see the report

cards, for in some schools, and at some grade levels, report cards are given to the child with the expectation he will take them home to his parents. They are not required to sign them, so the school has no way of knowing if they ever got there. Then there is the problem at the lower levels of not being able to understand what the report card means. Letter grades have been replaced by checks, simple designations that indicate if the child is above, at, or below grade level, or perhaps a brief paragraph telling parents about the child's progress. Many elementary schools do not feel it is helpful to assign letter grades, and parents who have learned what letter grades mean must guess what VG or NI would mean of a scale from A to F. Is VG (very good) equal to an A? Does NI (needs improvement) mean that the child is failing?

It should not be too difficult for a school to decide on a standard for reporting the progress of a student. Most parents take their child's report card very seriously. Many penalties are imposed because of the grade or mark on the child's report card. Schools that report the child's progress only twice each semester are not keeping parents informed enough to do much to help their child. A six week report is minimal, and it should be meaningful to parents. Secondary schools should allocate time in teacher's schedules for parent conferences, and inform parents about problems before the year is almost over. The parent who is interested in his child's progress wants more information from the school.

15. When the child is in elementary school and his parents are concerned about his progress, they can go to the school and usually find someone to talk with. His teacher or teachers are available, so is the principal, and many elementary schools have counselors who consult with parents and teachers. When the child is in junior high school, in some places called the middle school, the problem of finding someone to talk with is a bit more complicated. Parents may talk with the teachers, it is unlikely they will see the principal, and they probably will end up talking with the counselor. The counselor will contact the teachers and get a report, then contact the parents and discuss the reports from the teacher. As you can see, communication with the school is more difficult to arrange as the child gets older. When the child reaches high school, very often communication appears to completely break down.

Parents who want to understand what is happening to their high school child often find no one available to explain things to them. In large high schools, the principal is usually unavailable, and rarely makes an attempt to know his students by name. Many high school principals have become professional administrators rather than professional educators. The high school principal is surrounded by a large staff who carry on the business of the school in a manner similar to that of a large corporation. Rarely does he engage in professional supervision. When a youngster is having a discipline problem or is threatening to cause trouble, the child will be interviewed by the vice-principal or school counselor. The typical high school principal is burdened with the responsibility of a school whose enrollment is so large that it precludes taking a direct interest in the individual child. Instead of reducing his burden by decreasing the number of students in a school, the trend is moving in the opposite direction, by the planning of even larger and consolidated schools.

Parents can talk with the vice-principal, but they soon realize that his task is to calm them with reassurances and promises, or defend the school, often by subtly blaming the parents or the junior high school for the problems the child is having. When they ask personal questions about the child, the vice-principal will usually refer the parents to the school counselor, who, unfortunately, turns out to be no more help than the vice-principal. However, the counselor will at least make an effort to understand what it is the parents are asking.

The counselor's title is usually a misnomer. Parents suppose that the major task of the counselor is to counsel children. They imagine that if a child has personal problems that are interfering with school performance, he will seek out the counselor for help. Research has shown that this is usually not the case. Counselors are available to see children when their schedule permits. In practice, this available time is small in comparison to the time they are required to spend in carrying out routine clerical tasks and a variety of noncounseling functions (e.g. scheduling classes, testing incoming students, performing lunchroom duties, keeping records that a secretarial staff could handle). Frequently, their contact with the student is limited to relocating the youngster in a particular section of history or returning scores on college entrance examinations. Most counselors function as guidance personnel with an ill-defined role and a contaminated job expectancy. Their title suggests they are there to help children with problems; in most cases, they provide an information service to students, although many are trained to do more. When parents talk with the school counselor, they seek information and help. More times than not, they leave disappointed.

16. One source for informing parents about what goes on in schools could be the Parent Teacher Association. It was originally established to bring the parents closer to the school through an information and educational program that encouraged dialogue between the home and the school. It was developed with the idea that parents should understand what the schools are doing and how they go about doing it. Teachers want feedback from parents and the PTA was also set up as a way of accomplishing this. A few PTAs function in this manner. Most are fund-raising groups, concentrating on such things as where the chairman of the rosebush committee should tell her rosebush planters to plant the rosebushes the school bought from proceeds of the bake sale and bazaar. (They may also purchase a projector that the school needs and should be able to requisition from school funds.) Or, the PTA functions as a semi-political pressure group who feel compelled to attack administrative decisions and play watchdog over the Board of Education who was elected by the people, but for some reason can't be trusted.

The PTA can become a vital and effective means of communicating information to parents and, at the same time, provide parents with an opportunity to make a contribution to the schools. The average PTA suffers from gross apathy. A few parents are involved, and those who attend meetings do so more out of obligation than for the benefits they expect to receive. They want their child's teacher to see them at a meeting, feeling this is their way of showing interest in their child's schooling. Many teachers attend PTA because it is required of them. Often they are frustrated when parents want to engage them in conferences at the meeting instead of contacting them during the time set aside in the school day.

Interest in the PTA could be motivated if parents are offered something more than coffee and cookies. Parents want to know things about schools and about children in general. Many would like to participate in educational programs that could be conducted by members of the faculty, or in some cases by parents from the school who are in professional fields and have knowledge to share. A speaker on the subject of "The Hyperactive Child" may not be appealing to a large group. But, this same topic discussed in small groups that encourage interaction and group participation could be more effective. Study groups, panels of parents and teachers, or effective speakers will attract those who are interested in educational topics. Listening to debates on controversial issues, such as the merits of the open school, would be appealing to some parents, and hearing about the latest research on new math might interest others.

In short, the PTA can improve itself if it can first find out what parents want to know more about, then plan a program accordingly. An active PTA whose goals are to receive and impart information focused on the welfare of the child is perhaps the most effective way to bridge the communication gap between the home and school. A more appropriate name for this group would be a Parent and Teacher Information and Education Group.

Parent-Created Problems

The final area of school problems to be considered are those that parents create. In most instances, these are not deliberate attempts to stir up trouble, and, for the most part, parents are not even aware that what they do contributes to the problems schools have.

17. Parental pressure creates problems for schools. The irate parent who threatens to bring action against the school, or the angry group who demands that the school do what they want, both create pressure that makes school personnel uneasy. Pressure has become a common denominator in schools today. Children feel pressure from their parents and teachers; teachers feel pressure from students, parents and the principal; the principal feels pressure from parents and the superintendent; the superintendent feels pressure from parents, principals and the Board of Education; and the Board of Education feels pressure from parents, who are the voters and taxpayers.

Because administrators dislike pressure, one of the tasks of the school principal has become that of trying to keep all factions happy and appeased. This means that the schools have fallen into the same trap with parents as some parents have with their children. Schools are trying to be all things to all people and, in the process, they are losing their direction and respect. Giving in to one group of parents who are angry may cause problems with another group of parents who are not angry. Schools must learn what parents have painfully discovered: yielding to pressure does not solve problems or build respect. It creates more problems and solves nothing.

Case Illustration Number 19

To show what happened when one principal tried to respond to parental pressure: A junior high school faculty deliberated and agreed to initiate a program on sex education. It was to have been introduced in the seventh grade with a bit more concentration in the eighth and ninth grades. A group of parents who objected to this decision came to the principal in a rage. The principal did not want to see this become an issue that could involve the superintendent, so he agreed to reconsider the sex education program and after deliberation with his faculty, it was decided not to have one. However, another group of parents who had supported the original decision now became upset and went to the principal to protest the change of plans. The principal was trapped. He had committed himself to one group to discontinue the idea and he was being pressured to abide by the wishes of the second group. After more deliberation, he came up with what he felt was the ideal solution: one that would make everybody happy. There would be a program on sexual information for any child whose parent did not object to it. It would not be compulsory and the school would make provisions for those children who were not taking part in the program. The principal felt that he had made a good decision: the democratic process had triumphed once again. He thought that he had been a good arbitrator.

In reality, that is all he showed himself to be. When he had the opportunity to assert professional judgment and provide educational leadership, he retreated in favor of peace and security. He failed to communicate anything of value to the parents, for apparently he never felt good enough about his own values to want to impart them to the parents of his school. His decision implied that the learnings from a sex education program are not important for all children, and he allowed nonprofessionals to make what should have been a professional decision. Parent pressure is especially rough on the insecure administrator.

18. Another problem created by parents is a reflection of parental attitudes towards schools and teachers. When parental feelings are negative, they may result in the child's showing disrespect to teachers and indifference to subject matter. Many parents feel they are better educated than their child's teachers, for more parents today are college graduates or have attended college. Any mysteries about the benefits of higher education are unimpressive to these parents, who may even look down on the training they think a teacher receives. The teacher today is not viewed as being an intellectual, nor does he command the respect he once did.

It is important that parents do not destroy the image of

teachers. If they are dissatisfied with what they believe is happening in school, they should discuss it with each other and with the teacher. Discrediting a teacher in front of a child may sanction his negative attitude about school. This is especially true for young children or children who seek a reason to dislike school.

19. Parents create problems when their child has not been adequately prepared for school. If education is a value of the parents, the groundwork for it must be established by the parents before the child enters his first classroom. The young child must be receptive to the prospect of learning, and this comes about best when the parents have attempted to develop a home environment that motivates learning. This should be done when the child is two, not five and about to enter school.

20. Parents create problems when they have been negligent in their parenting and expect the school to accomplish what they failed to do. For example, schools take the position that it is up to parents to teach their child about discipline and being respectful to others. However, parents who have not done an effective job of parenting and have a child who is difficult to control, often expect the school to correct their failure. What usually happens in the confusion of role expectancy is a mutual dissatisfaction between the school and home. Unfortunately, when neither the school nor the home is prepared to assume responsibility for helping the child overcome his problem, or when neither will take a firm stand on disciplinary requirements, the child rejects any attempts to alter his behavior.

Schools have gradually rejected the concept of *in loco parentis,* whereby the school takes it upon itself to act ''in place of the parent.'' Because of the age of the child, elementary schools are forced to be surrogate parents, but as the child gets into the upper grades, schools claim less responsibility to function as parents. Colleges have all but abandoned attempts to regulate the student's personal and social life.

It is not necessary for teachers to act as parents or the school to serve as a home away from home. But schools should have standards as to behavior that will be accepted and rejected. Schools cannot undo what parents have done, for when the parent has avoided his responsibility schools cannot be expected to fulfill their responsibility.

School Problems and Teacher Training

21.   There is yet one more school problem that should be mentioned. It involves teacher education programs and the impact they have had on schools. It seems that if schools are having problems because of their policies, practices, and curriculum, the programs of the institutions who prepare teachers and administrators, and the philosophies of the faculties who teach school personnel should be examined. Teacher training institutions have their problems too. Although teachers are largely a product of the training they have received, many say they learned how to teach after they were hired as teachers. Despite the fact that colleges that prepare educators are constantly evaluating their programs and making changes they feel are improvements, graduates of these training centers do not always feel that their academic programs have been adequate preparation for their job as teachers. They regard their student teaching as the most meaningful experience and tend to negate many of their professional courses in education as having been more demanding in busy work than in content. Many of their professors lack direct contact with schools and pupils. Programs that are engineered in laboratory schools or theoretical models are not always transferable to a school that is comprised of a different population of children.

In a push for creative and highly innovative programs, which often results in change for the sake of change, some teacher education programs have turned their attention away from fundamentals of how learning takes place, the optimal conditions for learning, and establishment of a relevant curriculum. Instead, they are interested in developing programs for the highly motivated and self-directed student, and have encouraged a trend that rewards the unmotivated student with candy or other gimmicks, in which the focus is entirely on what the child is doing, rather than on why he is doing it. Somewhere in the shuffle, the average student, who tolerates education, gets lost.

Quality education begins where the training takes place. Teacher education institutions must continue to evaluate their product in terms of the problems that schools are having.

What Can Schools Do?

It is easy to be critical of a situation and do nothing but complain about how bad things are getting. One should not take a helpless attitude and feel that nothing can be done to improve conditions. Although there is no panacea or cure-all that will magically remove problems from schools, there is reason to be optimistic about reducing some of the problems if the schools are willing to take an objective look at themselves and begin to ask themselves the right questions. Too often, we are inclined to seek answers to problems before the appropriate questions have been raised. For some educators, an appropriate first question might be, "Is there a problem?"

Many of the problems of schools are an outgrowth of more fundamental problems such as poverty, cultural deprivation, or the effects of an affluent society. The problems of schools cannot be considered separate from those of society. Educational reforms cannot succeed unless social reforms are being achieved at the same time. Equality in education, which is one needed reform, cannot come about until there is more equality in society. Control of the drug problem in schools cannot be achieved until actions are taken to control the problem outside of the schools. Yet, to refuse to act on educational reforms until comparable steps are taken to improve social conditions is a you-go-first policy that could result in nothing happening. If social reforms are not forthcoming, our educational system must assume leadership. Hopefully, by exposing social problems, schools can encourage social reforms.

Nevertheless, there are things the schools can do to reduce many of their problems. Discipline problems in schools could be reduced and the communication problem between the home and school could be lessened. Programs designed to prevent school problems can be developed for parents of preschool children, and parents can be directed to child guidance clinics when beginning signs of trouble appear.

More efficient utilization of school psychologists and counselors would provide supportive help to teachers as well as parents. School mental health programs that stress prevention and identification of early problems would be helpful and teachers must be included in such programs. Appropriate legal actions against parents who fail to assume their responsibilities might encourage some parents to become more interested in obtaining help in carrying out parental functions. A closer parent-teacher relationship on a professional level would bring the home and school together as partners in the education of the child.

What Can Parents Do?

Most children begin their formal education with a lot of enthusiasm that parents generate by encouraging their child to feel that starting to school is an important step in growing up. The day he enters his first classroom, the child has been told a list of dos and don'ts by his parents who want him to cooperate and benefit from his academic years. Some parents attempt to prepare their child for school, others send their child to school because he has reached the proper age to be there. The child whose parents did something to get him ready has an advantage over the child whose parents took school responsibilities for granted and waited for the teacher to prepare the child. Parents cannot do much to correct the academic, control, and staff problems in schools, but they can do some things with their own child that would facilitate learning and reduce problems for the classroom teacher.

What follows are guidelines for parents who want to help their child get the most from his educational experience. In general, they are designed to teach the child to assume responsibility for his academic achievement and encourage parents to help schools achieve their goals.

Guideline 1. *Prepare the child for school.* When a child develops a learning problem or begins to show disinterest in school, his parents become disappointed and look for explanations. Assuming a child has average mental ability, one of the reasons why the child could develop a learning problem or become disinterested in school is the attitude towards learning he brings to school. Although it is possible that school methods and teacher attitudes have caused or contributed to the problem, often the source of the problem lies in attitudes that were present before the child started school. The child's preschool attitudes towards school are largely the product of parental attitudes and priorities. When the child's early attitude to school is negative and he feels forced to go to school, he may maintain an antagonistic attitude throughout his school years. If the child views going to school as a sacrifice in which he must give up his play in return for experiences that are not as exciting, the child may resent school, for children's needs are present oriented, and education is both present and future directed.

The determining factor is not the amount or kind of pressure parents put on the child, but the importance parents have placed on educational objectives. Frequently parents who have high, and sometimes unrealistic, educational goals for their child, encourage activities that give a lower priority to educational objectives. The five-year-old who has been encouraged to play with toys and games that emphasize skills other than those which are seen in an academic setting will regard educational media as new and foreign. If all that a child has had to play with are toy machine guns, cars, footballs, and bicycles, it will be more difficult for this child to develop an interest in work that involves words, numbers, and activities that require him to sit and pay close attention to what a teacher is saying. The child who, in addition to having toys and games that require physical activity, has been exposed to stories, books, sounds, puzzles, numbers, and words, will have the advantage of a good start in school since his experiences are compatible with the objectives of education.

The correlation between the attention span of a child who can watch thirty minutes of cartoons on television without becoming distracted, and that of a child who is asked to listen attentively to a teacher for thirty minutes is low. The child who has had experience in listening to directions and following instructions is less likely to resist school procedures. A child's receptiveness to academic learning must be cultivated, and, as in other ways, parents are the child's first teachers.

To prepare a child for school, parents are advised to begin as early as age three, when the child's speech is becoming intelligible and he is becoming aware of things around him. In order to make the child's world more meaningful for him, parents can begin to point to signs and tell the child what the word says. In this way, the child begins to associate letters with words. The child should not be bombarded with signs, but he can become familiar with some of the more common ones, such as grocery stores, department stores, gas stations, and other signs he sees frequently. Many children could be reading simple words by the time they reach kindergarten if parents have taken the time to read to them, explain what signs say, what numbers are, and expose the child to alphabet-type books that do the same thing.

The child's early experiences in school will involve working with large crayons, large pencils, and wide-lined paper. Parents can expose their child to these things without teaching the child to make a good letter A. The child who enjoys drawing with a pencil and paper is also developing his fine muscle coordination. There are many forms of lotto games to teach the child to match pictures, dot-to-dot books that help the child learn about numbers and letters, and picture books that give the child practice in language skills. All of these things encourage the child to think and remember. Perhaps the two most important skills that correlate with success in school are thinking and remembering; the earlier they are developed, the easier it will be for the child to learn.

Parents should also be honest with their child about school. School is not fun, nor is learning easy. School can be interesting, enjoyable, and stimulating, but it is not fun, as the child defines fun. It is fun to ride a bicycle or go swimming. But, the child who has been told that school is going to be fun will be disappointed because he will not experience what he has been told to expect. Preschool programs that are largely unstructured and attempt to entertain the child are deceptive and potentially harmful if they condition the child to expect fun and games in school. The five-year-old child who has spent two or three years in what he has heard his parents say is school, and who has been allowed to run around and do anything he wants in the school, may have a hard time adjusting to a more formal program.

Learning is work. For some children it is hard work. The child who does not realize this will expect learning to be automatic. Many children do not learn because they are not willing to work at learning. In language the child can understand, he should know why it is to his advantage to learn and the reasons that learning is important. Being honest to the child about school is an important part of preparing him for his school years.

Guideline 2. *The child must see that education is a strong value for both parents.* It is not sufficient for parents to occasionally ask their child if he did his homework, or only show an interest in school achievement when report cards come out. If the child is to have a high regard for education, he must see signs of this in the actions and interest of his parents. Children are encouraged to read when they have seen their parents read; they are stimulated to seek answers to questions when they have seen their parents refer to an encyclopedia or dictionary; and, they are motivated to talk about school assignments when their parents show a sincere interest in what they are learning. The child determines the importance of school according to the importance his parents place on it. If parents allow their child to miss school frequently and without a justified cause, the child may not regard school as something meaningful. If household chores are given priority over homework, or the mother is always the one to contact schools and put pressure on the child to do his work, while the father stays out of things, the importance of education as a value will be reduced. In short, the parents must demonstrate to the child that education is a strong value for both of them. It may not be the most important thing in the child's life, but it certainly should be among the top three priorities of the parents.

Guideline 3. *Help the child start each day pleasantly.* The hours in the morning before a child goes off to school may determine the kind of day he will have. It is not always an easy task, but parents can help their child go to school with a better attitude if they are able to prevent arguments and unpleasant scenes in the morning before school. The child who is upset before the school day begins is not going to respond gracefully to the normal frustrations of the school day and may need to release his home anger in school.

For some parents, a complete reorganization of the morning routine may be required. The child who is always rushing to catch the bus may have to get up earlier, and go to bed earlier. Siblings who fight in the morning may have to be isolated from each other; the mother may have to get up earlier; or the father may have to assume some additional responsibility. If the mornings are typically unpleasant, parents will have to analyze the conditions that make them this way and take steps to improve things.

A good breakfast is important and should not be bolted down in front of a television set. Pleasant talk and a calm atmosphere should be the goal. If mornings are chaotic, disorganized, or rushed, it may take some time to correct the problem, but the morning routine should be improved.

Guideline 4. *Encourage the child to develop good study habits.* A quiet place, a comfortable chair (one that is not so comfortable that he can fall asleep in it) and good lighting are the physical requirements for studying. But, the proper mental attitude is even more important. Despite what some youngsters say, studying with the television or radio on does not assist concentrating or remembering. Studying is a discipline that most students do not learn until they are well into their college years. The average student in secondary schools does not study often, and when he does it is usually a matter of reading material one time. Cramming before an examination is the most common form of studying, yet the student who must cram has not studied properly.

The purpose of this guideline is not to discuss effective study techniques, for there are sources in bookstores and libraries parents can turn to for this kind of information. Parents can encourage the child to develop good study habits if they see to it that the house is quiet enough for studying, that the child has a place to study that gives him good light, and that there will be no distractions such as telephones, televisions, record players, or radios.

One of the biggest problems that parents have to overcome is the child's insistance that other children don't have to study. The parent who can appreciate this and still require his child to study conveys his value of education to the child. The child can select the time of day he wants to study, and parents can cooperate by freeing this time for the child. Study time should be viewed as an important time by the parents. Letting it slip by for a day or two allows the child to feel that it is not important.

Guideline 5. *Show the proper amount of interest in the child's schoolwork.* The child should be encouraged to talk about what goes on in school, but he should not feel he has to give a daily account of what happens. Too much interest may create pressure. Parents can show interest by reading or looking at what the child brings home from school, being a resource person when possible, checking homework occasionally, and praising achievements realistically. A child needs to know when he has done something well, but over-praising something the child has done gives him false security. Parents who praise in the superlative may encourage their child to think he can do no wrong. Eventually, the child may be embarrassed to bring home work that is not satisfactory. Parents who want to encourage their child to talk about what he has learned must be careful not to show their child a know-it-all attitude. Children like to feel that they can teach their parents something once in awhile. The parent who is in competition with his child denies his child this opportunity. Proper interest in the child's schoolwork often means letting the child tell the parents things they already know when they are things the child wants to talk about.

Guideline 6. *Keep expectations for achievement realistic.* Every child cannot get an A in each subject, and many children have to work hard to earn a grade of C. At some point in the child's schooling, parents should have a good idea of what realistic expectations are for their child. The parent who feels his child can do better in school than the report card indicates is often frustrated. When there is reason to support this contention, based on teacher impressions or standardized tests, the parent should be aware that his child may have a problem and consult with the school. But, many parents expect more from their children than they can produce. Because the mother got As in school does not mean her child will and because the child's best friend gets As is no reason to expect the child to do similar work. Nor is it always realistic to think that the child cannot do better than D work. There is just as much danger in setting goals too low as in setting them too high. When in doubt as to what to expect from the child, the parents can seek a conference with the teacher or a psychological evaluation. For some children, a C could indicate a problem; for others it could be an acceptable grade. The informed parent knows which it is.

Guideline 7. *Don't overburden the child with activities.* Between the months of September and June, the child who is in school has what amounts to a full-time job. He puts in about thirty hours a week on this job, plus a certain amount of time in homework. Adding too many other things to the child's schedule detracts from his educational goals. Some of the activities that children participate in make great demands on their time and energy, and though the child may enjoy these activities, there is a limit as to how much he can do without harming his schoolwork. A child needs free time. His parents may want him to learn to play the piano, study ballet dancing, get religious training, develop his talents for art, or play football, and the child may want these things too. But, parents should not lose sight of their priorities, and if education is the first one, other activities would have to either wait, or accept a lesser position.

Parents must decide how many activities, in addition to school, are practical for the child. The answer would vary for each child, and certainly one or even two things might not be a problem for some children. However, parents have to be careful not to allow the child to get so involved with out-of-school events that he neglects school work.

Guideline 8. *Try to make contact with the child's teachers.* Most parents whose children are in an elementary school will, at some time during the year, meet with their child's teacher or teachers. Unfortunately, these contacts are less frequent once the child is out of elementary school. Yet, there is as much reason to meet secondary teachers even though it is not as easy to meet them. Not only does it show the child that his parents are interested in his education, but it also gives the parents a chance to interact with their child's teachers. Through contact with teachers, parents can learn of behaviors that are not always reported elsewhere. It is helpful for the child because it provides parents with insights into teachers who, otherwise, would only be names. Even when there are no problems connected with the child's learning, it is a good practice to meet his teachers.

Guideline 9. *Don't discredit teachers or school personnel in front of the child.* There will be times when the child needs to be consoled because of an unfair action on the part of someone at school. When parents attack the teacher or principal in front of the child, the child often loses respect for the people he will have to face the remainder of the year. The child who has heard his parent call his teacher "stupid" may begin to dislike the teacher and justify doing poor work in school because he knows his parents will defend him and blame the teacher. When parents feel they have a legitimate grievance with a teacher, they should make an appointment to discuss the matter with the teacher. They should also remember that until they have talked with the teacher they have heard only one interpretation of the issue, and should go to school with an open mind.

Guideline 10. *Have reasonable expectations for what the teacher can do for the individual child.* To state this another way, don't expect the teacher to work miracles with your child. Classroom teachers are not private tutors and the amount of time they can spend with any one child is limited. Parents are sometimes quick to blame teachers when their child has a learning problem. There are many explanations for a learning problem, and the teacher is only one of them. Teachers must work with the ability and attitude the child presents to them. Teachers can often change a bad attitude, but they cannot extend the child's ability. They can only hope to encourage the child to work to his capacity, which, for some children, is lower than parents would like it to be.

Guideline 11. *Ask if the school can use your services.* Many mothers have spare time that schools could put to good use. Most schools welcome volunteer help from parents and utilize their services working in the lunchroom, helping the librarian, filing in the office, being teachers' aides, and reading to or working with children who have learning problems. The parent who is involved in the school is able to share some experiences with his child.

Guideline 12. *Take a positive attitude towards achievement.* Focus on what the child can do and what he has accomplished. Parents who look at a report card and only see the low grades are not giving credit where credit may be due. This is not saying that low grades should be praised when there is reason to feel the child could have done better, but parents should not overlook the chance to give the child positive feedback when it is possible. Achievements cannot be encouraged when they are belittled, and many parents make the mistake of demanding perfection from the child who cannot be perfect. Emphasizing the child's strengths will encourage him to correct his weaknesses, for the child likes praise and wants to hear it often. A positive attitude conveys to the child that his parents have confidence in his ability and are interested in seeing him do well in school.

Guideline 13. *Try to understand the child's reasons for disliking school.* Many children adjust to school and are comfortable with it. Many more dislike it. The child who dislikes school may be rebelling against his parents, resentful of his teacher's authority, unable to do the academic work, unhappy with his social relationships, or lazy, or he may dislike school for other reasons. It is important that parents attempt to understand why he is unhappy with school before steps can be taken to correct the problem. It is possible that the child cannot verbalize his reasons for disliking school, or perhaps he is embarrassed to discuss them. The child who dislikes school and realizes that he has many more years of it often becomes depressed and wants to give up. Such a child needs parental understanding more than he needs lectures, and encouragement more than punishment. What he wants to hear his parents say is, "We understand how you feel, and we'll help you work things out. Don't give up!"

The child who dislikes school lacks confidence in himself and sees more reasons to dread school than look forward to it. He feels trapped and sees no way to solve his problem. Parental reassurances are important and talking things out with someone who will listen is helpful. The parent can be that someone. In trying to view the situation as the child sees it, parents must realize how frustrated their child is and encourage him to solve rather than run from the problem.

Guideline 14. *Encourage the child to assume responsibility for his own education.* The young child's motivation to succeed in school is based largely on his need to please his parents. If his success is rewarded by the teacher or his parents, the child will acquire a positive image of his ability and begin to show pride in his accomplishments. As he matures, the child seeks success to please himself, in addition to his parents. By early adolescence, the youngster who has experienced success should have sufficient pride that he can be trusted to fulfill his academic responsibilities. He will still need an occasional boost from his parents in the way of praise and encouragement, but when the home has made education a high priority value, the child realizes that his job is to do his best work in school.

The youngster who is able to assume responsibility for his own education wants to do well for his own sake. He is not just working for his teachers or parents, even though he may want them to be pleased with his achievements. A less mature child feels that he can punish a teacher he doesn't like by allowing himself to fail or do poor work. Such a child has no internal motivation to succeed, but still guides his actions in terms of the attitudes of the adults he wishes to please or displease.

Guideline 15. *School is only one part of the child's life.* Even though education may receive the highest priority from parents, school is not the only thing a child needs for a balanced life. He needs recreation, free time, some planned activity, responsibility for doing work in the home, and one or more interests. Hobbies are good for children, especially when the child can work on them in the house on rainy days. Parents should provide their children with the opportunity to develop any talents or creativity they possess, and expose them to cultural experiences. Children need diversity in their activities, but as was mentioned earlier, they should not feel overburdened with extracurricular interests.

Our educational system offers the greatest potential for correcting the problems that trouble society. A number of changes are needed if education is to be successful in meeting the challenge. Any recommendation for change must begin as an idea, but pessimism and negative thinking can prevent or delay changes when the concern is one of fearing that the recommendation might not be acceptable to everyone or work for every case. If we must wait until a utopian educational program is developed before doing things to improve the present conditions in schools, there can be no change or a movement that might prevent an expansion of current educational problems. Any recommendations for improving something as large as public education must be content to make their initial impact on a small percentage of the total population involved. We must not forget that the leaders of tomorrow are sitting in the classrooms of today.

- 9 -

When the Child Marries

Ambivalence is the simultaneous wanting and not wanting something to happen, or both an attraction and a repulsion to an object or person. The mixed emotions involved account for many inappropriate and inconsistent reactions. Much ambivalence is unconscious; at other times, ambivalence is recognized but it is hidden or disguised. A child who is ambivalent about growing up may learn to perform the complex task of tying his own shoes, yet insist that his mother zip up a less complicated zipper on his snowsuit. An adolescent who is ambivalent about becoming an adult may do and say many things which suggest that he is seeking freedom and autonomy from parents, yet, given the opportunity to go away to college, prefers to attend a local college and live at home.

Parents can express their ambivalence in wanting to see their young-adult children grow up in what could be termed a let-go-hold-on syndrome. This is seen when parents are seemingly encouraging their young-adult children to plan for their future by contemplating marriage, yet devise subtle ways to make the child think twice about the dangers of marriage. Looking for flaws in the child's intended marriage partner can be one form of holding on, especially when the faults found are more superficial than real. The parent who says, "She's a nice girl, but someday she'll probably be as fat as her mother," or, "I think Bob is a fine young man. Maybe after you're married, you can talk him into getting an apartment near our house," is expressing ambivalence.

There are many valid reasons for parental objections to a child's marriage. They may be objections to the marriage itself or to the marriage partner. Objections to the marriage usually concern such factors as the timing of the marriage, the age of the bride and groom, the readiness of the child for marriage, the reasons for marrying or the loneliness the parent fears when the child marries. Objections to the marriage partner are usually more devastating to the parent-child relationship, for they involve dissatisfaction with the child's choice and consequently will bring out differences in judgment and values. A personal attack on the character and personality of the child's partner of choice places the child in the difficult position of choosing between the parents and the selected partner.

Some parents express their ambivalence towards the marriage of their child in a peculiar, yet, socially accepted custom: crying at the wedding! Often the tears that are explained away as being tears of joy are, in fact, tears of realization that letting go is a reality. The parent not only thinks "I'm losing my baby," or "My life will be empty now," but also offers a silent prayer, "Please, Lord, don't let my child forget me."

Even after marriage, many parents refuse to allow the child to break away from their hold, and many children are unable to make the break from their parents. This occurs when parents have either inadvertently or deliberately reared their children to be overly dependent upon them. A daughter who grows up feeling inadequate and dependent on her parents becomes the bride who has second thoughts about marriage, fearing that the new husband will not show her the same care and attention that her parents did. She could also feel guilty for leaving her parents. The son who cannot break away from his parents will not have the same doubts about getting married or feel as much guilt in marrying. His concern would be whether his new wife would be to him what his mother was to him. He is caught up between loyalty towards his parents versus loyalty towards his wife, feeling the need to prove his love to his wife, while simultaneously showing his devotion and gratitude to his parents.

When the parent insists on holding on to the married child, a reversal of dependence occurs in the relationship between the parent and the child. Whereas at one time the child was dependent upon the parent, the parent now becomes dependent upon the child. If the relationship between the parents has been unstable, the parent may turn to the child for attention and affection. Frequently, a parent's need for a child is as intense as the child's need for the parent. This would be termed a *symbiotic* relationship, and anything or anybody who might come along to interfere with this mutual, somewhat parasitic relationship would be viewed as threatening and upsetting.

The parent who feels he must hold on, and is also aware that he must also let go will often sanction a marriage that he feels he can control. In this way, the marriage will not change the parent-child relationship too drastically. This, however, sets up the potential for distress in the child's marriage. If the marriage does not alter the parent-child relationship, the new spouse will be distressed. If the marriage does alter the parent-child relationship, the parent will be distressed and work to return things to the former condition. This can be done in subtle ways by encouraging the child to feel guilty for having been a traitor to the parent. The child is put in the middle, feeling guilty if he neglects his spouse; guilty if he abandons his parent; and finding no acceptable compromise that will not offend one or the other.

Not every child who marries does so out of love and the feeling that the loved partner will become the source for emotional security. Many children marry because of a need to escape from their parents. Their motivation is a need to avoid a situation rather than to enter into a new type of relationship. Such *forced* marriages are brought about by unsatisfying parental relationships which have resulted from pressure, rejections or domination. Many children are impatient to be free from parental controls and use marriage as their escape to freedom. Some parents are delighted to see their children leave home, even viewing their child's marriage as a kind of punishment. "He ought to get married. It will serve him right! Let him see what it's like."

The purpose of this chapter is to examine some of the problems that develop when parents refuse to accept the fact that their child is married. In essence, these are problems that arise when the parents are not willing or able to redefine their role as parents. This is not a chapter on "How to Handle In-Laws," or "How to Muzzle Grandparents." It is a discussion of the common problems of parental interference and guidelines that can avoid or reduce family arguments. Many arguments between young married couples are over parents and in-laws. Parents can encourage such arguments by not taking actions that would allow the young couple to be relieved of decisions that must offend someone. An example will illustrate:

Case Illustration Number 20

Gary and his wife, Linda, had been married less than six months. They were on the verge of divorce, and had decided against having children because of the tenuous nature of the marriage. When Linda sought out professional help, Gary was willing to cooperate.

Gary worked for his father-in-law. This did not pose any major problems for him; he and his father-in-law had a good relationship with mutual respect. The real problem centered around the demands of Linda's mother. Linda and Gary were expected to attend weekly dinners, Linda was expected to call her mother daily and go shopping with her every Saturday afternoon. The mother gave a large amount of unsolicited advice on purchases and decorating, and felt rejected if the advice was ignored.

When Linda was abrupt with her mother, she would sulk, pout, and become sarcastic. The mother wanted Gary to submit to being mothered, but Gary wanted no part of it, and was often not tactful in expressing his displeasure. Linda resented Gary's attitude towards her mother. She could understand his feelings, yet could not bring herself to support her husband in place of her mother. "Try to understand her," she would plead with Gary. "She means well."

This was a serious problem for Linda and Gary. They fought over the attitude and actions of the mother. Gary was convinced that Linda needed her mother more than she needed him. There was no doubt that the mother was aware of the dissatisfaction existing in her daughter's marriage, and she even had insights into the reasons. Yet, in no way was she willing to alter her relationship with her daughter. Fearing the separation that could result if she were to relinquish her controls over Linda, she offered Linda sympathy and comfort, but no release from her distressful situation.

Parents who are selfish and possessive towards their children tend to maintain a selfish and possessive position, despite the knowledge that their attitudes and actions are seriously affecting the child to whom they profess love. This, however, is not love but dependency, symbiosis, or fear.

Redefining Parental Roles

Do you marry the family as well as the marriage partner? The answer to this question should be no if the newly married couple is to acquire feelings of independence, freedom, and commitment to one another. Only if the couple wants to put themselves in the position of feeling obligated to others, responsible for making families happy at the price of their own freedom, or placing the commitment to each other second to the commitment to keep peace in someone else's family, would the answer be yes.

Yet the no answer needs some qualifications. Although there is no reason to feel that you have married your partner's family, you really are related to them now, in a way similar to the relatedness you have towards your own family after marriage.

This relatedness should be defined, or the marriage may suffer and the families be hurt and offended. When the families misinterpret the need for freedom as a rebuff or rejection they feel hurt. But, the freedom from the parents is essential, for just as no person can serve two masters, no person can be child to parent and wife to husband simultaneously. Primary loyalties, fundamental responsibilities, and major commitments must be to the spouse, not the parents. Parents who have not redefined their role to their married children will either hurt themselves, or their child's marriage. It is the fortunate child whose parents have assumed the initiative to redefine relationships with their married children. However, if the parents fail to redefine their relationship to their child, the child is forced to do it for them.

The Parental Adjustment

Very little has been said about the adjustment that parents must make when their children marry and leave home. It is not the same as children going off to college, or moving into their own apartment. Until the child marries, he thinks of home as where the parents live. After marriage, home becomes the place where the new marriage will begin and, possibly, where their children will be initially reared. The former "home" becomes "parents' house." Before marriage, visiting one's parents is viewed as "going home." After marriage, seeing one's parents becomes a "visit to the *parents'* home."

The plight of parents is, at best, a somewhat lonesome one.

One man and one woman begin a relationship that culminates in a marriage. When they become parents, they are no longer two. They may produce several children, each of whom will eventually leave the parents' home, and when all the children have left the home to marry and start their own families, the parents once again are two; although in an algebraic way they may have generated life to an untold number of offsprings. Two can produce four, who in turn can produce sixteen. But the two who produced the original four will end up as two again.

Parents begin a family when they are young. They invest time, energy, work, worry, and money to bring the children to the point where the children can leave them. Parental rewards are pride and satisfaction, but these can be mixed with feelings of failure, regrets, guilt, and often dissatisfaction. Parents must first learn to adjust to the presence of children in the home, and then they must learn to adjust to their absence. The initial adjustment to having a child in the home comes at a time when the parents are young, enthusiastic, optimistic, and filled with hopes for the future. These factors help make the adjustment an easy one. Conversely, the adjustment to the absence of children comes at a time when parents are living in that future they had thought about during the early years. They are less optimistic, less enthusiastic, and more concerned with the present than the future. These factors make the adjustment to the absence of the children more difficult. Although attainment of a goal can be exciting and richly satisfying, it can also be depressing. The enjoyment of working for a goal is gone once the goal is achieved.

Separating From the Child

There is one aspect of parenting that is often overlooked; the attitude that parents should have concerning the time when their children depart from the parental home and establish a home of their own. It is called *child-weaning* if the parent does it for himself, or *parent-weaning* if the child does it for the parent. A separation of the parent from the child must occur. It should begin long before marriage, before a dependency has developed. It should be accomplished with determination and an attitude that conveys the necessity for such an action. The child-weaning process should be a gradual evolvement of an awareness that the child is maturing along social lines. Early dating indicates that it is time to be aware of the social development in the child that will soon lead to a separation. Frequently, the parents are the last to be aware of this social growth. The older adolescent may be thinking about his future as a prospective parent even if the parent is not.

This is not to say that parents should be braced for a marriage when their fourteen-year-old daughter goes to her first dance with a boy, or their sixteen-year-old son announces that he just gave his high school ring to his latest girl. These events do signify, however, that the "little" child may be only a few years away from wanting a graceful separation from his parents. The parents can aid or deter this eventual separation.

Ideally, parents should begin the weaning process from their children. Otherwise, the child must either initiate the weaning or maintain an overdependency on parents. If the child has to initiate the weaning, parents will typically interpret the child's actions as rebellious and ungrateful. Parents who will not go to bed until their older adolescent is home are communicating more to the child than their concern over his safety and welfare; they are requiring that he feel guilty for wanting to have fewer parental controls.

Child-weaning is facilitated when parents know they have given their child adequate preparation and guidance that enables them to feel comfortable with their child. If parents of a twenty-year-old do not have such confidence in their child, and if because of his past behavior they cannot trust his judgment, mistakes in parenting have resulted in problems that have been maintained for many years. Any attempt to separate this child from his parents would be abandonment. Weaning should not occur unless there is a readiness for separation.

The parent who had difficulty separating from his own parents will probably experience difficulty separating from his children. The parent who has been unhappy in the marital relationship and who has used the child as a love-substitute, will have difficulty separating from the child, as will the parent who has used the child to make up for personal deficiencies. Those who feel guilty about the kind of parents they were during their child's growing years will have difficulty separating from their child. This is especially true if a poor parent-child relationship improves shortly before the child prepares to marry and leave home. Finally, the parent who feels inadequate and helpless will resist any attempts to be separated from the child.

Unrealistic Expectations

Marriage in and of itself does not change the basic personality structure of the individual. The man who was jealous before marriage will be no less jealous after, unless he attempts to overcome his jealousy. The woman who was socially inadequate before marriage will not be automatically transformed into a socially adept and competent woman. There is nothing magical or therapeutic about the marriage ceremony that transforms a person from what he has been to what he would like to become. This is equally true for the relationship that exists between the child and the parents before and after the marriage. The demanding parent is still demanding. The emotional parent is no less emotional with the married child and may find more reasons to be emotional and more situations to which he can overreact.

Nor has the basic relationship between parent and child undergone any major change as a result of marriage. People who are newly married may say their marriage has improved their relationship with their parents, but the time and space that now separates the child from his parents might account for the perceived improvements. In this way, absence *can* make the heart grow fonder. A basically poor relationship may, on the surface, appear to be better, but with any prolonged exposure, the characteristic problems will emerge.

The Road Paved with Good Intentions

Much that could be termed overprotectiveness, domination, overpossessiveness, and overindulgence is committed by parents who have "good intentions." Good intentions, however, are not an excuse for poor judgment. No parents should be proud of being overly protective, dominating, over-possessive and over indulgent. The rationalization that these things were done with good intentions is only a half truth, the other half being that the behavior met the needs of the parents. Being overprotective meets a parental need, just as the child's rebelling against authority meets his need for independence.

In most instances, good intentions without good judgment backfire against the parent, who is left with mixed feelings about what he tried to do. In truth, he says, he was doing what he thought was best for his child. However, he usually failed to see the cues that would have told him that what he was doing was, in fact, producing and reinforcing the conditions he was seeking to avoid.

Parents err by not being able to evaluate the effects of their actions. Good judgment that accompanies good intentions is a more desirable approach. The criteria to be used in determining whether an action is wise could be, "Is what I am doing for my child going to benefit him in the long run?" In the case of Linda and Gary, cited earlier, good judgment should have enabled Linda's mother to realize that she was a cause of her daughter's marital unhappiness and that her continued demands on her married daughter and son-in-law would result in destruction of the marriage.

Another example is offered to illustrate, among other things, (1) good intentions that backfired, (2) poor maternal judgment through interference, and (3) manipulating behavior resulting in an alienation of the mother and daughter.

Case Illustration Number 21

Annette's mother was a very insecure mother. She shielded her daughter from reality, yet she also pushed her and tried to make her the person she would have wanted to be. She provided Annette with dancing lessons, piano lessons, and tutoring in weak subjects in school. She controlled her choice of early playmates and friends, and eventually dates. She sent Annette to a private school for her last three years of high school, despite her protests. When it came time to select a college, the mother took the initiative and got applications from the schools she felt would be best for her daughter. This, too, was done over the protests of the daughter, who was anxious to break away from her mother. Annette also resented the way her mother treated her father. Both the daughter and the father were aware that the mother was the power in the family. The father no longer talked to his wife, for the battles that resulted were not worth the effort to him.

Annette became negative toward her mother and went out of her way to displease her. The mother regarded her attitude as evidence of a lack of maturity, ingratitude, and selfishness, and continued to interfere in Annette's affairs.

She initially objected to Annettte's choice of a mate because of her age which, at the time, was nineteen. Annette planned to be married when she was twenty. The mother started a campaign to discredit the young man, only to find that Annette was becoming more determined to marry him *because* of her efforts to dissuade her. She soon realized that she was not going to be successful in convincing her daughter to change her mind, so she gave in with such comments as, "Well, you always have a home to come back to," and, "If it (the marriage) goes sour, I won't be one to say, 'See, I told you so.'"

Annette's mother was a very unhappy woman. She had seen the daughter she had pinned her hopes on disappoint her. The dancing and piano lessons proved essentially unproductive, and, an even greater disappointment, her daughter dropped out of college. To make matters worse, Annette showed no appreciation of her mother's attempts to help or advise her. The mother's marriage was never a good one, and her only hope now was that she could have a good relationship with her daughter after the marriage. To help insure this, she insisted that her husband pay all expenses for a luxurious honeymoon, later taking all the credit for the idea. Annette took the money but didn't see the strings that were attached to it. Only after the honeymoon did she realize that the mother, by giving the honeymoon gift, had selected the site of the honeymoon, chosen the hotel, decided on their method of transportation, and even determined the times for their departure and return.

Because of the poor relationship between mother and daughter, Annette did not allow the mother to interfere in the marriage. A complete separation came about when, in a moment of extreme anger, she told her mother to "stay out of my life once and for all!" Her mother was deeply hurt, and remained that way. She blamed her daughter and pitied herself. On the surface, Annette was pleased with the break and maintained a limited contact with her family through her father. In her mother's mind, the daughter was completely wrong because the mother felt her intentions were good. The serious complication in this case was that the mother also thought her judgment was good.

The New Relationship

The characteristic feature of the redefinition of parental roles after the child marries is the recognition that the relationship between the married child and his parents is one of equals. Before the child marries, his parents may feel responsible for his welfare, regardless of his age. The child's relationship may still be based on some degree of dependency and his parents may therefore impose certain restrictions and expectations on him. For some parents, these expectations would mean, "As long as you are living under our roof you will be expected to listen to us." Other parents voice their concern by saying, "We still worry about your safety and would appreciate knowing where you are."

The unmarrieds who live away from parents may still have a need to regard home as the place where parents live, to which they could return if they so desired.

After marriage, this picture should change. No longer should the child be dependent upon parents. The needed strength and reassurances should come from the spouse. Parents can still be reassuring and comforting, but their contributions to the welfare of their child should now be secondary. They can become excellent resource people because their experiences are greater than those of the child. But, they should not expect the former status quo.

After marriage, the parents have no authoritative rights over the child. Obligations take on a new meaning. The mother may want her daughter to take her grocery shopping as she did before she was married. With marriage, however, come a number of new responsibilities along with changes in routines. If the mother is able to shop for groceries without the daughter, it is apparent that the mother wants the daughter for companionship and does not really need her assistance. The new schedule of the daughter should dictate whether the weekly shopping trip is continued or discontinued. If the mother is unable to shop because of physical limitations, she needs the daughter's aid. Mutually convenient times will have to be worked out, bearing in mind that the daughter's schedule is no less important than her mother's.

In a relationship the parents and child can become good friends. The same components that underlie good friendships should be practiced between the parents and the child: mutual respect for one another, consideration of feelings, cooperation, and a feeling of closeness. There is a great deal of personal autonomy in a friendship. The needs of a wife or husband have priority over the needs of friends. Friendships are worked around family schedules. A friendship cannot be based on demands or the manipulation of behavior. When asking your friends to dinner, you do not demand that they accept. If they cannot accept your invitation, you do not become nasty and put the relationship on the line. You respect their decision and assume that they have a good reason for saying no, if they are really good friends. You might feel disappointment, but not anger.

Before a parental relationship based on equality can be achieved, it is necessary that the children view the parents in a proper perspective. Parents should be viewed as people, flesh and blood, neither perfect nor all-knowing. The young child ascribes omnipotence to his parents. The parents make a point to impress upon their child that they know best. Many children grow up looking upon their parents as the standard for what is good and appropriate. As children grow into adolescence, they should become aware that their parents are real people who, like themselves, have weaknesses and doubts and can make judgmental errors. Putting parents in perspective is seeing them as humans who are mortal and subject to the same stresses and fears as any other person. Seeing parents as superhuman creates a barrier to an equal relationship.

When the child marries, he will have more in common with his parents. When the child becomes a parent, the experiences in common will increase. The fact that parents are older is not a reason for feeling that equality is not possible. The young lawyer has much in common with the experienced lawyer, even though the latter can point to hundreds of clients and hours spent in court rooms. The young lawyer may defer to the judgment of the older man, use him as a resource person, and model after him; but he is no less an equal. Experience does not, in itself, negate equality.

To repeat, it is important that the primary commitment of the newly married young adults should be to each other. Once this is understood, the young couple will have taken the most vital step in redefining the role of their parents. The parental relationship after marriage should be expected to be different from what it was. Things *are* changed, and what was, no longer is.

The love for parents will not be less than it was, but it will be different. The part of the child's love that was based upon his needs being satisfied will decrease. The love for parents is different from the love for husband or wife. Love of child is not the same as love between husband and wife. Each close relationship would necessitate a difference in the quality of love.

Reasons for Poor Parent Relationships

The relationship between parents and their married children is usually a carry over from the relationship that existed prior to the marriage. A poor relationship can be due to the actions of either the parents or their child. Not all children seek a better relationship with their parents after they are married; some may view marriage as freedom from parental controls and avoid a relationship out of fear that parents will maintain power over them. The relationship that exists between many young married couples and their parents is one of tolerance. For some couples, even this would be a better relationship than they now have with their parents.

Parents can create a poor relationship with their married children if they:

— are unwilling to let go of the parent-child relationship
— refuse to accept the changes that are brought about by the marriage
— expect the pre-marital conditions to exist instead of the new relationship
— make selfish demands on their child
— try to be possessive of their child
— interfere with the decisions made by the newly married couple
— contrive to manipulate or control their child's marriage
— offer excessive unsolicited advice
— make their child feel guilty for leaving them
— are overly critical, negative, or offensive to their child's spouse

The young couple can be responsible for the poor relationship with their parents if they:

— do nothing to encourage a relationship
— use their parents only when it is convenient for them
— reject their parents
— misinterpret parental suggestions as criticism
— overreact to parental opinions
— are quick to become defensive or argumentative
— reject advice because it is advice
— make unfair demands on their parents
— harbor feelings of resentment or hostility towards their parents
— fear parental interference (hence, avoid a relationship)

Many problems between parents and their married children could be avoided if each person would respect the other's right to live his own life. This requires a mutual letting go, and problems develop when either the parents or their children take it upon themselves to tell the other what he should do. And yet, there is no reason why the child must become defensive, or the parent offended when advice is offered. How the advice is offered is critical: tactful suggesting rather than commanding is essential. If the mother says to her married daughter, "If I were you, I'd take a course in cooking," the defensive daughter might respond with, "Well, you're not me!" A more tactful approach might be to say, "Have you ever considered enrolling in one of the cooking courses I've seen advertised in the paper?" Of course, if the daughter is going to be defensive, she can resent any advice, regardless how it is offered.

Mutual respect does not mean isolation. The way to build a relationship is not to avoid one. Parents who are possessive and selfish, or have a martyred attitude will force isolation and alienation despite their desire to build a relationship. Possessive parents place demands on their child for time. Selfish parents take more than they give and expect their child's loyalties to remain with them. Parents who have a martyred attitude in their new role as parents of a married child are asking for pity and try to make their child feel guilty when they are not at the top of his new priority list.

There can be no resolution of differences without a willingness to understand things from the other person's point of view. Nor will a positive relationship develop if either parents or their married child allow themselves to be easily offended or extremely defensive.

Guidelines for Newly Married Couples

Although the guidelines that follow are for newly married couples, they could be used by any couple who want to establish a positive relationship with their parents. A good relationship takes time to develop and needs the full cooperation of all involved parties. Problems occur when the parents and their children do not have similar goals for the relationship. The newlyweds may want a more distant relationship; the parents a closer one. It is usually more difficult for the parents to adjust to the new relationship than it is for the child to adjust to his independence from his parents. These guidelines were developed to establish the separation from parental influence and yet maintain a comfortable relationship with parents.

Guideline 1. *Discourage parental interference.* Marriage involves a major change in the lives of the husband and wife. Interference will jeopardize the adjustments that have to be made. The first year of marriage should be relatively free from outside pressures or demands and the couple should decide when they are ready to include parents in their lives. If relationships prior to marriage have been good, this decision could come very soon. Otherwise, it should come when the couple feels they have learned to function independent of parental influences and when they have established loyalties to each other.

Although parents may be ready for the relationship sooner than their children, it is the young couple who must decide when parental involvement can take place. Although this seems selfish on the part of the young couple, it is their way of establishing their new lives together and solidifying their commitment to each other.

Guideline 2. *The parent-child relationship must be redefined.* This has been stated earlier, but it is important enough to repeat. Once the child is married, his relationship with parents is one of equality. The married child should be prepared to have an independent relationship with his parents and feel free from their controls; he should no longer expect to be dependent upon his parents. Marriage does remove some security, for no longer can the child expect his parents to protect him the way they may have prior to his marriage. Parents are free to be generous to their married child, but he does not have the right to expect it. In the redefined relationship, the married child is free from obligations that were formerly related to parental authority. This is not the same as being free from responsibility, for the married child as well as the single child has a responsibility to parents.

It is not possible to establish an independent relationship with parents if the child persists in treating parents as nonequals. Deferring to parental judgment instead of making an independent decision is an example of maintaining a nonequal relationship. The married daughter who asks her mother "Do you think we should buy this sofa?" is not far removed from the little girl who asks, "Can I invite Alice to a slumber party?" The married child who seeks to be free from parental controls must show this independence by relying on personal judgment, rather than a parental decision. Asking for an opinion is logical when there are doubts about something. But, soliciting a parent's opinion should not be confused with asking the parent to make the decision. The way the married child phrases a question to his parents will indicate whether an equal or dependent relationship is being encouraged.

Guideline 3. *Don't live with parents.* Unless it is completely impossible to do otherwise, newlyweds should not live with their parents. They are better off living in a tent that is theirs, than living in a mansion that is not theirs. Many marriages that have ended in divorce and others that are unstable can trace their difficulties to the problems that developed when the couple decided to share a parent's home. The newlyweds must establish an independent household.

There are times when a parent must move in with a married child. This is not as bad, for if the young couple have established something they call home, it is their home that the parent is living in, and they are in charge of it. Even so, it is best if the decision to have a parent move in with the married child can be delayed until the couple feel they have adjusted to each other as marriage partners.

Guideline 4. *Be careful not to overreact to parental advice.* Young married couples are often intolerant of parental advice and feel threatened when they are criticized. They feel the need to oppose advice on the basis of principle regardless of the wisdom of the suggestion. They respond to a suggestion as if it were a command and become resentful of unsolicited advice. Because young married couples are inclined to be defensive, they misinterpret the comments of their parents, who are trying to be helpful, and use such comments as a reason to avoid a good relationship with them. Everyone is entitled to an opinion, and the newly married couple should regard their parent's opinion in much the same manner they would the opinion of a friend. Whether they act according to the suggestions that are offered is another matter, but the child owes his parents the courtesy of letting them express their opinion.

On the other hand, if parents become offended when their child does not take the advice they offer, they are not acting as friends and are inviting problems in the parent-married child relationship. If parental advice is excessive and unsolicited, they can be asked to refrain from giving it, but when unsolicited advice causes an over-reaction, the person giving the advice is being rejected more than the advice itself.

One of the things that parents have to learn as part of their adjustment to their child's marriage is not to advise or criticize as they did prior to the marriage. From the parent's position, this could mean discontinuing a practice they have done throughout the child's life. It may take parents time to remember that they are no longer expected to play the role of parents as they once did, and children should understand and appreciate that this is not easy for parents to do. The young couple should be prepared to listen to suggestions from any source, knowing that they will make their own decisions. Parents who take a, "You'll be sorry," or an "I told you so," approach encourage an overreaction to their advice.

Guideline 5. *Establish family traditions of your own.* The newly married couple should feel they are in the process of establishing a home and traditions that are no less important than those of their parents. Problems will develop if they feel required to decide which parental invitation they will accept for a traditional celebration. When both sets of parents invite the couple to a Thanksgiving dinner, one set of parents will probably end up feeling hurt. It should not be a matter of who invited them first, for one set of parents could offer the couple a standing invitation a year in advance. Nor is taking turns in successive years a satisfactory solution, for the couple may feel obligated to appease parents and postpone their own traditions. The couple should be free to accept or decline invitations without feeling guilty, even when there is only one set of parents involved.

Solid marriages are built on pleasant memories. It is exciting to recall the first apartment, the first car, and especially the first child. It is also pleasant to remember the first Thanksgiving dinner, the first holiday dinner, and the first of other traditional ceremonies. Some couples prefer to wait until they are parents before starting their own traditions, others are eager to begin right away. The choice should be theirs.

Guideline 6. *Stand united.* The newly married couple should present a unified position to parents. When parents are aware that the couple is united on an issue, they are less likely to attack the child or the issue. It also informs parents that the couple will not permit anything to come between them or allow anyone to play one against the other. If the couple disagrees on an issue, the place to settle differences between the husband and wife is in the privacy of their home, not in front of their parents. In a stable marriage, partners must protect each other in public. If, for example, the husband cannot agree with what his wife is saying, it is better for him to say nothing, than antagonize, embarrass or ridicule her in front of others.

Guideline 7. *Remain loyal to your spouse.* Whenever a husband or wife is put in the position of having to choose between parents or spouse, primary loyalties must be to the spouse. It is unfair for either parents or spouse to ask a marriage partner to make such a choice. An example of being put in the middle could occur if the husband's parents are displeased with their daughter-in-law and are critical of her to him. If his wife is equally critical of her in-laws, the son is caught between his parents' disappointment and his wife's resentment. The son will have to discourage his parents from speaking against his wife and, by supporting and reassuring his wife, convince her that she does not need to feel threatened by things his parents say.

The son is not responsible for what his parents do or say, nor should the wife take out her resentment of in-laws on her husband. If the son has a good relationship with his parents, he can explain to them the position they are putting him in and how this can have a harmful effect on his subsequent relationship with them. On the other hand, his wife would be unfair if she expected her husband to sever his relationship with his parents because they said something that offended her. The son cannot be asked to abandon his parents, but he can be expected to protect his wife. When strong loyalties are established between a husband and wife, there is also trust.

Guideline 8. *Arguing with parents is unproductive.* Arguments with parents do not resolve problems, they only create and intensify a bad relationship. No one really wins an argument, and the price for satisfaction is not worth the regret or guilt it may cause. It should be possible to disagree without getting into a heated or prolonged argument. When discussion starts to sound like a verbal battle it is time to stop the discussion, change the subject, or acknowledge a stalemate. Usually, an argument is predictable, for both the child and his parents know what issues are almost certain to produce an argument. New arguments are rare, and since it is apparent that previous attempts to solve the problem by arguing were unsuccessful, it serves no constructive purpose to rehash what has been said before. When two people have different feelings about an issue, and both feel justified in their thinking, the most productive thing that can be done is to agree that each person has the right to disagree, and then drop the subject.

Guideline 9. *New grandparents may need an orientation to the parents' training rules.* In time, the newly married couple become parents and their parents become grandparents. The relationship that develops between grandparents and grandchild is determined by what the married child-parent relationship has been. Grandparents have the right to define their own role and act according to what is comfortable for them. They may choose to become very involved with the new grandchild or have infrequent contact with him. This is their choice; but, what they do with the grandchild should be determined by the infant's parents. Parents must not permit grandparents to undermine their authority or go against their training of the child. If grandparents spoil their grandchild, it is because the child's parents permitted it. It may be necessary to tell grandparents what rules have been established for the child's early training and require them to respect these rules.

Guideline 10. *Remember the golden rule.* What is fair to expect from parents is fair to expect from the newly married couple. If the young couple insist on privacy and discourage their parents from dropping in without previous notice, they must respect their parents' need for privacy and not drop in on them unannounced. The same could be said for other limits and restrictions the couple place on their parents. It is inconsistent for married children to resent parental advice, yet turn around and advise parents. The married child must be consistent and fair to his parents. Positive interactions between parents and their married children are facilitated when consideration is shown to each other and when the relationship is built on fairness and mutual respect. The young couple should remember that some-day their own children will grow up and marry. To rephrase the golden rule: Treat parents as you would want your children to treat you someday.

When the child marries, he takes the first step toward repeating the cycle that reproduces his species and perpetuates his society. In our culture marriage forms the basis of the family unit from which relationships are developed. When these relationships are close and compatible, the child, who is a product of the family, learns to interact unselfishly and positively with his environment. When the child marries, he is confronted with a new group of problems which require solutions and involve decisions. One of the problems is that of rearing a child in a society that places many obstacles in the child's path; one of the decisions is deciding on the best way to accomplish the tasks of parenting.

Man is like a tiger. He cannot always be trusted, for he has been known to attack others when he is frightened or desperate, and attack himself if he is troubled or lonesome. He continues to be the animal that is feared by others, and because he is aware of his own power, he is often afraid of himself. In order to protect and maintain some control over himself, the tiger has learned to hold on to his own tail. Only the tiger who does not fear himself is free to let go.